the new Parisienne

the new Parisienne

THE WOMEN & IDEAS
SHAPING PARIS

Lindsey Tramuta

PHOTOGRAPHY BY JOANN PAI

ILLUSTRATIONS BY AGATHE SINGER

ABRAMS, NEW YORK

For L.D. and the women of Paris.

CONTENTS

The Storytellers

The "Taste"makers

The Visionaries

Their Paris

"There's a whole image around the Parisienne that needs to be reconstructed because it's been a long time since she's looked like Brigitte Bardot or Édith Piaf. Paris is one of the most multicultural cities of Europe."

—ROKHAYA DIALLO, JOURNALIST, FILMMAKER, AND ANTIRACIST ACTIVIST

opposite Rainbow crosswalks in the Marais, an initiative by Mayor Anne Hidalgo to show support for the LGBTQ community.

INTRODUCTION

A LOT HAPPENED IN THE NINE MONTHS following the release of my first book, *The New Paris*. Writing a book can change a person, but so can the exchanges that emerge from its existence in the world. It connected me with readers and travelers from all over, but it also introduced me to people right on my doorstep, many of whom were incredibly inspiring women. I've had the opportunity to write about some of them, and the more I did, the more important it became to me to share stories about the lives of women in and around Paris—how they were shaping society and culture, even in the most subtle of ways.

Simultaneously, coverage about Paris—the city, the brand—carried on at a steady pace. For every article that explored the changing city were five that reinforced old narratives about the capital as an immaculate, living museum and repackaged the same must-see lists. Along with them came an uptick in stories about how French women (consistently conflated with *Parisian* women, as if identical) were doing everything better from powdering their noses to defying nature with ageless beauty techniques.

I wrote the first book because I felt the city deserved better—a more complete picture of what makes it a destination for some and a home for many others. Similarly, the idea for this book was sparked at once by my desire to capture a more representative image of the Parisian woman, in all of her diversity, and by a feeling that the *how to live like* canon had reached its expiration.

At its core, this book is about recasting the image of how one of the most commodified and romanticized groups of women is actually living today: how

---

opposite A different view of a familiar city from the Parc des Buttes-Chaumont.

she finds happiness and seeks fulfillment, how she weathers adversity and the indignities that may be thrust upon her, and how she's contributing to the city in her own way—one dish, film, boxing match, art exhibit, podcast episode, and jewelry collection at a time. But it's also about stepping away from a restrictive set of stereotypes that have defined this one woman for generations—a woman whose aura is seemingly impossible to dispel but must endlessly be dissected—and offering a new image and a set of stories to go with it.

MYTH MAKING

What do you see when you close your eyes and think of Paris? What about when you imagine the women of Paris? Chances are, she's familiar. In fact, she's as familiar to us as every other Parisian icon, branded and brandished like a symbol of national grandeur. Yet for all of her familiarity, the Parisienne isn't what she appears to be.

Seduction, style, beauty, and attitude have been seen as the marker and measure of the Parisian female mystique for generations. We speak little of her mind, her ambitions, her career, or her life experiences detached from her physical body. Instead, we focus on her collection of handbags and striped sailor tops, her innate ability to ride a bicycle across town in heels or let her hair loose with uncalculated abandon. Even the mundane of the everyday takes on a mystical élan, her face magnified by the deep, red lip we're told she sports as a sign of her boldness, whether she's picking up the dry cleaning or heading out for dinner.

It's an engineered, pervasive, and deeply troublesome myth that impacts not only the foreign women who are meant to consistently feel lacking and continue buying (literally) into the idea that a cream, top, or hairbrush will put them on the path to betterment, but the local women who don't hew to the mold popular culture has co-opted. It's an archetype that effaces black, Asian, disabled, trans, and other countless segments of the population with such ease that you, the consumer and traveler, come to Paris and are slack-jawed by the diversity. The Parisienne has been flattened to caricature in a way that does as much harm to her as everyone aspiring to be her.

For this issue, we can thank brands, marketers, women's magazines, and books, the greatest proselytizers of the branded Parisian woman. Even some of the most famous Parisian faces have capitalized on what they know to be a mirage to sell a fantasy. And it's worked: This hegemonic figure—intellectual, perhaps, but mostly seductive, chic no matter the circumstances, *always* perfectly composed—has sold billions of dollars' worth of perfumes, lipsticks, entire wardrobes, and even attitudes.

Today, there are a staggering number of brands that have been created to *sound* and *feel* French. French Girl Organics, Glossier, Ouai Haircare, Être Cécile, and La Garçonne, among others, are all designed to deliver on a lifestyle ambition that itself has been implanted over generations and run exclusively on perceived value.[1] All over the world, the average reader and consumer falls victim to the illusory truth effect—the idea that the more we're exposed to something, the more likely we believe it, whether or not it's true. And in this case, the Parisian beauty ideal trumps all else.

Even as far back as the eighteenth century, the stereotypes of the Parisienne were well established—Jean-Jacques Rousseau and work by his predecessors had already begun sketching images of the Parisienne whose reputation was intricately connected to her proximity to the royal court. But it was largely Rousseau, in one of his most widely read works, *Julie, or the New Heloise* (*Julie ou la Nouvelle Héloïse*), published in 1761, who depicted the Parisienne across social classes as inordinately concerned with fashion and artifice as a symbol of status, preoccupied with drawing attention to herself, and talented in seduction,[2] laying the groundwork for many of the associations that developed later.

Parisian elegance and refinement in dress, appearance, and manner, as it became prized (and embellished) in the following century, wasn't reserved for the elite. That emphasis trickled down to the most modest working-class girls. The rise of structured prostitution up through the Belle Époque largely fed the myth of the *erotic* Parisienne, an association that evolved further with the rise of pleasure houses and hedonist theaters. And the first modern department store, Le Bon Marché, cannot be overlooked for its role in cultivating the image of the modern, modish Parisienne, and spreading it beyond French borders.

The store, opened in 1852 by Aristide and Marguerite Boucicaut, revolutionized the retail experience and established a model of modern commerce that laid the foundation for stores all over the world, from Macy's to Selfridges. M. Boucicaut incited desire by allowing women to touch and try products. Prices were fixed, and he ran occasional sales, replenished stock, and rolled out seasonal fashions that inspired the Parisian woman to reinvent herself incessantly.[3] As a result, women from outside of Paris flocked to the store, some even applying for jobs. The Parisian woman was now admired for the multitude of representations that writers, painters, and popular culture built around her, and those images would follow her in various forms up to and after World War II. With her *garçonne* style, Chanel stepped in and rocked fashion by freeing women from corsets and oppressive garments, and Brigitte Bardot, the inveterate coquette, anchored the Parisienne to an image of sexual

revolution and liberty in the 1960s and 1970s that has yet to be shaken off for a foreign audience.

A combination of those long-standing associations carry over into the modern image of the Parisian woman that's played out over and over again, set to the backdrop of her city, equally as romanticized. Paris is Kate Moss's costar, for example, in the ad campaign for Yves Saint Laurent's perfume Parisienne, the two myths—city and woman—converging into one unmistakable image: luxury, elegance, femininity, money. "The myth retains its power, even finding ways to be reinvented, through its legacy and a database of images and clichés used by the industries of fashion, advertising, and tourism,"[4] writes historian Emmanuelle Retaillaud-Bajac. In other words, it doesn't matter if there is truth behind the stereotypes; there is enough material to keep the lore alive.

LA PARISIENNE TODAY

Where does that leave us today? With what Nigerian novelist and feminist Chimamanda Ngozi Adichie calls the single story, when complex people are reduced to a single narrative. While she used the misconceptions of Africans as her primary example in her viral TED talk, "The Danger of a Single Story," she noted the universality of a limited perspective. The pernicious, narrow view of Parisian women as white, heterosexual, thin, seductive, and concerned with superficial matters is capitalized on, repurposed, and recirculated as novelty by tourism boards, magazines, books, and brands. And it is dangerous for the same reasons that Adichie highlighted in her talk—"[T]he problem with stereotypes is not that they are untrue, but that they are incomplete. They make one story become the only story."[5]—it strips people of their humanity.

For Alice Pfeiffer, the Franco-British journalist and author of the book *Je ne suis pas Parisienne*, which looked at the myth of the Parisienne in fashion history, it's a story that fits the image the country *wants* to portray. "It works in France's favor to keep whitewashing its image. Then they don't have to address their colonial past," she says. And the ideal, today? "The May 1968[6] pre-maternal body, reflected by figures such as Jane Birkin, Françoise Hardy, or France Gall, became the one face of liberation that stuck forever, which virtually no one can attain." Or at least, it hinges upon only a select few actually being able to mimic it, but everyone else absolutely believing they might be able to.

---

opposite La Rotonde Stalingrad, a popular hangout for many women in this book.

This creates a distorted standard of personal worth where the unachievable is perpetually presented as the golden ticket to happiness. For too many years, I genuinely believed that if I just followed the trends, and bought that scarf and that bag, and pushed myself hard enough at the gym, I'd blend into the mold and become the ultimate version of myself. It's hard to say what the bigger betrayal was—the lies I was told about the way Parisian women behaved and lived or being hoodwinked by them for so long.

The danger in anchoring the Parisian woman to a white, heteronormative standard, whatever the ill-founded reasons may be, is that it leaves little to no room for the rest of the population. Society has reached an impasse in the way women are portrayed universally. If women are actively demanding change around the world, why should it be any different in Paris? Why should an entire set of the French population be reduced to one or two qualifiers?

When I look around me as I navigate the city, almost none of the women I observe resemble the effete avatar so neatly painted for us. The woman I see is white, black, Arab, Jewish, Muslim, Asian, African, South American, slender, curvy, petite, and sky-high. Some are in wheelchairs. Some have style; some are indifferent to whatever the Western ideas of style imply. Some believe makeup is a form of self-expression; others shy from the unwanted attention it may bring. They are teachers, shopkeepers, entrepreneurs, mothers, mentors, writers, singers, artists, innovators, chefs, and all far more than the sum of their experiences. They are Parisiennes—not necessarily born in the city or even born in France but residents of the city of Paris and its bordering suburbs.

The women in this book, like the millions of other women that walk the city with them, aren't *new* in the sense that they are novel; they've always been here. But rarely do they get the spotlight or the megaphone they deserve.

ABOUT THE WOMEN

I've never been a deeply religious person, but I do believe in fortuitous connections, some of the purely professional variety, others more spiritual. Such encounters inspired this book. So in thinking about who I would include in a project meant to reflect but a small sample of the extraordinary women in Paris and Greater Paris, I first looked to my own circle. I saw that I was surrounded by many inspiring entrepreneurs, experts, creatives, and change-makers, among them Elena Rossini, Rahaf Harfoush, Nida Januskis, Julie Mathieu, Muriel Tallandier, and Ajiri Aki. Then I thought about the women whose work I had long admired,

"A woman's appearance is part of the country's source of national pride and therefore her body belongs to the national gaze." —ALICE PFEIFFER

read about, stumbled upon, or felt inspired by in some way (whittling down that list was painful!). The final collection includes both women I've known, to varying degrees, for years and have gotten to know on a much deeper level through our conversations for this book, and women I've had the immense pleasure of meeting for the first time. In most cases, I have chosen to weave in my connection to and impressions of each woman for clarity and transparency.

Not all of the women I spoke to have had felicitous lives or grew up with great ease. But all of them, like every woman I know, are battling something or working toward something, guided by their own moral compass and those of the women who uplift them. What I have found inspiring and nourishing is to learn how other women channel their pain and frustrations into greatness—their own personal greatness, whatever that may look like.

This selection is by no means complete—if I could, I would have interviewed hundreds of women from other industries and backgrounds. But I hope this will be the beginning of a new way of thinking about not only the women of Paris and the way they are inhabiting the city, but about women in general. I've learned a lot about myself and my home from all of these women. Not only about the city's challenges and shortcomings but about its everlasting power to transform. May these stories be as edifying for you to read as they were for me to uncover.

AND A PRACTICAL NOTE . . .

Each woman has shared a handful of places and spaces in the city that she loves, which you will discover throughout the book, including through the photography. Much like *The New Paris* was meant to be a window to seeing and experiencing the city from a new perspective, it was important to me that this book also include a practical component: travel advice that invites visitors, new and returning, to explore Paris differently and support women-run businesses along the way. A complete list of those addresses can be found in "Their Paris Guide" on page 306, which I hope you'll let inspire your next visit to the city.

following spread L'Officine Universelle Buly, cofounded by Victoire de Taillac (see page 102).

ABRICOT

Officine Universelle
Buly
fondée en 1803

LAVANDE

Officine Universelle
Buly
fondée en 1803

BEFORE YOU BEGIN: A CULTURAL PRIMER

THERE ARE A NUMBER OF THEMES, terms, and ideas that are evoked throughout the profiles and conversations featured in this book that may be unfamiliar to you. I've included background and context below to help you navigate some of these concepts as you read. Feel free to refer back to this page as you go along.

LAÏCITÉ

Study French culture or spend any length of time living in France and you'll quickly understand how strongly the French feel about the separation of church and state, or *laïcité*, as their version of state secularism is known. But it's more than secularism; it also refers to the "role of the state in protecting individuals from the claims of religion."[7] A sacrosanct principle of republican universalism, it's both fiercely debated and protected.

While the concept's roots can be traced back to the French Revolution, the theory wasn't written into law until 1905 and was initially introduced to keep religion, specifically the Catholic Church, out of the affairs of the state while also guaranteeing individual religious liberty.

Among the guiding principles, as stated in Articles 1 and 2: *the republic ensures freedom of conscience but does not recognize, promote or subsidize any religion.* In order to promote the freedom of individual conscience, the state must maintain a position of neutrality to protect citizens' ability to practice or maintain atheistic beliefs. Public workers of all kinds, from schoolteachers to transportation agents, town hall officials, and even nurses, must refrain from wearing anything overtly religious.

---

opposite A café institution in Belleville, a neighborhood where many cultures, religions, and ways of life collide.

As Islam has emerged as the country's second most prominent religion, certain critics have noted that extensions of the 1905 law have been seen less as necessary to ensuring the freedoms of French citizens but rather as attempts to suppress the perceived threat of Islam on the nation. Since 1989 (the first *affaire du voile*), French debate has hotly contested whether young girls could wear the head scarf in schools. This led to the now-infamous 2004 law prohibiting "conspicuous" signs of religious affiliation in public schools, like large crosses, head scarves, kippahs, and turbans, and followed seven years later with the 2011 ban on sporting burkas and niqabs in public places. France was the first European nation to make this prohibition official.

It was a recurring topic of conversation during my interviews, particularly with Sarah Zouak, Rokhaya Diallo, and Delphine Horvilleur, who believe that the principle of laïcité is just but its meaning has been lost or distorted, in some cases to enforce assimilation and segment swaths of the population.

Why this obsession with the head scarf in the first place? There are entire books written on the topic, but the answers offered by Joan Wallach Scott in her work *The Politics of the Veil*, for example, highlight that the reasons run far deeper than the perception of the veil as an "emblem of radical Islamic politics" or oppression. The ban on the veil, she says, is about the "desire to eliminate rather than address the growing challenge to French republicanism posed by the aftermath of its colonial history."[8]

Other theorists, like Andrew Aguilar, a doctoral candidate at Sciences Po Paris and a fellow at the IC Migrations think tank, believe the issue expresses traditional growing pains exhibited by all nation-states. "While framed as a crisis to the pre-existing political order, almost all developed nation-states experience this issue in one way or another as minority populations begin expressing new values or demanding additional rights," he told me by email. "The French state has engaged in extensive efforts to improve the living and educational situations of migrant populations and while it is not perfect, it is far from saying the state wants to eliminate cultural diversity."

The term, as you can see, is more loaded than what *separation of church and state* might suggest, so I have chosen to use *laïcité* whenever the idea is discussed.

IDENTITY

Crystallizing what it means to be French has been a looming preoccupation among the country's philosophical and political elite, one that can certainly be traced to the devastating Algerian War of Independence from France (1954–62). There was a great migration of Algerian families to France after independence (though that was not the first; it began in the run-up to World War I) and a feeling, still experienced today by second- and third-generation Algerians born in France, that they are outsiders. But it wasn't until the 1980s when, in response to both the antiracism movement and the emergence of the far right as many decades of North African immigration became more visible in the public sphere, a panel of philosophers and historians, which included Marceau Long and Dominique Schnapper, developed an understanding of national identity.[9] While the historical tradition of republicanism often emphasized the importance of civic engagement, this panel crystallized the specific historical and cultural dynamics of French citizenship. Since, the understanding has been that to be French connotes civic duty more than ethnicity. This is also deeply intertwined with the next two themes.

RACE, MODEL MINORITIES, AND THE ISSUE OF *COMMUNAUTARISME*

Communautarisme (or *communalism*) emphasizes that the individual cannot exist independently of their ethnic, cultural, religious, sexual, or social affiliations. It has been defined as "the priority of the group over national identity in the lives of individuals."[10] In essence, it is the multicultural model embraced in countries like the United States, England, and Australia, where individuals "derive a strong part of their personal identity from their backgrounds and histories"[11] and still live together as part of one nation. It's also a word in heavy rotation in France and always employed as a pejorative.

Multiculturalism in the American understanding, as cited above, is largely seen as incompatible with the more narrow conception of French identity, which favors "a single indivisible republic that makes no distinction among its citizens."[12] You are French before you are anything else—Jewish, Muslim, black, Asian, Arab, Hispanic, lesbian, trans—which should remain parenthetical along with all other affiliations.

In this universalist theory, everyone is equal and equally French; "any division of the Republic into individual identity groups"[13] must be prevented. As a result, the state does not conduct censuses or collect data on race, ethnicity, or religion (in fact, such statistics are associated with Nazi Germany and collaborationists).[14] It is believed that emphasizing ethnoreligious differences in its citizens is dangerous to the country's values and "only serves to distance them from their essential Frenchness."[15] If France is color-blind, then it follows that there is no need to categorize the population and therefore no issue with or basis for racism. This hinges, however, upon not only "swearing allegiance to the nation but by assimilating to the norms of its culture."[16]

Of course, color-blind the country is not. Because of this flawed universalist approach, serious issues of discrimination and racism run deep, and absent are the tools to measure and combat them sufficiently. Adding fuel to the taboo race debate was the removal of the word *race* tout court from the French constitution in 2018 (a campaign promise by former president François Hollande).[17] Gender replaced race in the first article of the text, now reading that France "shall ensure the equality of all citizens before the law, regardless of origin, gender or religion."

Critics viewed the change as yet another sign of deep "discomfort with evoking race," not only in France but across Europe. Denying the very existence of race, says Rokhaya Diallo (see page 47), doesn't eliminate racism or the discussion around it, but means "denying the reality of racial discrimination. The constitutional framework has a deep impact on the policies that are defined by the government. And there is nothing more dangerous than a country that refuses to see its most obvious issues."[18]

There's an important disjuncture between the idea of Frenchness as best demonstrated by an immutable loyalty to the republic and the reality wherein minorities are often treated as inferior whether they've assimilated or not. The examples are numerous of French men and women of color being treated as equals when they are "exemplary"—winning football matches, saving babies from falling out of windows, excelling in academics—but instantly being reduced to their origins when they fail, fumble, or fall in with the wrong crowd. The crushing pressure to be a "model minority" to justify their legitimacy comes up in conversation with Leïla Slimani (page 181) and Sarah Zouak (page 130), both of whom are French citizens.

On paper, the French don't expect or require the effacement of another identity. Emigrating from Senegal or being born in France to Senegalese parents, for example, doesn't mean a person must abandon all connections to their origins. But for the former French ambassador to the United States Gérard Araud, roots are "an individual reality." That's what he wrote in a letter to comedian Trevor Noah after the *Daily Show* host joked on air that the French team winning the 2018 World Cup was, in fact, a win for Africa, given that 80 percent of the players were of African descent. Araud explained his rationale, saying, "By calling them an African team, it seems you are denying their Frenchness. This, even in jest, legitimizes the ideology which claims whiteness as the only definition of being French."[19] Where the multiculturalist American model allows people the freedom to be different but still be American, in France, assimilationism remains the dominant stance on diversity and immigration.

But assimilation and citizenship aren't inherent protections, which Grégory Pierrot addressed in a powerful essay on navigating France as a Frenchman with a mother from Martinique. "No matter how French I actually was, no matter how well I knew French history, how well I spoke or wrote, how beholden to French values of *liberté, égalité, fraternité*, how connected to culture I was, there would be Frenchmen to fly the *Drapeau tricolore* in my face as a reminder that for them, against all aforementioned values, my skin alone was proof that I would never quite be French."[20]

Central to the debate about who gets to be French today is a philosophical quandary on identity that was never actually resolved by those philosophers—what is innate, what is genetic, and what is inherited? Some of the conversations in this book highlight how painful the discussion continues to be, particularly for those who find themselves dangling in the discomfort of *presque* Français (almost French).

ANTIRACIST

Several women in this book, including Rokhaya Diallo (page 47), call themselves antiracists. This can be understood as anyone "of any racial or ethnic background who takes a personal, active role in challenging systemic racism."[21]

FEMINISM AND AN INTERSECTIONAL APPROACH

Feminism in France has evolved considerably since Simone de Beauvoir published *The Second Sex*. Many of the feminist activists in this book have made it clear that the word alone, slowly but surely, is shaking off its taboo. Still, feminists find themselves having to reiterate that feminism is not about gender wars but about a social movement fighting for equality and against sexist oppression. And they're doing so in a variety of different ways.

Today, there are as many interpretations of feminism as there are women, with micromovements within that fight for equality. Clear distinctions in ideology, however, can be made. When it comes to the self-identified feminists in this book, they generally adhere to an intersectional approach. While they are among the most vocal, they know they have yet to tip the balance and become the majority.

French feminism has long had a reputation for universalism and gender essentialism (and therefore has been generally aligned with patriarchal ideology). Its most prominent figures have been white, bourgeoise, cis-gendered, and able-bodied and share the opinion that the fight is, more or less, the same for all women. In the eyes of feminist fashion journalist and author Alice Pfeiffer, the particularity of these French feminists is that they are more interested in speaking for their privileged class (and maintaining their positions within it) than speaking for their entire gender. As she puts it, the dominant contingent "is against the head scarf; pro-sex in a way that seems apologetic to male sexuality; anti-pornography and prostitution; believes that dressing sexy is a sign of gender betrayal and that feminism should have limits" (cue the 2018 Catherine Deneuve- and Catherine Millet-signed manifesto in *Le Monde* denouncing #MeToo and defending *une liberté d'importuner, indispensable à la liberté sexuelle*—how men should have the freedom to "bother," a concept indispensable to sexual freedom. In other words, a man's "right" to seduce).[22]

This philosophy is perhaps best represented by Élisabeth Badinter, among the country's most widely known universalist feminists and intellectuals and the most mainstream insofar as her books, often controversial, on the culture of motherhood and women's independence, have been national bestsellers. The causes she has championed over the years have also been subject to controversy, particularly her public support for the 2005 head scarf ban and the 2011 burqa law, as she believes these dress codes are oppressive largely because they are "traditional."[23] In an open letter to Muslim women at the time of the vote, Badinter wrote, "I believe that what's good for me—liberty—is good for you."[24] Which is another way of saying the traditions of "other" cultures are necessarily an impediment to women's freedoms and therefore this must be done to protect them.

The emerging generation of feminist voices, some of whom you will meet in these pages, insists that it's not about wearing the head scarf or opting not to, rejecting cosmetics or adornment, losing weight or gaining it, surgically transforming our bodies or leaving them be, having five kids or five cats, pursuing a career or staying home to raise children—it's about having the freedom to *choose* without judgment. They are adamant that intersectionality, a theory developed in the United States in the late 1980s by civil rights advocate and scholar Kimberlé Crenshaw that only found a footing in France in the last few years, is the only way forward.

In feminism, intersectionality suggests that the fight for equality isn't created equal by nature of the disadvantages and inequalities that many nonwhite, nonbinary, non-able-bodied women face. Those oppressions take different forms and often compound themselves, as does a person's ability to resist and navigate them, but are largely based on constraints that attend one's class, race, sexual orientation, nationality, and religion. Recognizing and understanding these different dimensions, says Rebecca Amsellem (page 55), is an act of solidarity.[25]

---

opposite A busy corner in Belleville, a dynamic and multicultural neighborhood.

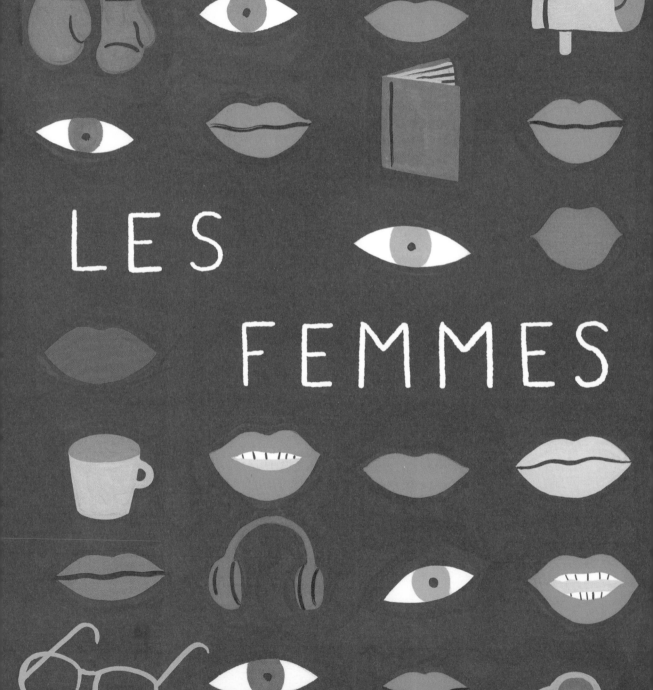

LES FEMMES

Hé toi
Qu'est-ce que tu regardes ?
T'as jamais vu une femme qui se bat
Suis-moi
Dans la ville blafarde
Et je te montrerai
Comme je mords, comme j'aboie

Hey you
What are you looking at ?
You've never seen a woman fight ?
Follow me
In the pale city
And I will show you
As I bite, as I bark

—CLARA LUCIANI, VERSE FROM THE SONG "LA GRENADE"

Leading the new wave of French feminism

LAUREN BASTIDE

CREATOR AND HOST OF *LA POUDRE* PODCAST

SHE IS AMONG THE MOST PROMINENT mouthpieces of the current generation's intersectional fight for equality (see pages 27–28 for more on this concept). In fact, even people only tangentially familiar with Lauren Bastide and her podcast *La Poudre*, which stoked the popularity of podcasting in France, know she represents the intrepid group of modern feminists having frank conversations about gender, race, class, and sexuality. It's through early adoption and strategic use of digital platforms that she has been able to give an unfiltered voice to the underrepresented, cultivating a group of resisters one episode and Instagram post at a time.

We meet in the leafy courtyard of Hotel Amour, a café that doubles as her secondary office when she's not at the headquarters of Nouvelles Écoutes, the podcast network she cofounded in 2016. She sets her blue baseball cap on the banquette, shakes out her wavy blond hair, and thanks me warmly for taking an interest in her story. That I've been following her work with interest since 2009, when she was still a journalist at *Elle* magazine, would be understating the truth. At the time, I was dipping my feet into the Parisian fashion pool and looking for insights on the Parisian woman in all of her complexity. I didn't care deeply about fashion designers, but I was eager to understand the role that material culture and aesthetic arts, craftsmanship and style played in the everyday life of the Parisienne. And even then, Bastide's name surfaced time and again. She was the woman to watch.

Bastide was born and raised in Orléans, a moneyed Catholic town an hour from Paris that she describes with the kind of aversion that comes from being made to feel like an outsider in your own home. "People held balls organized by their aristocratic descendants so that their children could marry amongst each other," she describes, raising her eyebrows as if to say, *See what I mean?* Ideologically and

"I don't know what else to do with the mic but give it to someone who doesn't have one."

demographically, she didn't fit in. "My social status was a handicap in my school. Everyone was classist because my parents weren't as educated as theirs were; my family owned shops and hair salons downtown and I stood out among the children of doctors and teachers." The women in her family gathered on the weekend to flip through the pages of French *Elle*, fantasizing about runway shows and the grandeur of Paris. Where religion and tradition characterized the community around her, she felt pulled toward aesthetics and art. Her place, she knew, was somewhere in Paris.

Despite the confines of her environment, she always marched to her own drum. That trait ultimately served her well, throughout journalism school and the ten years she worked for *Elle*. By the time I discovered her, she was on her way to becoming editor in chief and was known for having her finger on the pulse of Parisian society— its preoccupying cultural stories, its next big disruptors (she prophesied the rise of bloggers and the "influencers" that would follow)—and emphasizing the human side of fashion, not its frivolity.

She brought journalistic rigor from her training in news reporting and was always engaging to read. There was heart where for other writers there was obligation. "Foreigners know *Elle* as a monthly glossy but as a weekly in France, we covered news and reported stories. We could write about Balenciaga and the burqa in the same issue, which I liked." Still, she had even higher ambitions for the magazine. She wanted to cover the underrepresented for whom having it all was anything but a philosophical debate. She envisioned stories on police violence, racism, prostitution—more than the thorny concerns of the magazine's imagined core readership: Parisienne born-and-bred, white, heteronormative, thin, and bourgeoise, with the trifecta of career, husband, and children. *La totale.*

"It's a violent double bind for the women who don't check those boxes," she says, adding that her political consciousness sharpened over time as she realized she was addressing a target audience that didn't actually exist and didn't represent the population. Where were the cosmetics reviews for darker skin tones, size twelve-plus ready-to-wear, and diversity in the models? She found answers for the glaring absences in representation in the teachings of influential thinkers Angela Davis and Édouard Glissant. By that point, clashes with a new editorial director ensued, pressures from advertisers mounted, and the idea of changing the system became pure fantasy. She knew it was time to go.

---

opposite A clear view of the Sacré-Coeur from South Pigalle in the 9th arrondissement, Lauren Bastide's home turf.

"La Parisienne is from the suburbs or from foreign or immigrant parents. It's diversity that's going to shake up Parisian culture."

The turbulent year she spent next as a panelist on the late-night show *Le Grand Journal*, fighting to be heard on and off camera, only fueled the development of *La Poudre*. "It was a good day if they let me speak for sixty seconds. As maddening as it was, I didn't want to give them the pleasure of breaking me down. I spent my days with my Nouvelles Écoutes cofounder Julien Neuville building my show, creating the business, then I'd go to work at five p.m. with a big smile. I used all the financial stability I had from that gig to build the business."

While enrolled in a master's degree program in gender studies at the Université Paris 8, she set out to build an influential podcast network, the Gimlet Media of France. Her show *La Poudre*, now with over 2.5 million downloads, became its calling card, dominating the French zeitgeist in the manner of *This American Life* or *Serial*. By the end of season one, with greater confidence and a solid following, the episodes had a decidedly more potent urgency as Bastide discussed timely aspects of women's issues with artists, thinkers, and change-makers, her voice mellifluous but always firm. Within the intimacy of a Parisian hotel room, she has spoken to afro-feminist and documentary filmmaker Amandine Gay about growing up adopted and the fetishization of black bodies; she has discussed rape, mother-daughter relationships, and sexual orientation with author Sophie Fontanel; and she welcomed activist Daria Marx to speak about fat-phobia in France and the problems with the "body-positive" movement. In 2018, she launched the first English-recorded interview with the British bestselling author and journalist Reni Eddo-Lodge.

Ask her loyal listeners what makes her approach so refreshing—which she extends to discussion series and the moderated talks she hosts—and the answer is always the same: She sets up the discussion, asks the right questions, then takes herself out of it. She lets the other woman's voice lead. "I create something that appears to be cosmetic on the surface but the message is subversive and political. The voices I feature want revolution, like me. I give a megaphone to activist women who speak directly into the ears of young girls, many of whom listen from the best neighborhoods of the country." The way to raise awareness and enact real change, in other words, is by penetrating invisible boundaries. Bastide is a bridge connecting the fighters, the marginalized, the discriminated, and the privileged. With her help, the future for la Parisienne is an enlightened one.

Her Paris

FAVORITE WOMAN-RUN BUSINESS?
The Carreau du Temple (shown above), run by Sandrina Martins, who is brilliant. She leads a social and cultural space that is open and free to all Parisians.

PREFERRED NEIGHBORHOOD?
Around la rue des Martyrs, where I've lived for fifteen years. I've observed its changes and am part of its history. It's a little village: My kids give kisses to the baker; I run into people I know all the time, families with young kids who have "grown up" with me.

WHERE DO YOU GO TO BE ALONE?
I love going to exhibits alone. The Musée du Quai Branly, the Palais de Tokyo, and especially the Jeu de Paume are where I often find powerful themes that connect with the questions I'm grappling with.

Driving awareness for the emancipation of disabled people

ELISA ROJAS

LAWYER AND DISABILITY-RIGHTS ACTIVIST

ELISA ROJAS ISN'T BEING HYPERBOLIC when she says she adores Paris. Her eyes flicker and her smile widens the moment I ask her what moves her about the city as we sip macchiatos at Le Bistrot du Peintre in the blissful lull of August. She's not a big spender, she tells me, but loves to observe the way the upper echelon of Parisian society lives; the boutiques they frequent, the clothes they buy. "It's proof of the disparities that exist," she says emphatically. She loves beautiful things but wonders if one can be interested in the futile while being an activist. She doesn't have the answer yet.

After arriving from Chile as a child, she lived at the gates of the city before moving with her family into what she considers the bustling heart of real Paris, a unique pocket of the 12th arrondissement that both maintains the spirit of its working-class roots and draws in a mixed crowd for its ever-expanding culinary scene. "It's terrible to say, but I rarely leave—the neighborhood has everything I need!" It's teetering on the cusp of being too gentrified, though, and she says its diversity is fundamental to its soul. Still, this is home. Nowhere but this city fills her with what she calls a "stupid" level of pride. "I mean, look at it," she says, gesturing to the street as if no explanation was actually needed. "It's because we know we're associated with a city interconnected with beauty and culture that so many people dream of experiencing."

That profound love for the city and a desire to experience it with greater ease and access are among the things that Rojas, an employment lawyer, has in mind when she fires up her computer to write, tweet, and connect with an engaged community of activists. She is among the most sought-after voices on disability rights and uses Twitter, her blog, and the collective she cofounded, CHLEE (Collectif Lutte et

Handicaps pour l'Égalité et l'Émancipation, or the Struggle and Disabilities Collective for Equality and Emancipation), to raise a magnifying glass to the country's failures to enable disabled people to participate as full citizens in society.

It's a role she's not even fully comfortable with occupying—she dislikes being on camera and is discerning about the interviews she'll give to the press. Truthfully, she was initially reluctant to be part of this book. But when she considers that the unemployment rate sits at 18 percent among disabled job seekers, twice as high as the national average, and the median income of disabled individuals creeps in at 18,500 euros per year, more than 11 percent less than that of the able-bodied,[26] she sees her ability to fight and speak up as a luxury, a tool she must wield.

"Journalists have a tendency to perpetuate the image of handicapped people as either being sad and vulnerable or heroic for simply getting up and brushing their teeth in the morning," she insists. *Despite their handicap* goes the common refrain, as if a disability is fundamentally incompatible with a regular existence. "Wherever possible, we're woven into inspiration porn," she explains, adding that even her seemingly inexplicable success story—going to school, studying law, becoming a lawyer, using the tools she learned in school to defend her ideas—has the makings of an inspirational tearjerker meant to uplift the able-bodied. What she carries with her is a firm message: the words used to tell these stories matter.

They matter when she takes aim at laws that are passed but never enforced; at Sophie Cluzel, the secretary of state who represents issues relevant to people with disabilities under the prime minister, for her spurious ideas of inclusivity and barely veiled ableism seeping through each of her self-congratulatory tweets; and all those who couch their indifference in the plight of disabled people with moral platitudes and marketing campaigns that check boxes more than they drive real impact. She can be lacerating in her fury about the systemic dismissal of disabled individuals, like herself, and the denial of their humanity. She may roll her eyes at the casting of able-bodied actors in the roles of disabled characters but vehemently denounces prevailing representations of the handicapped body as abnormal or deformed. Worse yet are the representations of disabled women. "We're first infantilized and then perhaps seen as women and therefore infantilized a second time. But we're not even really recognized as women; we're perpetually asexual little girls." They are doubly burdened.

On paper, everything she's fighting for sounds entirely reasonable. Disabled people in France should be more visible. They should be able to live autonomously. Their rights should be equally as important to society and to governing bodies as

"We have to stop telling the able-bodied that becoming handicapped is the end, that it's the worst thing that could happen to them—there IS life to lead and we're working to make sure the conditions are good for those who are currently disabled and those who might become disabled."

those of the able-bodied. Concern for such rights and representation was even a pillar of President Emmanuel Macron's election campaign. And yet the progress toward achieving any of this is perhaps decades behind the United States whose disability rights activists and supporters have inspired action and antidiscrimination policy since the 1970s,[27] leading to the Americans with Disabilities Act of 1990. The law also helped lift handicap and disability out of a purely medical model of treatment (where the disability is viewed as a problem that concerns only the individual) into a social model. While an antidiscrimination law in France does exist, its shortcomings are legion, and the country lacks the power in numbers among activists to lead to any kind of long-term autonomous movement in defense of the emancipation of the disabled. "France still believes it's up to disabled people to adapt to life and not for the country to adapt to them. The real paradox lies not in the fact of being handicapped and living one's life but in not being able to do something because of well-documented systemic oppression that needs fixing."

The oppression she's referring to operates on several levels in France. There are the recent changes that have weakened a law[28] that was intended to ensure accessible housing in the construction of new buildings, and the most glaring discrimination, that which Rojas has made her cause célèbre in her fight for awareness: institutionalization. Since the 1950s, the medicosocial system has been designed around specialized institutions, managed by private nonprofit organizations that are largely subsidized by the state. These are pushed as the only path for disabled individuals. While the objective was supposedly to address their specific needs in the best way possible, the price to pay for those impacted is a total lack of freedom and autonomy. "The problem with these specialized institutions, beyond the perpetual conflict of interest between the management associations and the state, is that it leads to real social and spatial segregation." She speaks from experience—the first seven years of her life were spent in and out of one such institution.

It's not only an infringement of their rights, but it promotes abuse, which often goes undetected because these spaces are cut off from the world. "It's sabotage. The legal framework I acquired opened my eyes to the rights I *did* have that weren't being respected. The idea isn't actually to make us autonomous financially or professionally. That would mean a loss of power for these associations."

In 2017, preliminary observations by a visiting reporter from the United Nations Human Rights Office of the High Commissioner confirmed much of Rojas's own observations about the dysfunctions of France's paternalistic approach and concluded that the country must completely transform its system on the basis of human rights, with a focus on truly inclusive, environmental, and societal solutions that favor an autonomous life.[29]

As for life in Paris, infrastructural improvements are made but painfully slowly. "We don't have the same freedoms as other Parisians; we don't have the same choices. I can appreciate the beauty of Paris, but I can't take advantage of everything." But she highlights the salient point, the most obvious and yet the easiest to overlook, that she doesn't and will never know what it's like to experience the streets of Paris on her own. The city offers alternatives and solutions, but there is often something lacking—dedicated elevators in buildings that malfunction and are never repaired, ramps on public transport that a driver can't maneuver—that reminds her that the disabled population remains an afterthought. "Accessibility isn't just providing the equipment; it's making sure people are trained to use it properly."

The road is long, but her tireless efforts to ensure there is broader awareness and support among *all* citizens aren't in vain. And while she may only be an observer of some facets of Parisian life, she can embrace it if the laws and institutions help make her life, and the lives of all citizens, as fulfilling as possible. "I believe in us," she says, pushing her coffee cup off to the side. "We're capable of doing so much."

Her Paris

FAVORITE WOMAN-RUN BUSINESS?

The vintage shop Mamz'Elle Swing, which is run by a wonderful woman dressed head to toe in forties/fifties looks. She sells clothes and accessories. I love it!

A HAPPY PLACE?

Galeries Lafayette (shown above)! But not only for the mercantile side of things. When I'm there, I'm awed by the past, both the Art Nouveau beauty of the store and what I know of its beginnings, including the fact that it employed women in sales from all social and economic backgrounds, giving them financial emancipation.

YOUR CULTURE FIX?

I love to go to the Musée des Arts Décoratifs and the Centre Pompidou, but I don't go to learn something. I go to see what the experience stirs in me.

Fighting for racial, gender, and religious equality in France

ROKHAYA DIALLO

JOURNALIST, FILMMAKER, AND ANTIRACIST ACTIVIST

ROKHAYA DIALLO IS A WOMAN in the spotlight. As one of the guardians of new French thought, the multihyphenate talent—author, journalist, documentary filmmaker—is a regular commentator on French television and radio, hosts the show *Talk* on BET, cohosts *Kiffe ta Race*, a podcast that explores issues of race in France with personal stories and a dash of humor, and travels the world to speak about systemic racism.

More than one of the few prominent voices representing the black community, she has assumed the role of a bridge between France and the outside world. She pens opinion pieces on discrimination and ethnic profiling for the likes of the *Guardian* and the *Washington Post* (how I initially discovered her), speaks at conferences—including those hosted by the United Nations—and creates films that find captive audiences abroad. Her documentary *De Paris à Ferguson: Coupables d'Être Noirs* (called *Not Yo Mama's Movement* in the US) explored the parallels and distinct differences between the racial tensions and issues of police brutality in the US and France in the wake of the deaths of Trayvon Martin and Michael Brown and the Black Lives Matter movement that followed, and premiered to wide acclaim at Harlem's Schomburg Center for Research in Black Culture in 2016.

So impressive are her credentials one would think she was born into antiracist activism. But when we meet at Le Grand Marché Stalingrad on one of those mild, devastatingly beautiful September afternoons to talk about her journey, she speaks instead of a series of inspirations and then a political awakening.

Born in Paris to Senegalese parents, Diallo spent her early years in the 19th arrondissement and her adolescence in the diverse suburb of La Courneuve, where her skin color was a nonissue. "It was so mixed around me. I was hardly an anomaly. It wasn't until the end of my studies and the beginning of my work life in Paris that I realized I was always the only black girl," she explains matter-of-factly. That's when the *where are you really from?* questioning began and never really stopped. For the first time, she understood that others perceived her differently. "If I'm being asked where I'm from, that means I don't exist in the collective imagination. I'm associated with what is foreign, not French."

Unlike her interest in feminism and alter-globalization, a global justice movement that is "attentive to labor and minority rights, the environment and economic equality,"[30] which developed from following the work of activists and theorists Naomi Klein and Aminata Traoré, the racial question emerged organically. This was the early 2000s, when the debate about the head scarf was intensifying and ethnic profiling was prevalent but had yet to be the incendiary issue it would become. And then it exploded in 2005. The preventable deaths of two French teens of color, Zyed Benna and Bouna Traoré, who had run and hid from police fearing yet another stop-and-search, triggered three weeks of revolt that underscored the deep racial and social divide plaguing much of French society. It also set Diallo's activism into motion.

By day, she worked in production for Disney Television France, and on the side, she contributed to the causes she believed in. In 2007, she cofounded Les Indivisibles, an organization that deconstructed prejudice and discrimination through humor and parody. "We even created a ceremony to award each year's most racist remarks in the media. No one was safe!" she recalls, cracking a wide smile.

It's at this point in the conversation that I become acutely aware of how quickly Diallo can go from terribly serious, with an almost mournful glint to her eyes, to joyful and light. And she speaks swiftly, like a woman who's been cut off one too many times. This emotional range and expressiveness in her convictions are part of what drew notice from the casting director of a television network who invited her to speak about her newfound activism on a show. A spark was lit: With incredible ease on camera and astute commentary, she soon received other invitations to speak, write, and develop her ideas. Before long, she left her day job to become one of few black journalists visible on mainstream media platforms, from RTL radio to BET and LCI television networks, where she could debate the defining sociopolitical issues of her generation each week.

But it's a journey that has been met with considerable resistance.

The core of her work is fighting for racial, gender, and religious equality to make France the inclusive country she still reserves a touch of hope that it

"France can't address race at home but they can talk about race in the US; they'd vote for Obama but not Mamadou. Black Americans benefit from the cachet of the United States—it erases the fact that they're black. But us, here? We're associated with otherness, and so in the collective imagination, we are inferior."

can become. In the face of rising populism, she calls into question the ability of the republic to serve and protect all French citizens with its values of unity. She tackles identity in all its discomfiting and controversial truth in the French context—like how "if you are Arab or black, or merely perceived as Arab or black in France, you're twenty times as likely to be subject to identity checks by police. That's what I call state racism [the term is *institutional racism* in the United States],"[31] she explains.

Therein lies her trouble: She brings race into the discussion of French identity where it was intentionally left absent. In doing so, she upends the established narrative. When she spoke about institutional racism in France, she was immediately reproached. On Twitter, where she is perhaps the most vocal, she opines on simmering racial discrimination, calls out the failings of the justice system, and encourages people to see beyond the neatly codified understanding of Frenchness. As a result, not a day goes by where she isn't the target of verbal abuse and cyber harassment.

Her critics, cowering behind their computer screens, anime avatars, phony usernames, and, often, political credentials, call her a radical *communautariste* (see pages 25–27 for more on this concept). And they do so from the comfortable remove of white privilege and a steadfast belief in the universalist vision of France. I've watched as the tweets come at her like an avalanche, goading her to take responsibility for the incivilities and bad behaviors of blacks, Arabs, and any number of marginalized individuals to justify her stance on injustice. And they rebuke her when they assume she hasn't taken a public position on any number of world events or catastrophes. "They get filed under #ouetiezvousrokhaya (#WhereWereYouRokhaya), to try to find some element of humor in all of this," she says, though I know she wishes she didn't have to.

In cases of online harassment with bigoted or abusive remarks, the sequence of events is usually the same: Someone crosses the line, her supporters report the

"I feel so much more Parisian and French when I travel than when I'm at home. Here, I have to justify myself."

abuse, and the accounts often get suspended. But when attacks come from the mainstream media or public figures, the jousting can go on for days. In one such instance, an old clip of Diallo speaking on the show *C Politique* resurfaced on Twitter. In it, she explains how difficult it is for people of color in France to find certain products adapted to their skin tone. "I said, 'It's a permanent issue to live in a country that gives you the impression that you don't exist because nothing is created with you in mind; not Band-Aids, not hairdressers, not foundation. We can't buy our cosmetic products in the supermarket.'" When one user suggested she try invisible Band-Aids, she responded factually: The compress is white and therefore visible on darker skin. The exchange went viral and devolved into a barrage of mocking, racist, and misogynistic tweets from the usual trolls to even the (far-right) mayor of the southern town of Béziers—*Is she offended by her white teeth too? What other household objects might Rokhaya claim as racist next?*

This behavior persists because there's nothing more dangerous and primally terrifying to the established order than a woman with a voice. For centuries, society has expected women not to defend themselves and to, instead, repress their anger. And as a black woman who is repeatedly told not to rock the boat or complain but feel grateful for having "made it," Diallo goes against decorum. She fights back, knowing that her words matter and draw attention to the failures the country has tried and continues to try to sweep under the rug. And so she remains a thorn in the sides of any and all who, as she says, "aren't ready to confront the truths they don't want to see."

Still, she's not overly concerned with making enemies nor with the seriousness of the threats made against her online (among the most heinous, that she should be handed over to the KKK)—mostly because she doesn't believe they're much more than posturing. Still, when she can't speak freely at home, she speaks abroad. "France is stuck in an identity crisis," wrote Diallo in an opinion piece for the *Guardian* in 2018, following the news that a student union leader wearing a hijab was attacked by the media, "unable to recognize all its citizens and apparently frightened of its own multicultural reflection."[32] If her words find a willing foreign audience, it's

---

opposite Minoi (Faubourg 43), one of Rokhaya Diallo's favorite clothings stores.

because they're accustomed to discussing issues like race and discrimination more openly. As an observer, particularly one accustomed to the discussions around race that exist in the US, I can't say I've ever found anything unusual or especially polemical in her activism—she is firm but respectful; factual and well researched; constructive in her critiques. Even with all that I know about the French context, I still find it perplexing that one woman can provoke such outsize anger, particularly from institutional sources. Diallo offers an explanation. "They're afraid of what I represent—the possibility for change. Young people are getting active. France is changing. It's the end of a certain comfort and could mean the loss of privileges for [the] elite," she says confidently. "Other voices are forcing their way through in the media space, and that makes them crazy."

As much as Diallo is unflinching in her confrontation of injustice, she is not without hope. "Where there is dialogue, there is possibility."

Her Paris

FAVORITE WOMAN-RUN BUSINESS?

I love the African wax clothing stores Mansaya in the 11th and Minoi (Faubourg 43) in the 10th, which offers pieces made-to-order.

PREFERRED NEIGHBORHOOD?

The 19th arrondissement. It's where I grew up and live now. I think it embodies the best of Paris—the Jewish and Muslim populations, the cultural diversity, the artistic scene. There's so much life here!

SOMETHING YOU DO TO RELAX?

Go to the movies! Right in the neighborhood at the art-house cinemas MK2 Quai de Seine or Quai de Loire (shown above), which sit right across the canal from one another. They show an incredible range of independent and blockbuster films.

Driving the feminist movement of tomorrow

REBECCA AMSELLEM

AUTHOR AND FOUNDER OF *LES GLORIEUSES*

LIBERTÉ, ÉGALITÉ, SORORITÉ. It's the slogan that has defined each installment of *Les Glorieuses*, a weekly newsletter founded by Rebecca Amsellem, since it was first dispatched to subscribers in 2015. With a name that nods to the women, known and unknown, who have forged Amsellem's sense of womanhood, the emails read like missives from your tuned-in best friend, if that friend were speaking to nearly one hundred thousand readers and were regularly invited to comment on feminist issues on television and before the European parliament. Her voice is sisterly, meant to make the newfound feminists among her audience feel comfortable joining the intersectional movement without a deep knowledge of how far women have come and how far they still have to go. But her message also resonates with those who consider themselves enlightened, offering them insightful analysis on the news and current events through a feminist lens.

At its heart, it's a safe space that lifts the blame off women and celebrates them in all of their complexity. As she sees it, her newsletter pays homage to those whose words, sounds, and images remind the world of a woman's power and encourages action. Sporting empowerment merch may be good for the conscience, but what is it doing to help the oppressed? More than an email, *Les Glorieuses* has become a movement for pay equality, it's a book, it's *Les Petites Glo* (the first feminist and cultural newsletter for adolescents), it's a politically engaged group, and it's a club with gatherings organized monthly.

We spoke about her path to activism, the battles that lay ahead for women, and why she doesn't consider herself a figurehead of the movement.

"Around me, I see women who fight, some who decided to follow a traditional path, some who are civically engaged, some who want to make an impact in the world even if it means risking their personal lives. Detached from class, race, or religion, Parisienne is a state of mind."

Looking at your career, would you say you've done what young Rebecca had imagined for herself? I always knew I wanted to have an impact and dedicate my life to making other people's lives better, but I didn't know exactly how to do that. When I was around seven years old, I wanted to be president (obviously!) and even said so in school. My teacher reprimanded me and called in my parents, saying that I had mocked the academic system since my dream wasn't realistic.

So very encouraging of your teacher! How soon did you find yourself leaning toward activism? As a kid, I had a tendency to rise up against everything, without being able to put words to my anger. But I was also very shy. I preferred reading at home to going to birthday parties and sleepovers. My parents were cool with that and I generally had more fun with adults. I wanted to get older to have another view of things. I think my activism developed much later when I fully grasped the injustices and imbalances in society overall. Creating *Les Glorieuses* gave me a structure for my fight.

*The release of your book—*Les Glorieuses: Chroniques d'une féministe*—was timed to the fiftieth anniversary of the May 1968 protests. What would you say is the biggest difference between the feminist fight then and now?* It was really a struggle to be a woman in May 1968. Abortion was still illegal; contraception was legalized only a few months before. It had only been a few years since women could open a bank account in their own name and could work without permission from their husbands. Women were active in the worker and student revolts of '68 and went straight to the barricades. When they realized that nothing was granted to them after the fact, the MLF (*Mouvement de libération des femmes*) was created two years later. It was the beginning of a structured feminist fight to challenge the patriarchy and take control over their bodies. Today, there are a plethora of demands and a diversity of feminist movements. There's not one single figure of feminism in France, but overall it's a fight for choice, to have the best options available to us, and once those choices are made, to ensure there is sorority between women for those choices to be respected.

You've been most vocal about pay inequality. In fact, at the time of writing this, you were leading a campaign to highlight that as of November 6, 2018, at 3:35 p.m., working women in France were doing so for free based on wage inequalities, and that at this rate, it wouldn't be until 2168 that the pay gap would close. Do you believe this is the most critical issue facing women in France today? All fights for women's rights and their representation are critical. There is no issue that is more important than [another]. I decided to fight for economic equality because it is mandatory to shape social and political equality. Without equality in economy, all of our rights can be taken away instantly. With an equal distribution of wealth, we have power to demand more rights.

Do you think you are part of a select group who perceive these oppressions and discriminations against women, or do you think that mainstream society is waking up? In France, there's clearly a very Parisian bubble. When it comes to sexism and #MeToo, a survey conducted in the summer of 2018 revealed that 45 percent of French people hadn't even heard of the movement. But one year in, there were important discussions being had and there was a slight change in people's imagination. The fact that we even began talking about consent means it existed in people's minds where it hadn't before, and that's an important first step. When I talk about feminism, I have to talk about a revolution of the imagination because we cannot actually change society's behaviors for good if individuals don't change their ways of thinking. As for broader change for women—social justice, pay inequality, reproductive rights—the paradigm shift isn't going to come from us. As activists, we're here to create the ideal conditions for future figures of the movement to emerge. No new paradigm shifts come via the intellectual class— they come from the working class. And that's a good thing, because this isn't just a movement about women but a movement tied to race and class.

And you're trying to make sure that message is understood by a younger generation of women, with **Les Petites Glos.** It's interesting because at their age, I didn't even know the word *feminist*, but many of today's adolescents have laid claim to it. Their engagement fits perfectly with the adolescent tendency to revolt. What's more, I find that these young women think way beyond any binary concept of gender and have a far more open vision of the world than we do. My job is to make sure that the society they'll grow into will be ready to welcome their way of thinking.

That being said, has the word feminist *finally been freed of its taboo?* It's definitely become more mainstream, but that's where we all need to be very careful. It shouldn't become a trend; it needs to be a revolution. That nuance is structural. It's not enough to wear T-shirts with feminist slogans on them (even if it's important). There needs to be profound thinking, both realistic and utopian, about what our institutions and values will and should look like in the future.

One of the common criticisms of feminist activists relates to their inherent privilege. How do you respond to this and define your role in the movement? I work behind the scenes so that the people who have the strength, energy, and courage to stand in the spotlight can emerge and make their voice heard. My role is to use my community of engaged activists to put the spotlight on some crucial issues for the feminist movement: equality, parental leave, and menstrual poverty, among others. During those campaigns, I pass the mic to women who usually do not have access to this community. When someone is the victim of institutional racism, they don't feel welcome and must work so much harder to be heard. We help them accomplish both.

Do you foresee yourself influencing legislation? My colleagues and I are regularly asked to speak before the National Assembly and the European Parliament. But public decision-makers don't really take our opinion into account. They listen, but it doesn't go further than that. The president of the National Assembly gave up his perch to a woman on International Women's Day, as though that's a significant gesture—we don't care. Pass laws. Otherwise, it's all feminism "lite."

Do you think the city could be a force in the women's movement? I think Paris could be a catalyst, but I don't think the strength of the movement will or should come from the intellectual class. In the US, there are more activists from other classes. What bothers me there, however, is the *starification* of activists. It's important to have figureheads, but it's more important to have ideas. We just need to find them and make them heard.

Her Paris

FAVORITE WOMAN-RUN BUSINESS?

Make My Lemonade (shown above), the brick-and-mortar clothing and accessories boutique from DIYer and entrepreneur Lisa Gachet, a woman who has always supported other women. She created a wonderful space along the Canal Saint-Martin where we occasionally host events for *Les Glorieuses*.

YOUR PREFERRED NEIGHBORHOOD?

The 10th arrondissement, where I live and work. The rue du Château d'Eau is home to a multitude of cultures: bohemian, Yiddish, Israeli, African. It's very mixed and very special.

SOMEWHERE YOU GO JUST FOR YOU?

To the pool, at least once a week. I love the Piscine Georges Hermant at the top of the Buttes-Chaumont Park and the Piscine Pontoise, which stays open close to midnight most nights. And I go to the Centre de Danse du Marais for Frédéric Lazzarelli ballet classes. It's my breath of fresh air a couple of times a week.

*Advocating for a safer and more
inclusive home for the trans community*

CLÉMENCE ZAMORA CRUZ

TEACHER, SPOKESPERSON FOR INTER-LGBT, AND TRANS ACTIVIST

IT WAS EASY TO SPOT Clémence Zamora Cruz when I went to meet her at the Gare du Nord on an early November morning. She was standing off to the side, scanning the crowds for me with trance-like focus and looked just as she did in her photos—long silky black hair and piercing blue eyes that were impossible to look away from. We searched for a quiet place to talk, something of a feat in Europe's busiest railway station. We ended up with coffee and a snug spot among travelers inside the Brasserie L'Étoile du Nord, where she insisted that the fact that we were bookended by people who might overhear bits of our conversation wasn't a concern. And so she spoke candidly about her life, as if we were alone.

Her story begins in a staunchly Catholic family. Zamora Cruz was six years old when she announced that she was a girl. It wasn't so much a coming out as an affirmation of her identity. There was no wavering or confusion about it, no gender dysphoria—she knew. "My parents told themselves my longer hair and interest in girl's clothing would be a passing phase," she tells me. But one particular family dinner set a different tone. Her parents went around the table, asking her brothers and sisters about their futures, what they wanted to do and be when they grew up. "I want to marry my English teacher!" said Zamora Cruz proudly when it was her turn to answer. Her father rebuked the idea immediately. "You can't. Boys can't marry other boys." She shot back, "Well, there's no problem, because I'm not a boy."

This was the early 1980s in Mexico, which was then, like now, one of the most dangerous countries in the world for trans people (currently, it is the third deadliest after the US. Brazil ranks first, according to reports by the Trans Murder Monitoring [TMM] research project).[33] Gender identification issues were heavily stigmatized and either conflated with sexual orientation or treated as a form of mental illness.

"Conversion therapy" and other medicalized care aimed at convincing trans individuals to identify with the gender they were assigned at birth was systematically recommended as "solutions."

Distraught by Zamora Cruz's revelation, her parents took her to see a psychologist, who prescribed "strict masculinization"—no more folk dancing, no more drawing, no activity that could be construed as feminine. "They pushed me into football, which isn't a problem in principle, but I wasn't interested in it at all."

Roadblocks and humiliation followed her through her academic life. Her school's director considered her to be the source of the problem, provoking unwanted attention and abuse with her long hair and feminine clothing. But they also blamed her parents for their questionable child-rearing and their inaction in "fixing" the problem, as if it were as simple as slapping a Band-Aid on a gash and waiting for it to heal. "As bad as things got, it's hard for me to blame my parents—there was no support for what they were going through. There were hardly any specialized centers in Mexico or even in countries that were supposedly more 'advanced' on the issue,"[34] she can say now with great magnanimity. The weight of the social pressure was intolerable and led to harassment not only in school but at home, where verbal and physical abuse abounded. Her siblings blamed her for the bullying they had started to incur by association, and her parents felt helpless. "People often forget the collateral damage that coming out trans can have on a family. It was [an] unhappy place for everyone."

The transphobia she encountered within her own family isn't uncommon. Households that reject or deny a young person's identity or sexuality often compound the sense of alienation they feel at school and a lack of support puts them at great risk; many choose to emancipate themselves by leaving home but end up homeless (an estimated 40 percent of the homeless youth population in America is LGBTQ),[35] and the prevalence of suicide and suicide attempts is "much higher among transgender people than the general population"[36] (in France, two out of three transgender adolescents consider taking their own lives and one out of three act on it).[37] At fifteen, Zamora Cruz was pushed into making such decisions as transphobic tensions at home came to a head. It was the night of Christmas. "Insults turned into shoving, then slapping, then hitting, until finally I hit back. I knew I couldn't stay. I left home and slept outside in Puebla's main square. I spent the night talking with other 'social rejects,' young people who had left home for

---

opposite Along the Canal Saint-Martin, a happy place for Zamora Cruz.

similar reasons, and took the first bus out to Mexico City the next morning," she tells me with great composure.

She lived in the streets for over a year, a time she reflects on now as a blessing in disguise. "It gave me a closer look at the social injustices that exist. Even though it was hard at home, I always had a roof over my head and food on the table. That year taught me solidarity, about figuring things out and getting by," she says, closing her eyes briefly in gratitude. "But also about the kinds of oppressions that others suffer, not just gender or sexual identity but economic and social injustices." It was also a crash course in women's rights and the issue of prostitution, which is typically discussed from a moralist stance. "I was a sex worker for part of the time I was out there. Many transgender people are refused jobs and become prostitutes as a means of survival. Yet white feminism will try to say that it isn't an acceptable way for women to liberate themselves," she says, realizing this period in her life was the catalyst to her intersectional feminism.

As much as it forced her to grow up, she was still a teen runaway and the police eventually found her. Her parents were notified, but when she returned to civilian life, it was instead under the protection of her grandmother, who took her in and cared for her despite their estrangement. "She respected me even if she didn't understand me. She gave me all of her support so that I could go forward," says Zamora Cruz. "She encouraged me to go to college. She taught me survival rules—never isolate myself, always come home from school accompanied, for starters." Combined with the defense mechanisms she learned in the streets, she was on a stable path—for a time. Her grandmother helped her get an apartment in Puebla, and she worked toward a degree in tourism administration, despite experiencing hostility from professors. She pressed on, graduated, and landed her first job. By this point, she had also become an engaged human rights and political activist, regularly participating in student demonstrations calling for democracy.

"In the beginning, I was left alone during protests and marches. But as police oppressions picked up again, I started being harassed. The Dirty War wasn't really over," she explains. If she left home again in 1996, it was because no amount of survival skills could protect her from the increasingly hostile and dangerous political climate. "I was approached at a bus stop one morning by a group proclaiming to be the police. They placed a revolver to my head and told me to leave or they'd come after my family." Was it because she was trans or associated with the student movement? I ask her. "Surely both. But it didn't matter—I had to flee."

With a French boyfriend at the time, applying for a visa to France presented itself as the best option. But the fight was far from over. She went through a grueling

"Paris is a lot of things. It's a fragmented melting pot city and a refuge city for people who come in search of a better life. It's a city that regenerates as much as it crushes. It's a living paradox, just like the Parisienne. There's an image and a lifestyle that isn't in line with reality."

interview process for a student visa that concluded with a meeting at the French Embassy with a senior official who held her fate in his hands. "I told him that if he didn't issue the visa, he'd be condemning me to death. He stopped taking notes at that point, and we had a very frank, human conversation," she says, knowing that he was pivotal in the decision to approve her application. "I've found natural allies along the way. They haven't always declared themselves as such, like that man, but they've protected me when I needed it." She considers herself lucky.

When she finally arrived in France, Zamora Cruz thought that life was going to be easier, that she'd have greater rights and more support. In her imagination, she was settling into *le pays des Droits de l'Homme*—the country known for its Rights of Man. "And in one way, it was. But it was primarily the rights of the white man," she begins. "Even if the violence in France isn't necessarily physical or overt, it's almost more vicious." She describes a litany of discriminations, from deadnaming, to pathologizing doctors, and bias-based harassment, or discrimination from police who brushed off reports of violence. She recalls a particular moment in her university class where she was ignored by her professor while giving a presentation. When she confronted him, he simply said, "People like you don't interest me."

"I wish I could say that life is better for the trans community in Paris [compared to Mexico], but it depends on a variety of factors. You have to consider it from an intersectional point of view—often, trans people live through other oppressions, be it their race or class, and find themselves in a permanent state of precarity," she tells me, specifying the difficulty that persists in employment, housing, and health care.

While the country has made inroads in terms of rights and ranks high on the Rainbow Europe Index—France was the first country to remove transgenderism from the classification of mental illnesses in 2010 (the World Health Organization recategorized "gender incongruence" in 2018 from a mental disorder to a sexual health condition)[38]; antitrans discrimination was entered into the penal code, and since 2017, transgender people can legally change their gender without undergoing sterilization or proof of medical treatment, long considered a human rights violation[39]—Zamora Cruz and her fellow activists say the efforts don't go far enough. "There remains a barrier to accessing many of the services and rights that exist. Legislation on its own doesn't protect; it needs to be accompanied by awareness, training, and education. Practical measures, not just theory," she explains. A police officer may have the responsibility to take violence against trans people seriously but lack the competency to do so without amplifying discrimination.

If things are going to improve in France, she believes it will be through education. Gender stereotypes need to be broken down from an early age. I ask her if she believes it's possible—can Paris be a leader for LGBTQ rights? Only on the condition that it devotes the resources to it and treats the issue intersectionally, she says. "Paris needs to be at the forefront of anti-discrimination efforts overall. The city has to allocate more funds allocated to LGBTQ rights and to the collective fight." The question she asks herself now is how the state can combat the institutional LGBTQ-phobia, as they insist they are committed to doing, if budgets are being cut in education and teachers are losing their jobs.

There may not be a good answer for that, but she remains committed to her activism. In her volunteer roles as spokesperson of the Inter-LGBT organization and copresident of Transgender Europe, she is working to make conditions better and safer for future generations. Part of that fight involves advocating for gender self-determination so that trans people may modify their identity documents through a statutory system, not the court system. As part of the transgender organization *Pari-T*, Zamora Cruz gives French lessons to trans migrants, and as secretary of the nonprofit *Au-delà du Genre*, she helps trans youths and their families combat transphobia. "We can't fight with our words forever."

Now, twenty years after arriving in France, she no longer experiences the same level of discrimination, nor is she afraid of putting herself at risk. She is happily married and, in the last several years, happily in contact with her family, whom she hadn't seen since she left home as a teen. When she finally reconnected with them in person, all the transphobic clichés they harbored fell away, one after the other. They not only accept her, they respect her. But she also knows it's because she fits into their binary conception of the world. "They see me as I am: a woman," she says. "And so in the binary of man and woman that they find reassuring, there is a place for me."

Her Paris

FAVORITE WOMAN-RUN BUSINESS?

Marina, an Italian restaurant in the 10th arrondissement. I've always loved going there with my husband. The owner is welcoming, and I know her to be a real fighter.

A SOLO RITUAL?

Walk or cycle along the Canal Saint-Martin (shown above). When I lived nearby, it's where I would go almost daily to recharge.

YOUR HAPPY PLACE?

The library at the Sorbonne. It is a magnificent space with frescoes and lamps. But it's not a place everyone can go—you must be a researcher or a student. The library will always be an important place for me—it saved my life. As a teen and as a university student in France, it was one of the few safe places I could go.

the
Creators

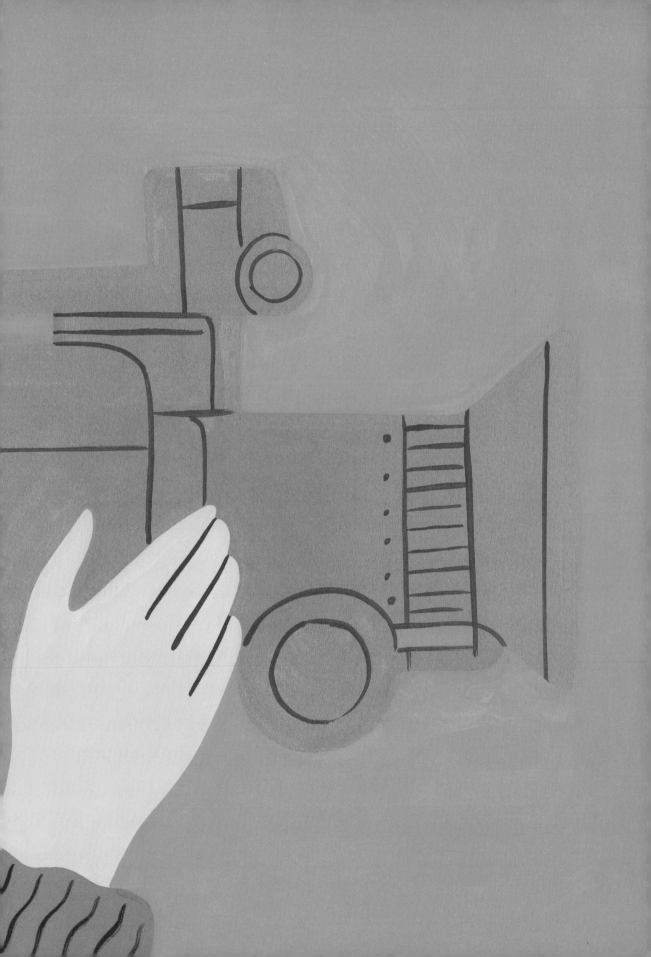

Building on the past to create meaningful spaces

ALINE ASMAR D'AMMAN

ARCHITECT AND DESIGNER

IF I WERE TO PINPOINT THE first flutter of excitement I felt for a story that could eventually take shape into a book much like this one, it was the moment I met the polymathic architect Aline Asmar d'Amman.

It was summer 2017, and I was touring the freshly reopened Hôtel de Crillon, the iconic eighteenth-century-palace hotel overlooking the place de la Concorde, for which Asmar d'Amman oversaw the artistic direction. I was brought into the Grands Appartements, commodious suites designed by the late Karl Lagerfeld, and there was Aline in one of the living rooms, readying the spaces for yet another magazine photo shoot. She was wearing a crisp blazer, fitted jeans, and vertiginous heels. The heels, I'd later learn, are an Aline trademark. Petite with golden skin and a disarming honey voice, she shook my hands and looked me right in the eyes as she said how thrilled she was to meet me and show me the rooms herself. I wondered if she had confused me for someone else, a luminary that merited such a dignified welcome. But such was her gracious character; she's a woman who believes deeply in her work and its power to connect her to people.

That and her benevolence also come from a place of genuine care for forgotten gestures and niceties, the small but impactful acts of kindness that endear her to those she meets. She sends lengthy handwritten missives and thank-you notes on namesake stationery (I received one, myself, after our first interview) because it's personal; the personal makes her happy. It's also how she caught the attention of Karl Lagerfeld, a man she didn't know prior to working on the hotel project, but whom she approached to get involved by appealing to his own affection for the written word and eighteenth-century arts. She wrote and deposited a letter for him at 7L, the bookstore he owned in Saint-Germain-des-Prés, and crossed her

fingers. Within twenty-four hours she was in contact with him directly and he was on board.

"Before you go, I have to show you the bathroom!" she announced excitedly, leading me into the apartment's striking bathroom done up entirely in black and white marble. I was in her company for maybe a total of ten minutes, but I felt instantly drawn to her. There are people who are unforgettable for their work, their eccentricity, or even their ingenuity, but Asmar d'Amman is memorable first because her very presence is radiant. She pulls you in with her buoyant energy and enthusiasm for what seems like her craft but really is all of life, and then you can't see anything but her multitude of talents.

The magnetism I felt during our first encounter only intensified the next time I saw her at Culture in Architecture, the firm she established in 2011 with offices in Beirut and Paris. The meeting room and atelier where we spend hours talking is a cabinet of curiosities, exploding with textures, materials, and immaculately arranged books on design, literature, and fashion. At the back sits a piece of the hulking black marble console that was featured in the first collection of functional sculptures she developed with Mr. Lagerfeld. The windows, stretching from one end of the room to the other, kiss the city's horizon and draw the eye up to the Sacré-Coeur. For a woman who grew up in Beirut to the sound of bombs falling and windows shattering during the war, her everyday view in Paris is well-earned creative inspiration.

French-educated and raised in a family of bibliophiles, Asmar d'Amman essentially read her way out of the trauma of war. Her mother, a French teacher, instilled in her a love of French literature and insisted that nothing, not even the chaos surrounding them, would stop them from immersing themselves in the arts, in the latest fashions, in living. She didn't have time to be afraid. The abiding rule in the family was that everything was okay so long as they were alive; they were to behave as if things were normal, and they strove to establish routine. "Creating normalcy was key—it shaped our character. My mother always found a sense of celebration in the everyday, and that kept us alive with dignity when everything was trying to bring us down."

She learned to find beauty in destruction. Soon, seeing the vestiges of a fractured city would no longer be something to overcome. A breathtaking ray of light on a wall riddled with bullets would awaken a sensitivity that led her to architecture. "I couldn't help but want to be part of the reconstruction of my country and I approached architecture studies as the start of a lifelong commitment," she says. If words were her shelter as a child, they became the foundation and philosophy of her work.

"Architecture is a responsibility, a political act. I believe that it plays an important role in our psychology. We can become better people if we're enchanted by a space."

"Every project needs a story," she explains. "Emotion can't be created without the legitimacy of a proper story. And it has to be real; it has to have meaning because we're polluted by so many messages today." Her company's logo reflects the pillars of her creative vision: culture, architecture, and emotion. They exist together, never alone. Mixing literature and architecture in the reconstruction of a devastated land was a powerful sensation for Asmar d'Amman that confirmed she was on the right path.

After winning two prizes for her final studies project at the Académie Libanaise des Beaux-Arts by the Ministry of Culture and the Order of Architects and Engineers of Beirut, she apprenticed for award-winning architect and urbanist Jean-Michel Wilmotte between New York and Paris. Then she went out on her own and began taking on residential projects in Europe and the Middle East.

All of her work, from private homes in Lebanon to luxury hotels or historic landmarks, bears the hallmarks of a visionary unencumbered by, but respectful of, the past. In the tumbled concrete and rough-hewn character of a postwar Beirut, she saw tremendous beauty. That duality of the raw and precious is what fascinates her and what she seeks to marry in the spaces she builds.

As dream projects go, the overhaul of the Hôtel de Crillon was the opportunity of a lifetime. Over the course of four years, she and the team of designers she handpicked took the stiffness out of the hotel's former iteration, while preserving most of its heritage details—mirrors, marble floors and mantels, and historic salons. That included the Marie Antoinette salon and suite, which she designed herself and for which she commissioned the work of several women artists she admired to supply new pieces—Helen Amy Murray produced the carved leather nightstands, Lauren Collin created delicate paper sculptures, and Zoé Ouvrier carved a long wood cabinet etched with branches. "Marie Antoinette had an opinion, a voice. She took risks of being disliked, not knowing that she'd be admired for her extravagance hundreds of years later," she tells me, pointing to the sketches of the salon in her studio. "These women conveyed her spirit; strong women who work and fight in a man's world [of architecture and design]; it was important to me to showcase their talents." The result is indulgent and opulent in a way that would have certainly bewitched the royals were they to take up residence today but also fits seamlessly into a contemporary context. And it will be timeless because that's what she strived for.

To be sure, the journey wasn't without its obstacles. As the only woman leading the project and as someone uncompromising in her convictions—in the design decisions, in the materials to use, no matter how rare, in the artists to bring on board—she came up against resistance from competing interests. "There's management, finance, economical factors. But it's really that it's never easy for a woman to be right; there always has to be something wrong," she tells me, adding that Mr. Lagerfeld was the one to raise her spirits and remind her that without battles along the way, their jobs would be uninteresting.

Still, her work reviving an iconic landmark for the city was wholly embraced and naturally became her calling card. It led her to bid for other ambitious projects like the refurbishment of the Jules Verne restaurant on the second floor of the Eiffel Tower, which was unveiled in 2019. There, she tapped into the feminine power and innovative legacy of the landmark itself to imagine a space whose elegance comes from contemporary decorative arts and the talent of French artisans, including the work of Ingrid Donat, one of the most influential living bronze artists in the world today, and Marie Khouri, who designed stunning sculptural candleholders for each table.

Her contribution to Paris, and arguably wherever she designs something new, is creating beauty. "It's a universal value that connects all the cultures and religions of the world in an ever chaotic society," she says. And once she creates it, she lets it go to live on its own. Nostalgia simply isn't part of her way of working or living. "I never planned anything in my life. I've just always tried to live intensely and find the joy in every instant. I raise my sons to understand that accomplishment is about an accumulation of experiences," she says with great wisdom. "Live freely and good things happen."

---

opposite A cabinet of curiosities: Books, materials, and sketches provide creative inspiration for Aline Asmar d'Amman at her office and atelier space in Saint-Germain-des-Prés.

Her Paris

FAVORITE WOMAN-RUN BUSINESS?

Liza's eponymous Lebanese restaurant on rue de la Banque: it's delicious any day of the week.

PREFERRED NEIGHBORHOOD?

Without hesitation, Saint-Germain-des-Prés. It's where I first landed in Paris twenty years ago in a small studio on rue Bonaparte, and where the Parisian offices of Culture in Architecture are located. I love the artistic and literary spirit in the neighborhood. My favorite workout is to stroll the streets hunting for treasures at the galleries of the Carré des Antiquaires, pass by my favorite bookstores (7L on rue de Lille or L'Ecume des Pages), then come back to the office recharged and fully inspired.

SOMEWHERE YOU LOVE GOING AS A FAMILY?

Museums and bookstores, but also the flea market at Saint-Ouen, where my two boys, Lionel and Raphael, are used to going and getting spoiled by the kindest *antiquaires* with candies and marvelous little objects from their collections.

Campaigning for stronger representation of women in the arts

ELENA ROSSINI

FILMMAKER, CINEMATOGRAPHER, AND ACTIVIST

WHAT DOES A FILMMAKER LOOK LIKE? How about a cinematographer? Search for either term in Giphy, a database of animated GIFs, today and you'll come across more than 150 images of women and minorities, from directors Haifaa al-Mansour to Ava DuVernay.

That they are instantly visible on platforms saturated with male talent is entirely thanks to the efforts of Italian documentary filmmaker Elena Rossini. On August 11, 2017, she announced on Twitter that she had an idea about how to harness the power of the Internet to give more visibility to women directors. One month later, a handful of women had already been elevated into top search results on Giphy, Twitter, and Slack. Since then, she's created a line of T-shirts prominently featuring the names of directors and budding filmmakers to celebrate the artists as agents of change.

"The images we are exposed to have a profound influence on the way we see the world—and ourselves," she writes to introduce the project. But this very thought can be said to be the animating idea of all her work, whether it's exploring the commodification and globalization of beauty in her critically acclaimed feature-length documentary *The Illusionists* or uncovering the insidious dangers lurking behind technology and social media in her new film and interactive education platform *The Realists*.

We spoke about gender inequality in the film industry, the activism that drives each of her films, and a few of the Parisian women that have inspired her since her early days in the city.

Before we get into the crux of your work, I wanted to ask: Is there a link between filmmaking and all of the LEGOs I see around your office? When you think about it, "maker" is a key component of the word *filmmaker*. I fell in love with LEGOs when I was a kid because they allowed me to be creative, building small worlds with bright, colorful blocks. I used to build entire LEGO cities with my childhood neighbors and create elaborate stories about their inhabitants. Then after a while, we would disassemble the bricks and build new structures. The work of a director—a filmmaker—is fairly similar. It's all about teamwork and creating elaborate virtual worlds.

I've been a passionate advocate for representation, and one of my favorite LEGO creations is a film set with an all-female crew: from the director, to the cinematographer, the boom operator, and the assistant director. It makes me smile every time I see it.

The films you have chosen to make carry very strong messages. Was there a catalyst in your personal life that motivated the sociological focus of your work? When I was in film school, I was actually interested in fiction and was only pursuing fictional narrative projects. But when I moved to Paris after graduate school in Boston, nobody took me seriously when I introduced myself as a filmmaker. They'd say, "Oh, are you a film student?" And "Ah, what kind of short little videos are you making?" I had made a feature film when I was in school and I was really shocked by the juxtaposition between the encouragement from my professors and peers who recognized my talent, and then coming to Paris and being judged based on my age, gender, and physical appearance. Credibility became the number one barrier I went up against repeatedly. Later, I ran into this in a big way with several television networks to whom I presented my film. I won a competition with a new network, presented to their CFO and CEO, and the first thing they said was, "Congratulations! We love your pitch, fantastic project, but before we continue, please let us know if we can help you find a *réalisateur* (a male director)." And I was dumbfounded—every page of the proposal carried the words "written and directed by Elena Rossini." But they wanted me to be in the film, in front of the camera, and get a male director. It was maddening!

Women behind the camera and in technical roles are a minority (about 4 percent of hired directors for the one hundred top-grossing films of 2018 and 3 percent

---

opposite Details from Elena Rossini's home office, her creative sanctuary on the left bank.

"The Parisian women that I have always been drawn to are activists and change-makers, pioneers in their profession who are not afraid to go against the grain to change society."

of cinematographers for top live-action films from 2016 to 2018).[40] Unpleasant experiences like that meeting with the network executives encouraged me to devote my work to the issue of representation, gender inequality, and social injustices. My modus operandi has always been to turn frustrations into creative projects—because I think that simply airing grievances doesn't lead to change. You have to put in the work. Networks and production companies didn't believe I could direct a documentary? Fine! I decided to embark on the journey on my own and enlisted help along the way.

And that was the beginning of your work on **The Illusionists.** Exactly, I set out to make a film about the beauty myth in particular. I explored how physical appearances are impacting the lives of women and girls. The trigger was seeing all the billboards around the city featuring young women that carried the implicit message that in order to be successful, you need to be a young woman who looks a certain way. Although when you are a young woman, no one takes you seriously.

From that starting point, my research led me to expand the full scope of the message to include a look at the economic system that supports corporations, brands, and media companies in their quest, not to improve anyone's lives, but to keep women, men, and, increasingly children, in a constant state of anxiety and insecurity about the way they look for profit.

Numerous studies show that sad people are bigger spenders. Someone who is perfectly satisfied with the way they look won't need new clothes every month, expensive creams, or cosmetic procedures. Yes, sex sells, but insecurity sells so much more. My work on *The Illusionists* aimed to cast a critical look at consumer culture, break illusions related to beauty, and ultimately create more empowered citizens and empowered consumers.

The media have repeatedly shown us one variation of the Parisienne, and brands play up the stereotype. What about in film? When you think of movies, especially American movies that are filmed in France, the women that they cast always fit that idealized image. Why is that? I think it goes back to most creators and directors being men of a certain age. They're not interested in showing the real lives of women or an authentic depiction of the beautifully diverse population of Paris. The Parisienne celebrated in movies is—with a few exceptions—a thin, conventionally beautiful Caucasian young woman. Women of color, members of the LBGTQIA+ community, and older women are virtually invisible in the fantasies concocted by foreign filmmakers and the media.

In what ways do you think this blind reverence for an unrealistic ideal is dangerous for women looking to Paris from the outside? It sets them up for unattainable life standards, as the photographer Sara Melotti says in my second film, not just beauty standards. This is something I'm addressing in the sequel, *The Realists.* Consider this: Instagram is used by more than eight hundred million people, and when you think of the most popular Instagram users in Paris, they all fit a certain mold: very attractive, young, and with a certain economic means that is apparent in the way they can dress and the places they can access. It's understandable how this could create a double pressure to look immaculate and elegant but also to have this idealized French experience that is, in fact, inaccessible to most people.

Something tells me you weren't hoodwinked by the clichés—what was the image you had in mind of the Parisienne before you moved to Paris? The Parisian women that I have always been drawn to are activists and change-makers, pioneers in their profession who are not afraid to go against the grain to change society. Women like Simone de Beauvoir and Agnès Varda, my ultimate role model, who made films and art projects well into her nineties. She had this curiosity for life, creativity, talent, and advocacy when it comes to the rights of women. Their work spoke for them, not the way they look.

If the first film looked at the dark side of the advertising industry in the globalization of beauty, your next film gives a starring role to the dangers of social media and technology. What do you hope to achieve with this project? My new project *The Realists* picks up where *The Illusionists* left off: my aim is to break illusions about our brave new world. If up until a few years ago people used to spend hours consuming traditional media—and desiring to emulate the celebrities promoted on television, in movies, and magazines—now people across generations are spending inordinate amounts of time on the Internet or on their smartphones.

They are comparing their lives to those of celebrities but also to the lives of their friends and neighbors, whose minutiae they see broadcast on social media. Comparison anxiety is widespread. Just like I did with *The Illusionists*, I would like to promote the importance of media literacy: understanding the market forces behind these trends. And I would like to create a movement, encouraging people to be more mindful and intentional with their tech habits. If you think about it, a small group of young, male, mostly white engineers in Silicon Valley have created tools adopted by billions of people around the world. They've revolutionized how we socialize, how we work, how we spend our leisure time, how we date. I'd like people to think more deeply about the designs of these platforms, what we gain, but also what we lose when we engage with the world virtually. I've called it *The Realists* because we have so much more to gain if we put more value in real connections away from a screen.

Do you think that Paris can become a center for more vocal rebellion against the systems in place that are exploiting its women? I do. The French, by nature, question everything and are used to fighting for their rights and preserving a way of life that is dear to them. It just takes time.

opposite A peaceful, meditative place. Elena Rossini's favorite spot in the Luxembourg Gardens, with a clear view of the Panthéon.

Her Paris

FAVORITE WOMAN-RUN BUSINESS?

I love Berkeley Books of Paris. Run by Phyllis Cohen, an American in Paris, this used and rare bookshop is like a safe haven for creatives. She organizes a lot of readings and concerts and was even inspired by me to start LEGO Sundays!

SOMEPLACE YOU GO FOR CREATIVE INSPIRATION?

I have a preference for the *rive gauche*, and my first apartment in Paris was within walking distance of the Luxembourg Gardens, so I still find it to be a really magical place. It's more airy and open than other parks. And there are certain films from the Nouvelle Vague [French New Wave] movement that actually took place there, so that certainly helps!

YOUR GO-TO FOR A CHANGE OF SCENERY?

I go to the avenue d'Ivry in the 13th arrondissement for a fresh perspective; it feels like somewhere completely different. It's part of the city's Chinatown, which is actually a neighborhood for Chinese, Vietnamese, Laotian, and Cambodian communities. There are incredible shops and restaurants, including the Tang Frères supermarket, itself a destination.

Healing through music and humanitarian actions

INNA MODJA

SINGER, SONGWRITER, AND ACTIVIST

WHAT DOES A SURVIVOR LOOK LIKE? There isn't a formula; she could be anyone. She is hundreds of thousands of young girls around the world. She is, in this case, Malian singer-songwriter and activist Inna Modja. That she feels comfortable talking to me about her childhood trauma and humanitarian commitments over a plate of truffle pasta is a testament to how far she's come through a complex healing process.

Modja is the sixth of seven children from Bamako and the last of her sisters to be the victim of female genital mutilation. She was five, the family was then living in Ghana, and the excision was carried out by a female elder, unbeknownst to her parents. Just as with her sisters, the family lived the experience as a collective trauma. "Each time it happened, it was done by some other member of the family. And each time, my parents felt like failures for not being able to prevent it from happening," Modja shares. Though the sting never faded, everyone in the family carried on without making it a recurring topic of conversation. "We knew our parents were opposed to it, but what could we do?" Up to 91 percent of all Malian women are excised without ever understanding why.[41] "It's a tradition that's gone on for generations so nobody questions why it's being done; it's ignorance. Traditions are like education," she begins. "In some villages, people believe that the rubbing from walking long distances to farms or to get water hurt a woman's clitoris. In other places, they say it's the male part in the female body and if you don't take it away, it can bring infertility to the man. They're all crazy stories." It's violence against women, she insists, for which there is never a justifiable reason.

It was only later, as a young adult pursuing her language and literature studies in France, that the inhumanity of what she experienced fully crystallized. The pain she had tucked away resurfaced but now with the contextualization to understand

its long-term effects. Shame wasn't on the spectrum of emotions she felt until the first French gynecologist she consulted told her, matter-of-factly, that she had been excised and there was nothing to be done. "She just said, 'This happened to you. You have a scar where you should have a clitoris. It's really visible.' I didn't know my own body. I didn't understand what had been done." Now she had the realization that a visible sign of the past meant that her story couldn't be hidden. She'd have to share that part of her with a partner, revisit old wounds. "I became so self-conscious after that. I retreated a bit. I'd wake up feeling worthless, worried that I'd never fully be a woman." She sits back in the booth and takes a breath, looking around the room and back over to her husband, who joined us for lunch. They smile gently at one another. He's heard her story time and again but comforts her as if it were the first telling. In that brief silence, it strikes me that her childhood was relatively free from the weight of the irrecoverable loss of what was so intimately hers—largely because she didn't fully grasp what had been taken. Instead, that pain seared the beginning of her adulthood. Would it have made a difference to have known before?

She says she doesn't think of it that way. The important thing was finding a way to heal. "That first gynecologist should have been the one to direct me to a doctor who could perform the surgical repair but she either didn't know about it or didn't care. A lot of doctors simply don't." In some parts of the international medical community, it remains taboo. It would take a few years before she discovered the French surgeon who would conduct the operation. "He not only developed the technique but fought to get social security to cover the costs of the operation—it's now completely free."

With the surgery came a newfound confidence and perspective on life. She reclaimed something she was told she'd never get back. "I felt like it gave me my personal power back. I didn't feel like I was less than anymore. So I said, okay now that I have what other women have, what are you going to be? No excuses," she tells me about kicking her music career into high gear. She had been writing music for other artists but stopped everything to focus on her own work. She had just enough money to pay rent and afford studio sessions, so she recorded a demo that she handed out to industry friends. Within a year, she had a contract with Universal France and would go on to produce three albums. Paris would become a grounding force after long stints abroad on tour. And in 2018, she joined the revival of Les Parisiennes, a quartet popular in the 1960s, and performed across the country.

The trauma against which she built a resilience could have easily destroyed her. But Modja is a fighter who took the weight of her pain and funneled it into her art, into optimism and advocacy.

It was inevitable that she channeled her experiences into activism, she says. While growing up, her mother ran a foundation to raise awareness around HIV and AIDS, educating young girls who came from Bamako or Malian villages who didn't know how to write. "I was raised to care," says Modja.

She began when she was twenty with the most personal of causes—working on campaigns for different organizations to bring awareness to female genital mutilation and the consequences it can have on women's bodies and overall health. At the UN, she has spoken about the blame directed at victims and the danger of a society that shames women for their abuse, and she continues to fight for a law in Mali to finally put a ban on excision. In her adopted home, she lends her time and support to La Maison des Femmes as an ambassador of Dr. Ghada Hatem-Gantzer's pioneering family justice center (see page 145).

More recently, she worked on *The Great Green Wall*, a documentary produced in partnership with the UN and Oscar-nominee Fernando Meirelles that explores something equally as close to home: desertification. "I come from the Sahel, a region that stretches from Senegal to Djibouti, that has been suffering from desertification. It's one of the reasons people migrate. It's climate change. Nothing is growing anymore; people can't live," she explains. "People see sub-Saharan African migrants on boats, risking their lives to get through Libya, and don't consider why they're fleeing in the first place. They see them as invaders and yet they aren't prepared to give up on the things that pollute the planet and put these people in jeopardy." The documentary aims to bring support to a project of the same name, an $8 billion ongoing initiative led by the African Union and the Food and Agriculture Organization of the United Nations to re-create and restore 8,000 kilometers (nearly 5,000 miles) of degraded land due to desertification and, hopefully, help to curb migration. "It's been ten years and only 15 percent is complete. We're pushing for other countries to get involved and for the rest of the world to see this as a priority. You can already see the results in places like Senegal," she says excitedly. "I've visited very arid areas and [seen] communities working together, building gardens, planting trees. They're doing what they can."

Buoyed by her political and humanitarian commitments, her music, and the itinerant life she leads with her husband, Modja can say unequivocally that she's happy. She uses her platform for more than music, just as her parents taught her,

and harnesses her voice not only as a creative tool, but as a tool for good. "Life is political, in every sense. I have to use the attention I've received for the causes I believe in," she explains. "Even if it doesn't appeal to everyone."

As engaged as she is and receptive as her following has been to her activism, she feels most at ease onstage, wherever in the world that may be. "It's still a safe, vibrant place for me to be. It wasn't always that way, but now I'm in total harmony with what I share," she tells me.

When she's been on the road for too long and aches for home, her original home, she remembers that the Niger River forever flows within her veins. Instantly, the desert warms her heart. It's this kind of sentiment she shares with her fans, reminding them with a smile and immeasurable strength of character that she is a woman of the world—always dreaming and always fighting.

---

above Coffee and florals come together under one roof at Peonies, one of Inna Modja's favorite woman-run businesses in Paris.

Her Paris

FAVORITE WOMAN-RUN BUSINESS?

Peonies, a spot that doubles as a flower and bouquet atelier and coffee shop. The owner is a friend, and I saw the process she went through to open the business, what she had to fight against. I'm so proud of what she has created!

SOMEPLACE YOU GO IN PARIS TO WRITE?

I like to spend hours at the Used Book Café at Merci. It's always a lovely spot to read, write, and linger.

PREFERRED MUSIC VENUE?

I love La Cigale, where I've done a few shows, and Folies Bergère (shown above), which is incredibly enchanting. It's one of the most beautiful places to sing!

Creating with purpose

AMÉLIE VIAENE

FINE JEWELRY DESIGNER

AMÉLIE VIAENE NEVER WEARS A WATCH. She doesn't like to feel the pressure of time. Instead, the jewelry designer lets herself be guided by the recess bells, the calls for lunch, and the pickup hour of the primary school that sits beneath her home and studio. For seven years, her hulking wood workbench sat facing the window of her turn-of-the-century apartment's second bedroom. It served as her creative cocoon, where she designed and handcrafted hundreds of one-of-a-kind jewelry pieces.

It is in her home—at her vintage dining room table in the next room—that I first sit down to talk about her life as a jeweler, one marked by family hardship and personal setback, perseverance, and deserved recognition. But it is in her very first atelier-boutique that the story comes full circle.

Viaene grew up in a tiny village outside of Troyes in Champagne, surrounded by nothing but great expanses of sky and farmland. "We had horses and chickens and there was a feeling of freedom in such wide-open country," she tells me. Her father was a skilled woodworker and single-handedly renovated their farmhouse, while her mother stayed home to raise her and her two siblings. It was a meaningful, if small, life. But her studies in applied arts at a specialized high school in a neighboring part of the region would pull her from home as a teen, giving her a first taste of independence.

At seventeen, degree in hand, she was considering fashion design school. But as she was planning her future, the health of her father sharply declined. "It was an incredibly difficult time for everyone. Finances were already tight, but they only got tighter. I certainly couldn't afford the university or the cost of living that would go with it."

Delaying her studies, she moved to Paris to work. Her shock of chocolate curls and towering frame—an obvious exclamation point—quickly drew attention from scouting agents who spotted her on the street. "I was signed by a modeling agency and started living life as an adult," she recalls. "I was hungry for independence and space amid everything that was happening in my family, but I never ended up settling into a place of my own. I jumped from one friend's couch to another—it was anything but glamorous." She doesn't romanticize the experience—there were positive moments, to be sure, with opportunities to get closer to the worlds of luxury and creative arts, but it was largely a means to an end, a way to support herself, not the start of a career. And it only lasted a few years. Jobs in retail gave her a regular salary and the stability she needed to get a lease for her own apartment and put down roots.

After the traumatic loss of her father in 2001, she resolved to return to the arts. She worked in retail by day and spent her evenings in jewelry-making classes offered by the Mairie de Paris, learning wax sculpting and gemology. "I had a fascination with fine jewelry, but I needed to make sure it was worth pursuing seriously, that it wasn't just a silly fantasy," she explains. A quick study with a deft hand, Viaene was strongly encouraged not only by her instructors, but also by the staff at the Haute École de Joaillerie in Paris, among the world's most prestigious jewelry schools. She was admitted on a scholarship and spent a year of intense training where she discovered a passion for the more traditional aspects of the trade—lost wax carving and the art of gouache painting.

"Creating jewelry from a wax model requires a kind of 3-D vision. I start with a sketch of the jewel, carve it, and then the mold transforms into metal by the process of lost wax casting. The method allows for the piece to be produced in one go, without welding," she goes on, removing her engagement ring and gently sliding it in front of me to feel the smoothness of its form. Her style is unequivocally contemporary—she plays with volume, proportion, and shape to create emotion. "I didn't immediately envision creating my own brand but I knew that I didn't want to work with the ephemeral. I wanted to create something that leaves a trace."

She reaches for her velvet box of jewels and picks out "*mon coeur*," a heart-shaped white gold ring with soft, elegant lines. "You see the heart now, but once it's on your finger, the shape changes; the heart becomes hidden. It was the very first piece I created."

She finally launched her namesake collection after working for the city's finest jewelry workshops, motivated in part by how much the experience stunted her

---

opposite Each of Viaene's jewels begins as a sketch and gouache painting in her atelier-boutique.

"I've only worn jewelry with personal meaning. Now, I'm encouraging the students I mentor to consider the role of jewelry in a world of overconsumption. What does it look like to design with purpose?"

creativity. "My first job was as a designer at an atelier, doing gouache out of a dusty closet. No matter what I drew, the craftsmen—and they were almost always men—deviated from my vision in production," she says. Not only was it a lonesome endeavor, but she and her fellow designers weren't respected. "We're squeezed like lemons and then replaced without hesitation." She wasn't meant to be hidden away in a windowless room expressing only a part of her talent.

Still, a solo venture presents a host of other challenges. There's something superhuman in the perseverance and faith required to pursue a business in Paris. Failure, no matter the context, is rarely considered a worthy risk, and in the jewelry trade, it's also an expensive one. When Viaene first began producing pieces of her own, she tested the market by presenting a small sampling at fine jewelry fairs. Many of the clients she met then, more than ten years ago, are regulars today. They bring in gemstones and family heirlooms for her to redesign or simply come looking to be enchanted by meaningful artistry. She considers herself among the lucky few to have made it this far. "This business is expensive. I wasn't born with a silver spoon in my mouth; I needed loans. The people who often succeed are those who come from affluent families or have large networks. That's fine, but it's not easy to make it without that foundation," she says.

What she did have was a solid work ethic, a fresh aesthetic, a signature style, and exquisite craftsmanship, which paid off in spades. In 2016, she was selected by Japan's Ministry of Economy, Trade and Industry and the French Department of Commerce and Craft to represent France at the G7 Craftswomen Summit, the first of its kind to focus on the role of women in artistic craftsmanship. In the same year, she was awarded the grand prize in the City of Paris's Artistic Craft Award (le Grand Prix de la Création de la Ville de Paris)—an important recognition not only for her but for other women looking to pursue a similar path. But most impactful to the future of her business was winning the Banque Populaire Fondation prize in 2017, which came with a grant she applied toward her first atelier-boutique.

On a quiet street in the 7th arrondissement, the atelier-boutique finally opened at the end of 2018, neatly coinciding with Viaene's twentieth anniversary as a Parisienne. She's beaming with joy on the morning I return to see her at her new "home." "Everything about my work is an exercise in patience," she tells me with a laugh. "My clients have to be willing to wait for me to create and I have to be patient with the process." Now that the schoolchildren and recess bells have been lifted from her creative environment, I ask her how she feels. "Free to consider what's next."

Her Paris

FAVORITE WOMAN-RUN BUSINESS?
Maison Aleph, Myriam Sabet's wonderful pâtisserie (see page 227). I called on her for my
shop's inauguration weekend! The flavors of her pastries are intense and delicious.

WHERE YOU LIKE TO GO WITH YOUR HUSBAND EN TÊTE-À-TÊTE?
Verjus Bar à Vins. Lola always gives a warm and friendly welcome, and my husband and I love
to meet up after work for a drink and a few small plates. We'd go weekly if we could.

A PLACE TO DISCOVER THE ART OF JEWELRY?
La Galerie des Bijoux at the Musée des Arts Décoratifs for its exceptional collection retracing
the history of jewelry from the Middle Ages.

above A selection of Viaene's one-of-a-kind rings, designed in her 7th arrondissement atelier-boutique.

Celebrating life and objects with meaning

AJIRI AKI

CREATOR OF MADAME DE LA MAISON

WHAT I NOTICE FIRST about Ajiri Aki are her shoes. Worn, tan sandals with multicolored straps that run neatly across her toes. She's paying for her coffee at Café Oberkampf, towering over the counter. She's tall, with her hair tied up and off her neck, and wears chunky rings that elongate her slender fingers. She sits next to me with her notebook, and I instantly wonder what she's working on. I contemplate commenting on her sandals to break the ice, but she addresses me first and eases into the kind of effortless conversation that makes me love city living (and spending so much of my work and leisure time in cafés). I learn that she's Texan, a fellow 11th arrondissement resident, an author—of the *New York Times* bestseller *Where's Karl?*, a mother, and a proud former New Yorker. Over time, I'd also discover that she is a woman of many great stories of hope and perseverance.

There was a threat of a menacing storm over Paris when we head over to the bar at the Hoxton hotel for an apéritif to talk about her life one early July evening during an insufferable heat wave. Her husband stayed home with her kids, Noomi and Baz, and we spent a couple of hours putting the pieces together from Ajiri the young girl in Nigeria to Ajiri the entrepreneurial woman in Paris who has built a company around values instilled by her mother.

Aki lived in Nigeria until she was five, when her mother brought her to the US to join her father, who had been completing a PhD in economics. "Immigrant families from Nigeria go wherever it's best for education and work, not necessarily where we'd find a community of faces that looked like ours," she tells me. That led them to Austin, Texas, where she was one of only four black girls at her school and struggled to make sense of her identity. Her family considered themselves Africans in America, not African American, and that was an important distinction she carried with her. She remembers riding in her mother's red pickup listening to Johnny Cash and Patsy Cline, thinking that the dissonance between her two worlds made her all the more different. "I'd go to school trying to fit in with the Jennifers and Sarahs and then come home to my mom cooking Nigerian food while singing 'Stand by Your Man'—she was a character, that's for sure. It's only now that I appreciate that about her," she says.

Aki compartmentalizes her life into before and after her mother died. Up until she was twelve, she was a natural-born leader. She joined the African Christian Fellowship and connected with other Nigerians every Saturday. She founded the Little African Voices, for which she choreographed and performed interpretive dance numbers, and made her own costumes, just like her mother would. She had big ideas, boundless curiosity, and a love for pomp and circumstance. She chided her mother for not using her wedding porcelain, especially since she knew her mother used to be just like her—inspired by spectacle. Then life took a dark shift when her mother died of congestive heart failure at thirty-nine. "She just got sick one day and died six months later. It was brutal. The Ajiri after that was worried about the disappearance of her culture," she says solemnly. Her father had no interest in upholding it.

She describes the disappointment in watching her father remarry swiftly and take a detached role in her life. By sixteen, she had asked her best friend's father to become her legal guardian, and she sought support in her high school coaches. Athletics saved her emotionally, she says. The unexpected and painful loss of her mother summoned survival instincts she didn't believe she had. "I always had to be scrappy after Mom died. I couldn't count on my father. The recurring theme of my life became fighting to make things happen for myself," she says. But along the way—through college, a bright career in fashion, and graduate work—the incredible generosity of women allowed her to stay the course. "There are a number of female angels who have come in and out of my life when I needed them most in the absence of my mother," she says, still incredulous.

There's Auntie Louise, who barely earned enough money of her own but paid to hold Aki's place at her university because she wanted her to have a better life; there's Dr. Sally Fortenberry, who refused to accept that Aki couldn't afford to continue studying after one semester and cosigned her loan even though she hardly knew her (years later, she'd pay it off without telling her); Shannon of the Costume Institute, who helped her pull together research for a last-minute application to Bard to pursue a master's degree (where she'd be accepted and given

"France makes you think that not everything is possible, but I will continue soldiering through the hurdles. That's what I want to convey to my kids. I want them to have the confidence to know that the hurdles can't break them down. I've had so many of them in my life."

a full scholarship); and there's Phyllis of the Museum of the City of New York, who gave her the chance to learn to conserve objects and become an assistant curator before she had even graduated.

Young Aki started to come alive again studying costume history and decorative arts. Her studies brought her to Paris, where she spent three months honing her repertoire in material culture and developing an encyclopedic knowledge of couturier Jean Patou, Coco Chanel's rival in the twenties and thirties. She spent another year between Paris and New York, completing her research and learning from archivists at the Musée des Arts Décoratifs and the Palais Galliera. But once she returned home, graduated, and faced the reality that jobs were scarce, she hit a wall. "I left fashion for academia, which I thought would mean something. But it was equally as closed off," she says. Feeling lost, she turned back to her contacts in fashion and and set up a fashion video production agency in New York City. That's when she met Thomas, a Swiss-German film producer based in Paris. "I swear I manifested that guy," she jokes.

They married in 2011 and moved full-time to Paris, where she held on to her company—the lifeline to familiarity and a sense of purpose—as long as she could. But then her daughter was born, her contacts moved on, and so did the work. Settling in Paris represented yet another reset for Aki. "I didn't do what my mother did when she moved to America. She found community instantly. I didn't have that. I had no family close by, no network. Being pregnant with Noomi was an incredibly lonely time," she recalls. She threw herself into the *Where's Karl?* book project with her friend and coauthor Stacey Caldwell, which helped for a time. But it would be several years, and after the birth of her son, before she'd land on her "sense of purpose," which also reconnected her to her mother.

It was during one of those *what if* conversations with friends at a country house one weekend when the idea for Madame de la Maison, her linen and antique tableware company, was born. "I was talking about how much I loved antiquing and decorative arts in general, how happy it made me, and I said, 'What if I could do this for a living?'" The *this* she's referring to is setting a scene, crafting a story and a sense of place through objects that she had already been collecting over the years. And she wasted no time in getting herself established. "I knew this was the project to pursue. I started a fully legal business right from the beginning. I didn't test the waters or approach it like a hobby. For me to build it, it needed to be ambitious from the start," she explains. Not only does she produce her own collection of linen napkins and tablecloths locally, but she sells and rents out all of her finds from antique markets and yard sales across France, from nineteenth-century silver fiddle-and-thread-patterned serving spoons to ironstone soup tureens.

Today, she's part of a new generation of antiquarians contributing to the resurgence of tradition by reviving objects with stories. She sees herself as a cultural bridge—unearthing the treasures of French culture and history, polishing them back to life, and finding them new homes, often with locals—and hopefully, as a source of encouragement for other women, particularly foreign women in Paris with ambitions of starting a business. "It's hard and tiring, and sometimes you'll have to strap your kid on your back like I do and get them involved, but it's possible."

As we're leaving the hotel, I ask her what she loves most about the pieces she uncovers from around the country, beyond their obvious beauty and history. "It's what they symbolize—gatherings, togetherness, family, friends," she begins. "Too often, people wait for a special occasion to use the things that bring them joy, like my mom, who died before that occasion came around. I don't store my favorite things away; I use them. They're a celebration of life."

Her Paris

FAVORITE WOMAN-RUN BUSINESS?

Racine Paris, a floral shop I love (shown above). When I was starting out in my business and needed to show what I could do, the owner set me up with dried flowers—she was helpful and made me feel like there was solidarity among entrepreneurs.

PREFERRED NEIGHBORHOOD?

The 11th arrondissement! It's a section of town with so much going on, and it's exciting to see it develop and grow, with so many people starting businesses.

SOMEPLACE YOU LIKE TO TAKE THE KIDS?

SUPER Café in the 20th arrondissement, which has a great terrace on a cobblestone square, plenty of dedicated play areas for kids, and a comfortable café for adults (plus a coworking space!).

Paving a new path for natural beauty

VICTOIRE DE TAILLAC

COFOUNDER OF L'OFFICINE UNIVERSELLE BULY

AS ONE-HALF OF THE PERIPATETIC DUO behind the cosmetics label L'Officine Universelle Buly, Victoire de Taillac is championing a paradigm shift in beauty, where standards aren't tethered to perceived shortcomings or flaws but the pure personal pleasure women *and* men can derive from caring for themselves.

In its short existence, the cult-favorite brand's old-world apothecary design codes and emphasis on raw materials has emerged as the alternative to overdone luxury. From oils, clays, powders, and creams to oral care, potpourri, and the industry's first water-based perfumes, she's helped to honor the best aspects of the past while innovating for the future. At her rue de Saintonge boutique, we talked about her career before Buly, her vision of beauty based around artisanry and crafted arts, and what sets her business apart in a saturated market.

Have you always been drawn to the beauty industry? Not at all—that came quite late, actually! Doubt has always been part of my way of seeing things, and as a teen and a young adult, I was never certain about anything. I studied contemporary history at the Sorbonne, and during my last year of school, my childhood best friend Sarah opened Colette, the concept store, with her mother. Quickly after opening, Colette asked me to work for them to handle communication in-house. It was my first job—I was twenty-two, Sarah was twenty-one, and we were adolescents in charge; it was nuts.

Knowing what Colette symbolized for Paris and the international design and fashion world, that must have led to vast opportunities. I launched my own PR firm even before leaving Colette, because I felt I had a real point of view. Colette

had hosted the launch of Kiehl's in France and later Aesop (before they were acquired), and I realized not only how much respect I had for the people who created these brands but how much I liked beauty and wanted to tell their stories. There is something universal about it: everyone can relate, everyone wants to feel their best, and I believe it enchants the everyday. Fashion is far more closed-off and elitist. There are more codes; it's extremely tied to means, status, and appearance, so that always interested me less. With my husband, Ramdane, who I met while working at Colette, we launched a cosmetics boutique called Parfumerie Générale. We were twenty-five. We had about forty different niche brands that weren't yet sold in Paris, in a contemporary shop in the 8th arrondissement. We set up the business with our best friends, with little money. Unfortunately, it all went from bad to worse after three years, and then it collapsed. I kept my PR business going for a long while after and then joined Ramdane when he had the opportunity to take over Cire Trudon, the seventeenth-century candlemaker.

And that was the gradual shift toward the world you navigate today. How did it happen? We then worked to revive a brand that had been bought by a French manufacturer who didn't know what to do with it. It had a beautiful heritage with a factory in operation since the eighteenth century (which is extremely rare), and they had been a longtime candle supplier for all the churches in France. After digging through the brand's archives, Ramdane decided to focus on aesthetics, creating a candle that looked unlike any other on the market, with green glass and a golden label, and, of course, the scents. Everyone had been copying Diptyque scents for twenty years, so it was time to get creative. It took off instantly—six months after we launched, the brand was distributed in thirty countries, in sixty by year one. I worked on the communication, the language, the catalogs, and press. We quickly learned that heritage brands are valuable when, and only when, they are managed right. In the end, we were bought out, and it proved to be another great adventure.

But timing was on your side because Buly sort of fell into your lap, isn't that right? By chance, an antique dealer friend of ours showed us a catalog from the nineteenth century, and it gave us the idea to relaunch an old brand of French cosmetics. We were living in New York at the time and came back to France to do the research and start from scratch.

"The image of the Parisian woman is stuck in the nineteenth century—white and thin. She was never updated."

By nature of its image and product focus, Buly already sets itself apart from the mainstream. How does it reflect your own personal approach to beauty?
Beauty is such a bizarre industry. First of all, everything hinges upon problems: half of the planet is told they are too dark and the other half that they are too white, and products are targeted toward problems one must absolutely resolve. But for me, beauty and skin care is simply about feeling good and taking care of myself. The idea isn't to be the most beautiful in the room—there will always be someone prettier, younger, smarter, and we can't live our lives in this constant competition for perfection. The beauty rituals should be incredibly personal and a way to soften life. I've never been able to relate to the ways that beauty and cosmetics are written about, particularly in women's magazines, which brings everyone down. As soon as we launched Buly, I knew that the catalog would be written differently.

Your book, An Atlas of Natural Beauty, *much like your illustrated catalog, carries a unique tone. How would you describe that editorial approach?*
Informative and well written. The more the client is informed, the better they buy for themselves. Beauty is personal, and each person has their routine and should make the right choices for them. The properties of each product, everything from the scented matches to the various powders, are described in detail in the catalog. Beyond simple storytelling, I wanted to give a cultural framework for the products—how to use them, what they're best for, where the plants come from.

You don't use alcohol in your perfumes, your packaging is sustainable (no plastic!), and you focus on oils, clays, and plant-based creams alongside a few nostalgic accessories. Do you see yourself as a disruptor in the industry? It's in our interest to be as creative as we can, to offer a different point of view on beauty and sophistication in self-care. We're not just a brand that makes lovely things but good-quality things. I think that the beauty industry made the choice to be utilitarian—use plastic, be mass-market—but that's not us. There's a pleasure in having the products themselves be beautiful—a beautifully crafted comb or a tube of toothpaste that's aesthetically pleasing. The shift away from purely utilitarian products in the beauty industry is slow, but eventually we believe that provenance, quality, and composition will be highly valued, like we see now in the culinary world. It's the little things that make a difference in life, so when we develop something new, we think as much about what it looks like as how it's made. They're becoming collector's items. Maybe in thirty years we'll even find Buly bottles at the Saint-Ouen flea market!

From the interiors of your Paris shops to the packaging design, there is an old-world glamour to the brand, which is an integral part of its appeal. Would you say Buly is a romanticized version of Paris? Of course—we wanted a very classic boutique where we could build a reinterpreted version of France that goes way beyond the brand, with a certain sophistication in service, attention, and expertise from our staff. I hope that the shops are places with a soul that feel unlike anywhere else. It's not just the retro and old-fashioned that inspires us but retro-futurism.

You have three children, including an adolescent daughter. What do you hope she learns from you? A lot of things! But most importantly (and not just from me but from having lived in Morocco, America, Japan, and France), I want her to know and remember that she isn't reduced to any obligations of physical perfection or a certain way of dressing. There are so many ways to be a woman.

opposite One of the many booksellers of Saint-Germain where Victoire de Taillac goes to feel rejuvenated.

Her Paris

FAVORITE WOMAN-RUN BUSINESS?
My wonderful baker at Secco on rue de Varenne, who I see every morning at seven. She's the first person I speak to, before anyone in my house has even woken up. I also adore florists, particularly the work of Clarisse from Vertumne, a space that completely matches her spirit.

YOUR CULTURE FIX?
The bookstore. Books, old and new, are my solution for everything. I love Chantelivre, which is for kids but has a well-managed adult section; L'Ecume des Pages in Saint-Germain, which is open late; and La Procure in the 6th, a gigantic bookstore specialized in religious, philosophical, and cultural books.

SOLO RITUAL?
Crossing the river! It's the closest thing we have to the sea. There's nothing better than the incredible light on the water, during the early morning or at sunset.

the Disruptors

Reinventing the capital no matter the obstacles

ANNE HIDALGO

FIRST FEMALE MAYOR OF PARIS

LIKE ALL PARISIANS, Anne Hidalgo is fiercely protective of her rituals. She runs errands at the same 15th arrondissement grocer, butcher, and cheesemonger that she's frequented for years, seeks reading suggestions from her nearby bookseller, and cozies up for dinner with her husband at her favorite neighborhood restaurant whenever her schedule allows. She attends as many of her teenage son's swim meets as she can and makes a concerted effort to free up time on weekends to reconnect with friends. Above all, she makes time to observe her surroundings.

She's a working woman, balancing a high-profile job with a private life she'd like to keep private, but those rituals are all indispensable, she says, to leading a city of 2.1 million inhabitants. "You have to first live the city to be able to run it. You have to know it intimately, as if it were a living person," she told me. "I love strolling on Sundays and seeing how fellow Parisians make the most of the city. It gives me plenty of ideas on what to improve when I head back into the office on Monday morning."

Our values need not align perfectly with those of Anne Hidalgo to appreciate her role in transforming Paris since she became the city's first woman to serve as mayor in 2014. Her governance revolves around social inclusion, innovation, sustainable development, and environmental issues, earning her a pioneering reputation among city leaders around the world for her steadfast commitment to climate action. In 2019, while chair of C40 Cities, a leadership network of the world's more influential cities, that dedication earned her a spot in the top twenty of the one hundred most influential people on climate policy by Apolitical.[42]

On Hidalgo's watch, Paris has committed to banning diesel engines by 2025 and phasing out all combustion-engine cars by 2030.[43] As of now, all gas-powered vehicles entering the city are required to display a sticker indicating their levels of carbon emissions. Under this Crit'Air antipollution program, older vehicles—from cars to tour buses and heavy trucks—are restricted between 8 a.m. and 8 p.m. The first Sunday of each month is car-free in ten congested areas of the city, including the Champs-Élysées, and the mayor intends to make the ban weekly if she's reelected (some twenty other neighborhoods are already pedestrian each weekend). She's expanded the city's beloved bike-share program Vélib' (and recovered from the misbegotten rollout of its updated fleet in 2018) and, faced with legal opposition from motorist groups, successfully pedestrianized large sections of the Seine's riverbanks. Bike lanes are proliferating, public transit is now free for kids under eleven (it was already free for senior citizens and disabled adults), and vehicular traffic has decreased, she tells me, by 20 percent in the last five years.

The war on cars isn't a panacea in the urgent need to reduce pollution, but it does help prepare citizens for the broader cultural and behavioral shifts that must occur. It may be uncomfortable and inconvenient, but the city's frequent bouts of smog (whose lungs can forget when the city outsmogged both Delhi and Beijing in 2016? Mine haven't . . .)[44] aren't going to disappear without collective action, something she reminds both the state and her constituents of regularly.

"In twenty years, Paris will still be Paris but in step with the times. We will get around predominantly by public transit, by bike, or on foot. Far from the era of car dominance, life will be calmer. Nature will take pride of place in the city, as it always should have," she explained. "There will be lawns in place of concrete esplanades, and green spaces in every neighborhood. We'll be able to swim in the Seine, and we'll continue to imagine and create the future with our skilled entrepreneurs, artisans, and artists"—the lifeblood of the city.

On the social welfare front, she's been a vocal champion of LGBTQ rights, transformed two of the illustrious salons of the Hôtel de Ville into a 24/7 refuge for nearly one hundred homeless women, established a social integration program that has put homeless Romani children back in schools and found shelters for their families,[45] established centers for refugees despite pushback from local residents, and created three times as many spots in urgent lodging for those in need as in her previous term. I could continue listing her contributions, but she says "there's so much more to do—solidarity is a big part of the city's identity. It was built over centuries by welcoming those fleeing war or misery. This tradition of welcome and openness to others must be preserved."

Born as *Ana* Hidalgo in the Spanish province of Cádiz to an electrician and a seamstress, the mayor and her family fled Franco's regime in Spain and settled in an underprivileged suburb of Lyon, France, where she was raised with her older sister. By fourteen, she became Anne, a French citizen. As she told Lauren Bastide in an episode of *La Poudre*, her upbringing with other immigrants and working-class Lyonnais instilled a sense of dignity inextricably tied to work. "Life was hard, but we always found joy. My parents left school very young but showed me that through work I would develop a sense of self; I'd understand who I was meant to be."[46]

Perhaps she sensed then that who she was meant to be was a woman in Paris who studied diligently, earned degrees, found recognition, and carved out her own place in society despite the socioeconomic barriers to ascension that existed then as they often do now. The city was, by her own admission, not only the future but *her* future—from one of France's youngest labor inspectors to heir apparent of former mayor Bertrand Delanoë, for whom she served as deputy mayor in charge of gender parity and later urban planning and architecture, until her own mayoral win.

As mayor, she has held one of the biggest and most visible roles in French politics and one nearly as scrutinized as that of the president. If she's been vilified for trying to improve city living and aggressively tackling the climate crisis head-on, it's not solely on account of her reforms and urban rehabilitation initiatives. Observing her govern these last five years, despite countless attempts to sully her reputation and accuse her administration of wrongdoing, has certainly reinforced the reality that women in political leadership positions are too often demonized simply for daring to step out from behind the curtain.

"When I was elected [deputy mayor] in 2001, the press said I had no influence . . . that my appointment was purely cosmetic. I was the loyal number two, the uncharismatic shadow of Bertrand Delanoë, whom I'd never be able to rival," she told *Marie Claire* in 2018, addressing the torrent of insults and threats she's faced in her political career. "Then I become mayor, I do my job, and suddenly I am a hardened authoritarian."[47] The delegitimizing of women in power is not unique to Paris or Mayor Hidalgo, but it is a constant, tiresome burden that displaces attention from the far-reaching and necessary work she's been doing for the city.

The specter of profound change to the way Parisians live their lives—bikes before *bagnoles*, especially—has attracted legions of critics. The most virulent have framed her as self-glorifying and opportunistic in her hard-line policies to curb pollution through pedestrianization; one of the attendant outcomes of ridding the city of cars is a sort of suburbanization and quieting of urban areas. With that comes the distinct benefit of increasing real estate prices for residents—values go up, taxes increase, and the city benefits. Happy pedestrians and homeowners can only help to shore up her chances for reelection.

There is also the feeling that while the greenification of the city contributes to an indisputably more pleasant experience, it invariably redefines who gets access to it:[48] what merchants can afford to operate and where; how easy it is for those living outside city limits to come and go. Opponents perceive these measures to be elitist and further evidence of Paris becoming *une ville de riches*—a city for the wealthy. And yet I'd argue that she's far more in touch with the needs of the people and the city's deeply cosmopolitan heritage than the aristocratic career politicians she's run against (such as Nathalie Kosciusko-Morizet) and will invariably face in the March 2020 municipal elections. What's more, the fact that over half of drivers in the city *only* drive in Paris and 80 percent are doing so for nonprofessional reasons[49] would seem to challenge the idea that limiting cars necessarily disadvantages those residing in Greater Paris.

I have always found Mayor Hidalgo to be likeable, warm, articulate, and thoughtful. Since she took office, the city has been faced with periods of tremendous turmoil and disruption. Through Charlie Hebdo, the November thirteenth attacks, ongoing *gilets jaunes* demonstrations, and the fire at Notre Dame, she was admirably self-possessed, a reassuring and unifying figure. When I think of her time as mayor, perhaps the biggest flaw I see is her utopian vision of the city, reclaimed entirely by its citizens, no cars in sight, and an overzealous desire to reinvent Paris, even if it means isolating members of her own party. She takes risks and stands by her convictions, even if they make her unpopular. But I also think we can challenge her politics without diminishing her commitment to the city.

"Paris is a city that is observed and scrutinized like few others in the world," she said. "Its future is to stay true to its history and preserve its singularity, all while being able to reinvent itself and meet the greatest challenges of the twenty-first century."

Ushering Paris into the future, as a global capital with the potential to drive broad and lasting change, means ensuring it becomes a more sustainable, ecologically sound, and inclusive place to live and visit. And she is unrepentantly focused on getting us there.

---

opposite Hôtel de Ville, Anne Hidalgo's office since 2014.

Her Paris

FAVORITE WOMAN-RUN BUSINESS?

I think first of the Palais de la Femme in the 11th arrondissement. Run by the Salvation Army in a hundred-year-old building, the organization takes in and supports women in need. I love visiting Les Canaux in the 19th arrondissement, which is overseen by a former member of my team who left politics to support entrepreneurs and start-ups in the social and solidarity economy. And I have to mention the Théâtre du Châtelet, which reopened September 2019. For the last two years, it's been run by Ruth Mackenzie, an incredibly passionate woman who was previously in charge of the Holland Festival and the Scottish Opera. She has a creative energy that commands admiration.

SOMETHING YOU DO TO DISCONNECT FROM WORK?

I devour the books I'm sent or happen to get my hands on. My local bookstore knows this about me and occasionally slips books into my mailbox!

A SOLO RITUAL?

I used to love to run, but an injury put a stop to that. Now it's by bicycle that I connect with the city.

Upending stereotypes and sexism as advertising's moral compass

CHRISTELLE DELARUE

FOUNDER AND CEO OF MAD&WOMEN AGENCY

"THIS IS WHAT I WAKE UP TO in the morning," says Christelle Delarue with a toothy grin, pulling aside her gauzy white curtains to reveal an unobstructed view of the Hôtel de Ville bathed in sunlight. The esplanade, which hosts everything from climate demonstrations to gay pride rallies, looms in her front yard. Just imagining the front-row seat she has from her balcony to the everyday bustle, the celebration, and the occasional chaos is exhilarating. "No matter what's going on, the energy gets me going," she tells me, stepping back into her living room as a gust of wind blows open the books neatly stacked on her dining room table, which doubles as her desk: Mona Chollet's *Beauté fatale* is propped next to her computer like essential reference material.

The apartment, with exquisite columns and stained glass, carries the spirit of activism not only in its proximity to the city's civic heart but in the double purpose it serves. It's Delarue's personal cocoon, her favorite place to read and write. And every Saturday morning, it becomes a safe space for women in media who have been the victims of sexual assault or discrimination to talk and receive guidance. Delarue is in a particularly good place to lead such a support group. The idea for her company, Mad&Women, France's first feminist advertising agency dedicated to fighting gender stereotypes, emerged after years of battling sexism in the industry.

That she has committed her work to effecting change for women—who, she highlights, influence 85 percent of the global economy, but 91 percent of them feel that advertisers don't understand them[50]—wouldn't surprise anyone who knew her as a child.

When we meet for coffee at Le Richer on a separate occasion, Delarue takes me back to the beginning. A self-described "hyperactive chatterbox," she was a precocious kid, aware of the world's injustices and forever incensed by them. "I was brought up to question *no*," she says. Raised in the Paris suburbs, she came from a culture of mutual support: you scratch my back; I'll scratch yours. She's the girl who'd give up her seat in the front row of the classroom for friends who had difficulties. When she couldn't dunk a basketball, she tutored her fellow players in math in exchange for help on the court. "That's how it was—we'll get there together," a radically different mentality, she insists, from Parisians who had more money, whose parents worked closer to home or not at all, who had more flexible hours, who were there to guide them. The idea of creating something together or helping others succeed because it helps you in return was fundamental to her upbringing. And it's a value that's always stayed with her.

As she got slightly older and spent her free time with her head buried in magazines, she was struck by the extent to which the messaging in ads left much of the population behind, herself included. "I distinctly remember feeling shocked by the expectations they created; I didn't feel represented at all. When I was twelve, I started cutting out the ads and repurposing them in a notebook with sketches and storyboards. I was re-creating the real story. It was cynical, but I was demonstrating the impact of advertising," she recalls proudly.

When she passed the final-year baccalaureate exam and got her driver's license, her sights were set on Paris where she, unsurprisingly, pursued studies in communication. "When women from the suburbs want to grow up, they go to Paris. There's a proximity to culture and education. Early on, we're encouraged to cross the Périph," she explains of the concrete beltway that runs around Paris, as much a psychological, ethnic, and social barrier between the city and the suburbs as a physical one. Through its fashion scene, gargantuan libraries, and cultural institutions, Paris was to be a form of social emancipation.

"The first time I stepped into the Panthéon, I told myself I wanted to die there," she begins, looking to the street and taking a hit of her cigarette. "It's sensational to be surrounded by so much beauty, diversity, and potential. A bit like when Parisians go to New York—these are world capitals that draw you in with their magic and the possibility for transformation." And it's transformation she knew she'd lead one day.

She ended up in New York City at the end of her degree to intern, and it proved to be the jolt she anticipated. She was curious and hardworking and quickly

---

opposite Inside Christelle Delarue's Paris apartment, her creative sanctuary and gathering place for women in the industry who need guidance.

blossomed. "I remember working on my first big international ad campaign for GM with a massive budget—it was surreal. My father had gotten me into race cars as a kid. I loved cars. I was thrilled to be on an automobile project because what I *didn't* want was for the work to be gendered. I'm female, and therefore I should work on a L'Oréal brand—no."

Once she returned to Paris, she realized that it's not only the brands and projects themselves that are gendered but the office relationships. Agency life in Paris hasn't evolved enough from the pervasive Mad Men–era codes of conduct where the white men in sharp suits (or tight jeans, tees, and blazers, as it were) are handed opportunity on a silver platter. Delarue's experience back in Paris mirrored much of my own observations while working for advertising and marketing agencies—they were hotbeds of patriarchal thought.

"I was constantly told to calm down, take it easy, stop pushing for more, be happy managing one client account. Isn't that enough? Meanwhile, all my male colleagues had access to multiple accounts. When I insisted, I was informed that I couldn't be pretty *and* intelligent in this industry," she remembers as if it were yesterday. She was steadfast in her refusal to be sidelined, but the reality was dismal.

As the account director at Buzzman, among the city's more bro-ish creative agencies, she was perpetually defending the role of women as more than the primary consumers for the household. "I was fighting against sexism at all turns, but it ran too deep." The behavior wasn't going to change, so out she went. By thirty, she had become the associate director of Marcel, an agency in Publicis, the world's fourth-largest communication group, and was still being asked to fetch coffee for meetings (worse, they were meetings she was leading). As one of few women in leadership, she had to be everything—a matriarch, a mentor, a change-maker, and a business driver. And she was perhaps the only one doing the hard work of questioning gendered codes and behaviors, challenging deeply embedded sexism that trickles down from the creative teams onto the campaigns themselves. "When it's done right, advertising has the power to influence social change. But that wasn't the case in either of the last two places I worked, so I left."

Fed up, she took six months off to travel and attend conferences led by industry experts around the world on transhumanism, the end of the digital era, and civil society in motion. She made connections, filled twenty-seven notebooks with observations, and considered the stereotypes that persisted. The experience crystallized what she had always known: more women were needed in advertising, and she could be part of making that happen.

"Brands and ad agencies ignore that they are partly responsible for the divisions that exist today. They have a responsibility to fix them."

"Women have the purchasing power but are stereotyped left and right. Why? For starters, only 11 percent of creative directors in the world are women.[51] Eighty-two percent of expert roles [such as doctors, lawyers, etc.] are represented by male actors,[52] even in ads meant to promote gender equality and women's empowerment. We need more women in strategic roles."

Since she founded Mad&Women in 2012, competing agencies haven't changed much, but she's observed an evolution in the awareness of her clients. It may have taken some convincing early on, but today it's easier to get everyone on board with the fact that feminism is a lever for gender equality. "If brands and companies hesitate, I let the numbers do the talking: nonstereotyped advertising campaigns generate a return on investment of more than 26 percent.[53] It's good for business and for women's representation."

And big brands and organizations are taking notice: LVMH hired her company to come up with an international campaign to promote their e-commerce website 24 Sèvres. Their tongue-in-cheek execution deconstructed common clichés (Parisians don't shave, they're always stressed, they only wear black) and offered a fresh take on a sartorial icon. Mayor Anne Hidalgo and her administration brought Delarue on board in their efforts to fight sexism in advertising in the public sphere (in a city campaign called *Pour un Paris sans Pub Sexiste*); she was named the expert advisor to UNESCO's gender equality division in 2019; and she regularly speaks at conferences about gender inclusion in advertising and fighting stereotypes in everyday life with concrete actions.

She says she'd be remiss not to credit #MeToo as a turning point in consciousness that has liberated expression, opened up the possibility for debate, and spurred a celebration of female-forward messages. Without question, that's a positive outcome. But while advertisers are more aware of the necessity to increase women's representation in campaigns, Delarue feels they've largely surfed on the movement as a marketing tool. "It's *femwashing*. Women may be more visible, but they end up confined to the same stereotypical roles," she explains. "We need real, considered action. We need women representing different bodies, skin colors, ages, and professions. Because if we

change the way women view themselves and the way institutions view them, we can reach greater equality."

Transformation must also extend to behaviors and overall work culture within agencies themselves. Following an investigative report in *Le Monde* in February 2019 revealing a deep culture of misogyny and accounts of sexual harassment and abuse at the agency Herezie, Delarue established Les Lionnes, a women's organization that aims to protect, defend (especially in court), and promote the rights of women working in advertising and communication. "The industry needs our talent and our voices more than ever," she wrote in an announcement on LinkedIn about her motivations in setting up the organization. "Now hear us roar."

Before we part ways, I think back to what she said about solidarity as a fundamental value and wonder how that plays out in her quest to end the objectification of women in the images we consume. "I don't carry this on my own. I'm bringing as many women on board as I can," she says firmly. "We're more powerful together."

---

above Inspirational reading on Christelle Delarue's desk at home.

Her Paris

FAVORITE WOMAN-RUN BUSINESS?

Ma Cocotte in Saint-Ouen (Sunday lunch!) in the middle of the Marché aux Puces. I often dream of having a huge house with a bunch of friends where we'd share simple but hearty meals together, and that's the atmosphere I get here. It's run by an extraordinary woman—a shape-shifting artist and a wonderful host.

SOMEPLACE YOU GO TO RECHARGE?

Anywhere on a horse! But when I can't do that, I lose myself in the parts of Paris I don't know as well, or I go straight to green spaces like the Buttes-Chaumont or the Luxembourg Gardens. I shut off my music and I observe people.

GO-TO SPOTS FOR AN APÉRITIF WITH YOUR FRIENDS?

I love the bar at the Royal Monceau. With a glass of white wine, I could stay for hours; it relaxes me. The terrace of Le Petit Fer à Cheval or Le Pick-Clops in the Marais or Le Pavillon Puebla, a suspended garden bar in the heart of the Buttes-Chaumont Park (shown above).

Leading innovation in aviation
and mentoring the engineers of tomorrow

DELPHINE DIJOUD

AERONAUTICAL ENGINEER

IN FRANCE, ONLY ONE IN FIVE ENGINEERS is a woman. Being part of that minority has never bothered Delphine Dijoud, a woman who has always marched to her own drum. She was one of few women in her graduating class from Les Mines, one of France's most prestigious engineering schools, and tried her hand at various industries, from automobiles to luxury perfumes, before landing in aviation. Recognized early on for her leadership potential, she has been fortunate to work for a company that has been a partner in her success every step of the way—a slightly different story from the one we often hear about women in male-dominated industries. When we met for tea on an autumn weekend, we discussed her rapid climb to leadership, the issue of parity in the workplace, and what she perceives as the remaining barriers for women to get ahead in aviation.

As a kid, did you know you wanted to become an engineer and what that implied? No, I actually wanted to be a doctor! I was drawn to the scientific and human side of medicine, but in the end, I had trouble seeing myself having to announce bad news on a daily basis. Fortunately, I was good in the sciences and in math, and was genuinely fascinated by how things were made. I had a family that really emphasized academics but, thankfully, left the career up to me.

What made you consider shifting to aviation? I was interested in technical products and then noticed a job opening for a position in an aviation company. Despite the industry having a reputation for being extremely masculine, I never felt that the hiring process was any different for me because I was a woman, which I greatly respected. Throughout all of my interviews and early encounters with

the teams I'd be working with, I saw people that were truly passionate about this field and open to me stepping in despite my having a more atypical background. And when I started, I discovered a super-exciting industry, from a strategic and technical perspective, and in terms of its global scope.

You were identified quickly as one of the talents to watch. How did that happen? After two years, there was a reorganization, and my manager at the time offered me a new role. You have to keep in mind, in a massive company like this, promotions and role changes don't happen very quickly. From then on, I was never really given the time to think or look elsewhere. I was singled out (in a good way) and encouraged. I also had a mentor: the adjunct technical director. She taught me a lot. She's someone who is very demanding; you have to really show her you're worth her investment. I guess I did that, because she was instrumental in me continuing to evolve.

In what ways were you encouraged? There was a difficult moment in my personal life, when I was going through a divorce, and it was clear I wasn't doing well. The head of HR at that time had me do different career assessments and interviews when they could've just closed the door on me. They knew how to guide me through a low period. They weren't prepared to let me go.

How does it feel to know you were seen as such a valuable asset? I'd be lying if I said it didn't present a bit of a dilemma. It's obviously wonderful to be esteemed in such a way, but I don't really have free will. For once, a woman is offered a wonderful, visible role! But is it really what I want to do? I don't want to suffer through it just because. I want to follow my own path. And there's the question of balance—these positions are never free of stress.

You're responsible for the development of future concepts. Is this a position you wanted? Yes, but it was also another role offered to me [*laughs*]. In this role, I'm heavily focused on innovation and agility. Everything takes ages to come together—we're in France, after all. It's motivating but time- and energy-consuming.

What makes you say that it takes ages? It's our Cartesian side ("Yes, but . . .") that slows us down. We see the risks more than we see opportunities, and we overthink concepts before we test them. And since I've seen how it works on the other side, working in the US, it's frustrating. But it's also through these French-American alliances that our work is strong—the marriage of a more entrepreneurial, risk-taking approach with that of a more cautious approach.

And to do this job, you're leading a sizable team. Do you enjoy being a manager? Before, I managed a team of one hundred people, but now, I also serve a representative role, which leaves me less time to manage directly, day to day, which frustrates me. The work in teams is important to me, and I draw a lot of my energy from those exchanges. I don't know how to stay calm in a corner. We're working on complex issues that require collective intelligence, and I think it's important to show people that they aren't just a number but a real part of the mix, making things happen. We'll see where I go from here.

How has the environment been within your company for women looking to get into the industry? It's been a real priority. On the education side, the company has been involved in an organization that shows the role women do and can play in the industry. I've also worked with the company on the renewal of their gender parity program and saw that the questions we needed to tackle were no longer about salary, but about the more insidious barriers—like, are we offering high-profile, highly visible roles to enough women? Regardless of what kind of work-life balance [accompanies] those roles, HR has to be in a position to offer them to women, including women with children. In this group, we also addressed another issue, which is how men will jump for some roles and women hold back from even applying. The barriers don't only come from companies but from all sides, and understanding that is crucial to creating an environment that works to foster lasting, substantial change.

You sound relieved that the company is a bit more advanced than you would have thought in handling such questions. Honestly, things have evolved tremendously. When I first started, people would still greet a room full of people with *bonjour, messieurs*. Today, we're not aiming for absolute parity but proportionality. You can't have 50 percent women when those numbers aren't even there in the engineering schools. Otherwise, it's positive discrimination, which I don't agree with.

How have you gotten involved on issues of parity outside of the office? I've been part of Frateli, an organization whose objective is to help brilliant students from underprivileged backgrounds. We guide and mentor them until they enter the workforce. And that's an important commitment. At work, I serve as an ambassador for the company to various schools and can help [students] as they consider their professional path. This isn't specific to women, but female students seem to naturally come speak to me. And when I see them, I realize there's still work to be done on equality and parity at an educational level.

Do you consider yourself a role model for other women who may look at you and think, okay, it's possible to climb to a leadership role in aviation? I should say first of all, that we've had a female managing director but never a woman in charge of production or technical teams. So there are still higher leadership roles that could still be filled by women, should they want them. As for me, I see my contribution in terms of the students I get to engage with and even with my team, who I can help evolve. It's actually what I love in management. I remember a young woman who was incredibly reserved, and we did a bunch of exploratory interviews about what she wanted to do and I helped reorient her. Since then, she's blossomed. That's where I can say, okay, I was useful! But I wouldn't go so far as to call myself a role model. I question my legitimacy every single day, and did even more so when I first started the role. Of course, that's a very common problem for women.

Where is there still work to be done? In two areas: I think the media has put a lot of emphasis in recent years on stories about female entrepreneurs and chefs rather than those in business and engineering. It's a shift that needs to happen—people need to see that women are visible in all fields. And engineering schools need to work harder to admit female applicants—the students of merit are out there!—by speaking to them early on and making sure they see the academic environment as an inclusive place.

Her Paris

FAVORITE WOMAN-RUN BUSINESS?

Le Servan, run by Tatiana and Katia Levha. I love their cooking, the Asian twist, the incredible ingredients they source, and the cozy atmosphere they've created.

SOLO RITUAL?

At least once every two months, I get myself a massage for stress relief. It might be a Thai massage at Ban Sabai or at Calma Paris, where they offer mood-driven massages.

WHERE YOU'D TAKE SOMEONE INTERESTED IN SCIENCE AND ENGINEERING?

To the Musée des Arts et Métiers and the Palais de la Découverte in the Grand Palais (shown above), where there are wonderful science experiments often led by PhD students.

SARAH ZOUAK

SOCIAL ENTREPRENEUR, FILMMAKER, AND COFOUNDER OF LALLAB

INCOMPATIBLE: THE IDEA OF two things or two people being so ill-matched and contradictory in nature that they couldn't possibly coexist in the world. We often think of the word in terms of amorous coupling, but what about when the elements of one's very beliefs are seen to be irreconcilably opposed and are refuted by society? Sarah Zouak, the cofounder of Lallab, a nonprofit organization, community, and online magazine that challenges existing narratives around Muslim women, was hearing that her identification with feminist values is incompatible with her Muslim faith long before she had even formally recognized them as feminist. When she proposed a master's thesis exploring feminism and the Muslim experience in Morocco, her professor told her it couldn't be done; the two topics were entirely separate, inconsistent, incompatible.

Such is the myopic notion shared by much of the world. "For one, it's always *la femme* Musulmane, never *les femmes*," Zouak points out. "We're described as a monolithic block, each of us identical in every way." How can Muslim women be feminist and support feminist principles when they are subjugated and oppressed, close-minded, and backward? So the questioning goes. "What's tough about growing up in France is being told incessantly that Islam is misogynistic and oppressive to women, when this wasn't my experience at all."

As destabilizing as the invalidation of her beliefs was, the moment with her professor marked the beginning of her formal quest to understand the feminist experiences of other Muslim women in the world.

When we meet, she's virtually glowing in the window seat of a small coffee shop near the Place des Vosges, still euphoric from getting married the week before. Glistening in the sun, her wedding ring casts a sharp ray of light on our table.

She feels energized, she tells me; her personal joy a welcome distraction from the critics who dismiss her work and from the flurry of Islamophobic missives she and her team field on a usual day. A little break to celebrate love keeps things in perspective, even for the most ardent of activists.

Zouak and her two sisters were raised to be socially and politically minded, academically driven, and heavily involved in extracurriculars, much like their parents were when they came to France from Morocco for their university studies. The eight-o'clock nightly news was sacred, a time to debate world events as a family and express their opinions openly. "They gave us space and freedom to develop as independent women," she says smiling. She and her sisters could, and would, pursue whatever they wanted.

Inside their home, Moroccan traditions kept the girls anchored to their heritage, and her parents' progressive values drove them forward. Never rely on men, Zouak's mother instructed. Together, their parents taught them to embrace their French-Moroccan identities wholly and peacefully, despite how torn they would feel at times between the two. Like many immigrant families, education was paramount, but so was the relentless, unspoken pressure to fold neatly into the dominant culture and to be "good" and "successful" Muslims—a feeling that builds up until the self-imposition of it all is effaced by the glaring reality that it's society as a whole that's expecting Zouak and citizens like her to be so very little.

Zouak's classmates, well intentioned though they thought they were being, would tell her she was the exception—unlike the others. She deviated from their expectations. But even that sense of acceptance was tenuous. "Children from immigrant families often think they have to represent their entire community, and that's a tremendous responsibility. Even if we apply ourselves, work hard, excel, achieve success like anyone else, all it takes is a Muslim to set off a bomb to sully our collective reputation," she tells me despondently. In a moment, she could be reduced to broad-stroke generalizations about an entire religion.

Even in business school, she knew her intelligence and merit weren't enough to prove she belonged, so despite her chagrin, she upheld the same charade, doing whatever she could to prove she was three times as funny and open-minded. She would not be reduced to a stereotype.

If she accepts who she is today—an amalgam of two nations and two cultures— she credits a particularly formative postgraduate experience. She embarked on a five-month, five-country tour to produce a series of feature-length documentaries aimed at reshaping the image of Muslim women and demonstrating how they live

"*Laïcité* is unfortunately misunderstood. I'm proud to live in a country where you can believe or choose not to believe. But it's often used to exclude."

out their feminism. The Women SenseTour in Muslim Countries took her to Iran, Indonesia, Morocco, Tunisia, and Turkey, and lifted any lingering doubt that the two states of being could coexist.

"The women I met changed my life. I knew I'd need to take the whole thing farther," she tells me, her eyes lighting up as if articulating the memory was enough to cast aside the hurt and frustration that tend to go hand in hand with any discussion of her life experiences in France. She had zeroed in on her calling, the one far greater than her and daunting in what it would demand of her—imperturbability and a boundless reserve of optimism, for starters. She would establish an organization committed to defending Muslim women against both sexism and racism, and in doing so, she'd be filling a glaring gap. "The country's largest feminist organizations and antiracist organizations weren't taking racism into account when, in fact, racism and violence against Muslim women are eminently linked. In France, 70 percent of Islamophobic acts are committed against women.[54] We can't dissociate the two," she says.

The problem, she insists, is the dominant universalist approach to feminism that believes it stands for and represents all women. "But so many women are left out. It's the whole point of intersectionality. Some of the Muslim women that come to our events aren't even thinking of pay equality; they just want a job—they're discriminated against for jobs and housing because of their names and appearances," she explains. As a result, Zouak officially launched Lallab in 2015 with her friend Justine Devillaine (an atheist) and got to work fighting the pathologization of Muslim women.

That means fighting a system—composed of intellectuals, press, politicians, and feminists—that spends inordinate amounts of time debating and politicizing the country's Muslim population. Specifically, whether or not the head scarf is a symbol of oppression or a violation of the nation's values of *laïcité*, while rarely soliciting the opinions of the women who wear them or opt not to. (Similarly, disabled individuals and lesbians fighting for the right to access IVF treatments are equally as absent from discussions that impact them.) Too often, Muslim women are silenced. When they're heard, they're demonized. Her organization is committed to giving Muslim women their voice and a platform so that, at long last, they can speak for themselves.

Lallab runs thematic discussion groups; hosts activities focused on personal development; provides resources and training programs to understand and resist stereotypes; produces documentaries; organizes antiprejudice workshops in schools; and leads talks on Islamophobia at the Senate and the UN, all in an effort to change the way Muslim women are seen and understood.

Zouak and her volunteers draft opinion pieces for Lallab's online magazine (where one can find stories like "The Top 13 Absurd Daily Conversations about My Hijab" and "Why I Decided to Remove My Veil"), *Le Monde,* and *Médiapart.* She gives interviews but laments being asked to address the same hot-take issues: the niqab, terrorism, and oppression. She's at the source of change, lobbying alongside those within the government who are actively working to make the country more inclusive. Sometimes she gets the sense that things are moving forward, but she's wary of Lallab being treated as a tool to clear consciences: "All of the biggest changes in history happen when impacted people mobilize together and make their voices heard, establishing their own political agenda. It's up to us to do this with our allies—Jewish, Christian, agnostic, and atheist women."

Despite the clarity of the organization's objectives, she and her cofounder have encountered resistance that has made solidarity slower to develop than they'd like. "We've been baselessly accused of being financed by the Muslim Brotherhood, we've heard that we're terrorists . . . and this from both the left and those in power. It's irresponsible. I shouldn't have to spend my time confronting lies," she says in rightful anger.

Is she optimistic? That's the question looming over us throughout our conversation. Naturally, I wonder how I would feel in her position. "Do you believe sentiment can change here?" I ask her, suspecting that it's her faith that gives ballast to her pursuit even when the odds are stacked against her. "I'm hopeful," she begins, calling out her solid support network of friends, family, and volunteers—her everyday champions. "But it's hard to fight each day for women to simply be what they want to be."

Her Paris

FAVORITE WOMAN-RUN BUSINESS?

La Caféothèque, a wonderful specialty coffee shop, and the feminist LGBTQ bookstore Violette and Co in the 11th arrondissement.

GO-TO NEIGHBORHOOD?

The 13th arrondissement! I did my prep studies near Tolbiac, and I spend a lot of time near the BNF (Bibliothèque Nationale de France, shown above). It's the Paris that people often don't come to see but should.

WHERE YOU GO FOR A DOSE OF CULTURE?

With my husband, who is an illustrator, we like to hit up lesser-known galleries like Arts Factory in the 11th arrondissement, which specializes in contemporary graphic art spanning illustration, digital design, and comics.

Challenging the traditional roles of women in the Jewish faith

DELPHINE HORVILLEUR

RABBI AND AUTHOR

AS ONE OF ONLY THREE female rabbis in France, Delphine Horvilleur is something of a controversial figure. Not because she is Jewish, but because she is a married woman with three children in a religious leadership position and dares to believe there is room for more liberal interpretations of Judaism and Jewish life that include women, in and outside of the synagogue. Her progressive values and commitments to interreligious dialogue are seen as an affront by the Orthodox majority and the Grand Rabbi of the Jewish Central Consistory, the state-authorized governing body of French Jews, who still does not recognize her rabbinical practice.

In no way, however, does that impede her quest to challenge traditional teachings, advocate for women's rights, and encourage religious faith to exist as part of a plurality of identities. Her humanism and tireless work fighting racism and anti-Semitism in Europe earned her the recognition as one of the Global Hope Coalition's five Heroes Against Extremism and Intolerance in 2018. We spent a morning in the Marais speaking about her personal journey to embrace her Jewish faith, the battle between tradition and modernity, and the complexity of religious affirmation amid French universalism.

Were you raised in a religious family? I come from a very culturally Jewish family but not a very practicing one. They adhered to a model of "Franco-Judaism," an identity entwined with both an incredibly strong attachment to France and its history, and to Jewishness. In other words, in my family there was a deep love for France and a profound respect for the secular values of the republic.

Was that duality ever confusing for you? From a very young age, I questioned the meaning of each aspect of my identity—Jewish, French, European—and how they came together and spoke with one another. On top of that, there's our family's double history. There's the story of my father's side—a French-Jewish family in France for centuries and saved by the Righteous Among the Nations during the war and forever thankful to France. On my mother's side, they were survivors of the concentration camps and lost everyone in the war. They rebuilt a family in which my mother was born. So I was living between two narratives: one of trust and one of mistrust. This cognitive dissonance definitely shaped me; I had to reconcile with two stories that were incompatible. Was my Jewish identity joyful or painful? Was it built on trust or suspicion? Would it create friendly or hostile relationships?

At seventeen, you left your small hometown of Épernay in eastern France, with very few Jews, for Israel. What were you searching for? I went to discover the country and work on a kibbutz before enrolling in the Hebrew University of Jerusalem, where I studied for four years. It was during the Oslo accords; we believed there would be peace. Yitzhak Rabin was prime minister, but then he was assassinated and that changed everything. Devastated, I went back to France and I changed directions to become a broadcast journalist and radio correspondent. The most extraordinary moments happen when we change our minds and reinvent ourselves. Meanwhile, I started studying the sacred texts. It always interested me but not as a traditional religious quest, more insofar as I was curious about what these texts could teach us about our history.

When did you realize you wanted to investigate this in a more structured, professional capacity? In Paris, in the early 2000s, I started to look for classes to study the Talmud but was quickly confronted with a problem: These classes were reserved for men. I was told, repeatedly, to go to New York. So I went for what was meant to be three months of study at a Yeshiva, and that turned into several years because I decided to begin a rabbinical program at the Hebrew Union College of New York. In 2008, I received my reformed rabbinic ordination. I moved back to Paris and have been one of the rabbis at the western Paris congregation of the MJLF (the Liberal Judaism Movement of France), a liberal synagogue, ever since.

What have you learned through this role? We're living in a time where people have the illusion that in order to live an identity faithfully, they have to identically reproduce something from the past. I think it's the exact opposite. Identity is fluid and shifting. We are what we are because we're no longer where we were before and there is something inside us that isn't the same from one generation to another.

This obsession with reducing individuals to their ethnic groups or families is a complete negation of the Enlightenment. We're trampling on an extremely important universal heritage of empathy that tells us we don't need to be the other to understand the other. I've tried to change things here, but it's challenging; we are, paradoxically, in a country that is both extremely *laïque* (see *laïcité* page 23) with fierce antireligious sentiment (religion is seen as the opium of the old-fashioned) and with religious voices that express themselves in the public sphere almost exclusively with a hypertraditionalist stance. This was especially palpable during the gay marriage debate, where we only heard from religious groups who opposed the practice.

It's because religion isn't all that important in France that we accept that religious leaders make remarks that are inconsistent with the convictions of civil society. This is a problem because whether we like it or not, this religious discourse is political and has an impact on the state.

Having said this, is laïcité still realistic as an ideal? I think that *laïcité* is a real blessing for French society, but we've lost sight of what it is supposed to mean. For some, it's a guarantee of religious freedom. But it's really a freedom of consciousness: Each citizen has the right to believe or not believe without being subjected to pressure from one's membership group. *Laïcité* is meant to ensure a neutral space and was established as a protection against religious pressure.

But it's certainly been amended in questionable ways, like to ban religious symbols. It's a gray area. There are places, like public schools, which can be called sanctuaries of the republic, that must remain neutral from all religious pressure, the suspicion being that food and clothing mask a kind of proselytism. Of course that can give rise to abuses.

Within the current understanding of laïcité, do you think that women who wear the veil are able to express themselves freely? When veiled women tell me that it's entirely their choice to wear the veil, I tell them that we cannot deny that their theologians see that bit of fabric as a tool for domination. And even if for these women it doesn't symbolize that, we cannot ignore the collective speech around it. I will always support women who choose to dress the way they want, but one cannot pretend that wearing a veil is a "feminist statement" as long as a very firm voice of

criticism against religious patriarchy isn't expressed inside that tradition. During the Fascist years in Italy, wearing a black shirt signified an affiliation to the Fascist movement. It doesn't matter if wearing a black shirt means something different for you. Our acts and our words impact more than ourselves. They can never be disconnected from a more general political discussion. Today, this needs to be fought in all religions.

You wrote "A Thousand and One Ways to Be Jewish or Muslim" with Islamologist Rachid Benzine. Are you both aligned with the idea that individual actions impact more than ourselves? Absolutely, we come together on these questions of refusing religious feminism. I stopped saying that I was a feminist Jew and instead that I am a feminist and a Jew because I think it's dangerous to lead anyone to believe there is feminism in our sacred texts. And we don't do these texts any favors by inserting our political agendas. We must commit to a critical reading of our texts and traditions, and that begins by recognizing that they are full of patriarchy.

This line of thinking has earned you a fair share of criticism. Why do you think you're considered a divisive, even heretical figure? The most conservative religious voices (particularly the Orthodox Jewry) see my self-expression and media exposure as a threat. The fact that I could possibly speak in the name of French Jews infuriates them because it legitimizes the feminization of the rabbinical function. Those who consider me a traitor are the traitors of tradition—they won't let it evolve as it needs to.

Your work questions a woman's place, but what can be interpreted from the historic texts themselves, if anything? It really depends on the time period, and this is true in all religions. That's why it isn't useful to ask if our religions are misogynistic or feminist: It depends on the time period and the voices. If you look hard enough, you'll find what you need to support your own ideology. The question is, is Judaism misogynistic in 2020? The answer is often yes, when it doesn't make room for women, physically or by representing their voices.

France has long had a reputation for anti-Semitism, and acts of violence have flared in Paris in recent years. Do you think the Jewish experience is unique in France? First of all, anti-Semitism is everywhere, not only in France. But France is particularly emblematic in this discussion because the country has been both

---

opposite A source of relaxation for Delphine Horvilleur: walking along the river.

a shining light and a terrible shadow for Jews. France was the first country to emancipate the Jews, to give them citizenship, but was also home to the Dreyfus affair. The first to have a Jewish governmental head, Léon Blum, in the 1930s, but also the home of the Vichy regime. So when we grow up as Jews in France, we are aware that this country can be both the best and the worst. It's a love-hate relationship, and that has a lot to do with its history: the French myth that it has something to bring to the world. It's what united France and America, actually. They are two nations that behave as though they have a mission to influence the world. But Jews also tell themselves the same thing.

Does the city do enough to combat anti-Semitism? The authorities do a lot but it is still beyond them. Anti-Semitism is embedded in the discourse of the masses; it's diffused, unlike the institutional anti-Semitism of World War II. Today, it's extremely taboo in the French political class. But in some rough neighborhoods, hate directed toward Jews grows in parallel with hate directed toward France. So when the state protects or stands up for Jews, it is seen to confirm certain conspiracy theories wherein the state is in cahoots with the Jews. When a synagogue is attacked and the state sends soldiers to stand guard in front of it, it's interpreted as further proof that the Jews are more protected than everyone else. We must step away from this conspiratorial rhetoric and competition of victimhood. We're all responsible for this: Parents, educators, religious leaders— everyone in a position to teach and educate must urgently promote narratives of resilience and self-reinvention. Young people must learn they are not victims.

Could Paris make this happen? Is it a suitable place to spread messages of religious harmony? By nature of its demographics, Paris is special: It has the largest Jewish and Muslim populations in coexistence in the world. That could make the city an unbelievable lab of exchange. But like France as a whole, its history is based on universalism and a rejection of communalism, and so we can never really talk about it in this way.

Religious affiliations or beliefs aside, what do you think it means to be a woman in Paris today? Refusing dogma to protect our way of life.

Her Paris

FAVORITE WOMAN-RUN BUSINESS?

Tavline, a very creative restaurant specialized in Israeli cooking that matches what I believe in: the coming together of tradition with a contemporary twist.

A PARISIAN RITUAL YOU COULDN'T LIVE WITHOUT?

Every morning, I go to a local café with my psychoanalyst friend to read the paper and debate the news. In New York, I missed this terribly—the morning café environment, where you remake the world and complain *à la française*. It's a space that's very inspiring, almost religious, for me. I write almost all of my sermons at these neighborhood cafés (like the one shown above), and it's one of the reasons I don't think I could ever leave Paris again.

WHERE DO YOU GO TO DISCONNECT FROM WORK?

There's nothing more relaxing to me than walking along the riverbanks or listening to the musicians playing on the city's bridges, especially on the Île Saint-Louis.

DR. GHADA HATEM-GANTZER

OB-GYN AND FOUNDER OF LA MAISON DES FEMMES

AT LA MAISON DES FEMMES, a rainbow-hued family justice refuge in Saint-Denis, a largely immigrant suburb north of Paris, women come for help, guidance, and a moment free from judgment. There are no victims here, simply women who know that their minds and bodies will be treated with humanity.

The thirty to sixty women who descend upon the center each day consider its founder, Dr. Ghada Hatem-Gantzer, obstetrician-gynecologist, something of a guardian angel. With a maternal smile and kind blue eyes, she and her team of specialists, from psychologists to sexologists and surgeons, are on hand every day to address everything from the most common concerns—contraception, family planning, sexual education, and counseling during pregnancy—to the most traumatic cases of domestic violence (including forced marriage), sexual abuse, genital mutilation, incest, and rape. They bring in self-defense coaches to offer free classes and run workshops on personal development and empowerment, creating a spirit of community and solidarity.

On any given day, the floor-to-ceiling windows of the center catch the slightest ray of light, brightening the space to match the warmth of the walls, adorned with vibrant colors. Each consultation room bears the name of a strong female figure—Gisèle Halimi, Malala Yousafzai, Frida Kahlo. For women who have suffered abuse or need guidance, the center stands tall as a beacon of hope, just as the doctor intended.

Born, raised, and educated in a Francophone environment in Beirut, Dr. Ghada Hatem-Gantzer came to Paris in 1977 to escape the war and pursue a medical degree, initially expecting to specialize in child psychiatry. "I couldn't do it. Maybe it's because I experienced how war affects kids," she says. It was her time interning in gynecology that sealed her future. "There's psychology, surgery, specialty—everything. I felt I could be useful there." Her plans after graduating were unclear, but she knew she couldn't go back to an oppressive atmosphere of war. Fate stepped in: she met a Frenchman and built her career and a family in Paris.

She tells me of her years as head of maternity at Les Bluets, the city's leading clinic, where Dr. Fernand Lamaze first introduced the method of "painless childbirth," followed by the eight years she spent overseeing the maternity ward at Bégin, the military hospital in Saint-Mandé. She treated ambassadors' and soldiers' wives and the women serving in the military. And it was there that the universality of domestic and sexual abuse occurred to her. "It isn't only the underprivileged who suffer through this."

An annex of the Delafontaine hospital in Saint-Denis visible from the street, La Maison des Femmes, opened in 2016 as a litmus test for the long-term viability of a dedicated center, the first of its kind in France. The idea was a response to the shortcomings of the hospital's family planning unit. "We couldn't keep up with the requests we were getting, and we weren't equipped to address the specific cases of abuse and violence we were seeing," says Dr. Hatem-Gantzer, who was awarded the Legion of Honor in 2015 for her work for women's rights and health. She estimates that 14 to 16 percent of pregnant women they were seeing had been victims of female genital mutilation; responding to that sufficiently required the right training and the right environment.

But would it work? The questions she faced were legion. Would women feel safe coming to them? Would they put their trust in her and her team? And equally as important a concern, would she be able to execute her vision with the funds she could secure—about 950,000 euros—largely from foundations and private donors? "While this was in the works, a new hospital director came along who was risk-averse and unwilling to devote much money to what I was trying to establish. But she couldn't stop the project from developing. I had to bring this whole thing to life without much support," she says. "But my strength is figuring things out. The Lebanese are good at that!"

And figuring it out was her moral obligation, for the sake of the women whose fates are imperiled and whose only source of information, support, and care would be Dr. Hatem-Gantzer and her team. Centralizing all of it was one way to make victims more likely to ask for help. "Our patients don't have to wait months to see a doctor—it's quick. And when there's urgency, we can act accordingly," she explains.

---

opposite A beacon of hope: Dr. Hatem-Gantzer's family justice center in Saint-Denis.

In her perspective, these are issues not only of injustice that needed attention but of public health.

She often reminds her volunteers and interns that domestic abuse and violence impacts women across all social and cultural backgrounds. As one of the most socially and economically distressed areas of the country, however, the department of Seine-Saint-Denis presents a great challenge, especially when it comes to the particular nature of a patient's circumstances. Dr. Hatem-Gantzer has seen every scenario—the undocumented who were abused while migrating to France; the women who have been forced into arranged marriages and into procreating against their will; the women who can't speak French to express their pain; those who are homeless because they are escaping abusive partners; those who are struggling to feed themselves or their children; and those who arrive to the center nine months pregnant without ever having had a previous medical consultation; among countless other hurdles she wants to help them overcome. "The concentration of suffering in Saint-Denis is unlike anything I would have expected for France," she says solemnly.

Today, the center operates on a budget of about 800,000 euros annually, but it's barely enough. Dr. Hatem-Gantzer admits to feeling perennially stressed about finances and the survival of the center. The team needs to double the size of the existing space, which they can't afford without another massive round of fund-raising from private donors, foundations, mayors, and regional funds. Whatever she can secure. "What we really need is regular public financing," she says with understandable frustration. President Macron was adamant about making women's rights one of the defining commitments of his presidency, but little has changed. Until something does, she soldiers on, tapping affluent personalities to step in as spokespeople and make sizable donations. And she insists on awareness building. She and fellow doctors visit nearby middle schools and high schools to speak about sexuality, protection, bodily respect, and consent.

"Care is part of what we're doing here, but education is going to be key to change and acceptance," she says. "We've had affluent interns work for the center who are bowled over by what they see and experience. That lasting perspective shift is important."

Her phone buzzes again. Last-minute decisions for another young woman—they're liaising with social workers. She thinks that's the last call for the day. Does she take these stories home with her at night? "Yes, of course. It's hard to escape them. But I'm doing what I'm supposed to be doing," she says confidently, offering a soft, reassuring smile. "I'm lucky—I'm alive. My three kids are grown-up. I can focus on caring for others now."

Her Paris

FAVORITE WOMAN-RUN BUSINESS?

The Théâtre de Poche-Montparnasse, which is overseen by two incredible women, Stéphanie Tesson and Catherine Schlemmer. I go to see performances whenever I can.

YOUR PREFERRED NEIGHBORHOOD?

I love the neighborhood around Le Bon Marché. I lived on rue de Sèvres when I was a student and spent time strolling the streets around Saint-Germain-des-Prés, around the Saint-Sulpice church (its fountains shown above), from the Seine up to Luxembourg Gardens. For me, it's quintessential Paris.

YOUR HAPPY PLACE?

The Musée Jacquemart-André, which was actually the home of a couple of passionate collectors. I was taken by their love story, the house, its magnificent winter garden, and the impressive permanent collections of Impressionist works. You can easily imagine the gatherings that were held there in the last century.

Advocating for gender equality in sports

SARAH OURAHMOUNE

OLYMPIC SILVER MEDALIST BOXER AND ENTREPRENEUR

TO SPORTS FANS, SARAH OURAHMOUNE is the tenacious athlete who wouldn't give up. She's the woman who beat all odds by returning to boxing after a career upset, temporary retirement, and the birth of her first child, regaining her strength and fighting her way to a silver medal at the 2016 Summer Olympics in Rio.

When Ourahmoune steps into the ring today, it's at Boxer Inside, the gym she set up in the 13th arrondissement to train hobbyists and amateurs of all ages and backgrounds. She applies her business training and status as France's most decorated female boxer to advocating for gender equality across disciplines in sports and ensuring inclusivity for locals in the run-up to the 2024 Summer Olympics in Paris. Before we toured her gym, we spoke about growing up athletic, the naysayers she encountered and overcame in her career, and the work that still needs to be done in changing the narrative around women in sports.

Tell me a little bit about the beginning. How were you first introduced to boxing?

I was always an athletic kid and tried my hand at everything. My older brother and I were the only Muslim kids in a Catholic school and were allowed to swap catechism classes for sports on Wednesdays. I first discovered tae kwon do in Clichy and loved it, but when my family and I moved to Aubervilliers, the local club had been burnt down. Instead, there was a beautiful boxing gym, and I ventured in out of curiosity. The manager, Said, had competed in the Olympic Games and knew how to sell me the sport: fencing with fists, the noble art, touching without being touched. In one session, he convinced me that it was more than brawling, and I kept going back to train.

Flash forward to when things get serious and you're a teen going to school, boxing on the side and training for competitions. Were you actively carving out your future as a career athlete? No, I loved competing, but it was never going to take priority over academics. I also didn't think it would be possible to make a career of it—especially since it wasn't until 1999 that French women had the right to box in a ring! Prior to that, fighting was outlawed. We could train if we found someone who would coach us, but even that was rare. If a woman went into the ring, then it was to be the ring girl. So it wasn't until 1999 that I had my first official fights, was part of the first French championship, and then the first French women's team by age sixteen. My rank was even bumped up so that I could fight in matches abroad. Only once I started winning titles did I feel like this could possibly be something big for me. Ultimately, I had found my place in boxing and quickly felt assured in my identity.

Would you say that's still true? Boxing was always a force. Without it, I would still be the self-effacing introvert I used to be. Boxing made me seen. That's also why it's so hard to stop because we risk losing that part of our identities. We turn the page and have to rebuild ourselves in another way.

You were a European champion three years in a row, a world champion in 2008, and a silver medalist in the 2011 European Championships. You were a rising star but walked away after the disappointment of not qualifying for the 2012 London Olympic Games. Did you really feel your career was over so soon? It was a tremendous failure. Four years of training to get to that point. And I felt strong. You get better at boxing with maturity, so I didn't feel ready to leave. But I also wanted to develop myself as a woman, as a professional, and it seemed like the right time. I went back to school, for a master's in communications from Sciences Po, in order to create my own business. I created Boxer Inside, the organization, in 2011 to give boxing lessons to mentally disabled individuals and to women who could bring their kids and place them in an on-site nursery. After being part of an incubator at Sciences Po, I started a company a year later to offer boxing lessons in companies, as well as boxing workshops and seminars on how sports can be a tool for personal development. It wasn't until April of 2018 that it all came full circle when I opened Boxer Inside, the gym.

---

opposite Back in the ring. Sarah Ourahmoune's 13th arrondissement boxing gym, Boxer Inside.

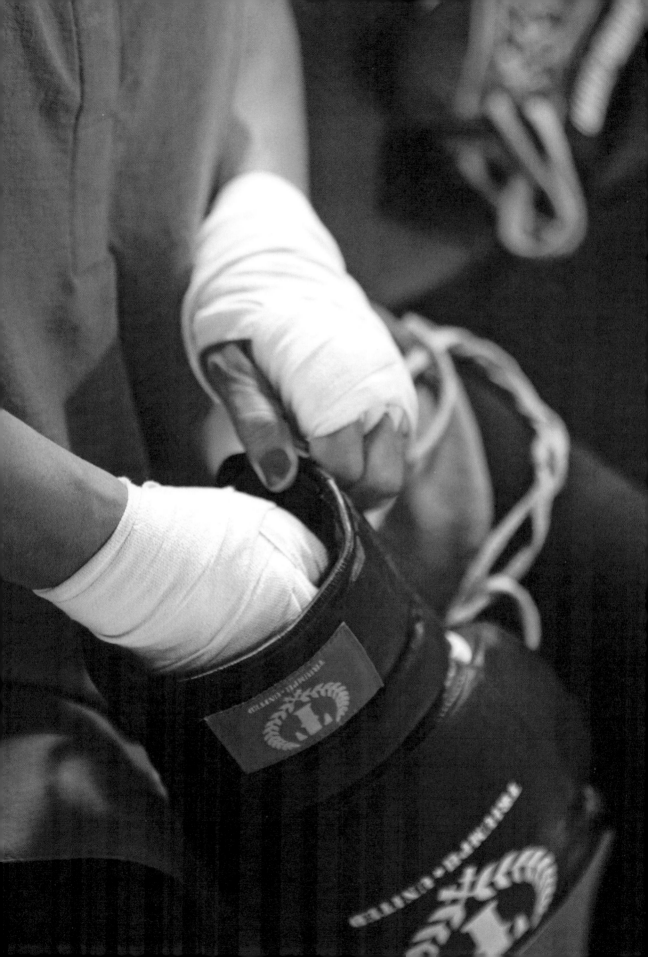

But that wasn't the end of your Olympic pursuit. Despite a lack of support from the French Boxing Federation, you got back in the ring and qualified for Rio. Was there a decisive moment when you knew you wanted to push through the opposition? I was thirty-two, I hadn't boxed in two years, my daughter was six months old—the odds were against me. But I was struggling to let go of the dream I'd had for so long. I came across a documentary about the French gymnast Isabelle Severino, who qualified for the Beijing Olympics at twenty-eight years old, at 1m70 [five feet seven inches]. With her age and height, she pushed the limits of gymnastics, and her story gave me the courage to get back in the ring after the birth of my daughter. And I felt even more determined once people kept telling me I'd never succeed.

What was it, your age or the fact that you had physically changed, that the Federation insisted made your comeback unrealistic? Age was definitely one of the factors. The Federation was preparing to send a preselected group of young, twentysomething girls deemed qualifiable to compete. They wanted me to guide them but not to compete. Maybe I had one chance out of a million to qualify, but I needed to try. First, I had to win back the title of French champion, which I did in 2015, which got me back onto the French team, but they still doubted my capabilities. I had to defeat the young boxers they were coaching to prove myself. No matter what, women have everything to prove in sports.

And they assumed your pregnancy and time away would have radically impacted your performance. Their thinking was that they've already let women into the sport, but a mother? That's asking too much. I won't deny it; it was physically challenging. It took me almost a year and a half to recover from my pregnancy. But for anyone, man or woman, who stops training for two years, it's the same struggle. Plus, the sport had evolved in that time. The criteria for evaluation had shifted from the power and physique of the athletes to an emphasis on technique. I had to adjust to those expectations. But I think my pregnancy gave me strength on an aerobic level on top of giving me greater maturity and experience. Motherhood gave me another perspective on the sport, on competition, and even on training. I only had one hour for my workouts because my daughter was with me, so I was more efficient, but I always really enjoyed that hour for myself.

---

opposite In the ring at Boxer Inside, Sarah Ourahmoune's 13th arrondissement boxing gym.

We know that sexism is alive and well in sports. How has that played out in boxing? In regard to uniforms, we had the same debate about wearing skirts in boxing as in tennis. We're lucky that so many boxers were willing to speak up and defend one another and that feminist organizations supported our position. No matter what we wear or how well we train, there is always a need to make the difference between men and women known. To give you an idea: Twenty years ago, women competed in three rounds of two-minute matches versus four rounds for men. When we inquired, we were told it was because women didn't have the physical stamina. Then men were given three rounds of three-minute matches and women four rounds of two-minute matches. They clearly maintain this gap to highlight that we don't perform at the same level.

Now that you no longer compete, how do you stay engaged in the sport, in addition to your work with Boxer Inside? There's still a lot to be done to fight against discrimination against women in sports in general, and that includes in leadership roles in federations and Olympic committees where there are still an overwhelming number of older men. I'm working to democratize sports through a number of actions. I'm in charge of diversity for the Comité National Olympique et Sportif Français [National Olympic Committee and French Sports], and we're only three women, mostly given the roles for the image. Our presence still isn't accepted enough. I'm also on the board of Paris 2024, where I'm working to make sure the games are inclusive for the residents of the 93 [Seine-Saint-Denis], the heart of where the events will take place, so that they can benefit from employment, housing, training, and the culture that surrounds the games.

You took home the silver medal at Rio—looking back, would you say that's your greatest accomplishment? It's certainly one of them. I wouldn't say it was more important than having children. This Olympic adventure was a family undertaking, and I succeeded because of them. It was important that my daughter understand what I was doing but not suffer from it. I felt guilty initially, but my absences were positive for her because she spent more time with her father, and they created a special bond. If my eldest is bold today, it's because of the values we've exposed her to: that anything is possible.

Her Paris

FAVORITE WOMAN-RUN BUSINESS?

I like that I'm constantly discovering new ones, actually. Like a restaurant in the 2nd arrondissement called (V)ivre, opened by Caroline Savoy. I loved it!

A SPORTY SPOT YOU LOVE?

The pool at the Molitor hotel is beautiful. They have a yearly membership or you can go for the day or have access with a spa treatment, and then stick around for a drink. I love the mix of sports, street art, and culture in one place.

A SPECIAL OUTING WITH YOUR HUSBAND?

Have dinner on a boat cruising the Seine (as shown above). The journeys last around two hours, and you'll see the beauty of Paris illuminated at night. It's a wonderful moment.

on Image

and Representation

IN THE BOOK *BEAUTÉ FATALE*, published in 2012, bestselling author and essayist Mona Chollet writes that the Frenchwoman isn't just a national treasure, she's a registered trademark. "Her noble mission is to perpetuate the elegance associated with the country, even if only to serve the international influence of the two French luxury giants, Moet Hennessy Louis Vuitton (LVMH) and Pinault Printemps Redoute[55] (PPR)."[56] It should come as no surprise that her text doesn't differentiate between the French and Parisian woman because the luxury brands make no such distinction. They are interchangeable—a problem in itself. Promoting a singular image of French beauty hasn't only been a bankable strategy for big groups; authors have capitalized on the opportunity too. When it comes to the absurdity of Mireille Guiliano's *French Women Don't Get Fat*, a worldwide bestseller, Chollet speaks of the more insidious effect of prescribing a balanced diet of bread, champagne, chocolate, and love: "It exploits the American fascination for clichés of French art-de-vivre, women's obsession with diets and 'secrets' (because they need them, poor things)."[57]

As for a quintessential image of the Parisienne—well, Chollet believes she hasn't evolved much since the days when supermodel-turned-author-entrepreneur Ines de la Fressange personified her on Chanel catwalks and even on a national stage, as the face of the Marianne statue, the symbol of the republic, in 1989. "Mention the word Parisienne, and a certain woman leaps to mind: hair tousled, face bare, in an elegantly understated outfit," wrote Oscar-winning French actress Isabelle Huppert in an essay on her personal style in the October 2018 issue of British *Vogue*. "The details might change—replace a trench with a navy blazer; add or subtract a *Gauloise* [cigarette]—but in the most fundamental of ways, the picture is always the same." Is it, though?

"My mother, a survivor of the Armenian genocide, arrived in France from Turkey in 1924 dreaming of being Parisian. Now there are heaps of prescriptive books and businesses around that very thing and the women shown are too often white and affluent. Meanwhile, the city's best dressed, most beautiful, and most alluring are those from mixed backgrounds. To forget that is to not have understood anything about Paris, a city [that] has integrated foreigners and people from provinces into a population of Parisians."

—SOPHIE FONTANEL, AUTHOR AND FASHION JOURNALIST

It isn't only the foreign media that perpetuates a monolithic image of the Parisian woman; it's a depiction that's bolstered at home as well. The Parisian woman's homogeneity in the collective imagination matches her inadequate and unrealistic representation in all forms of local media. For minorities, POC, disabled, overweight, and LGBTQ women, their invisibility and, in many cases, complete erasure, can have detrimental effects, "provoking an even greater self-loathing."[58]

When Sarah Zouak (page 130) was a little girl, she dreamed of being one of the hundreds of tall, thin white women she saw paraded in the pages of *Madame Figaro* magazine. Today, she still occasionally straightens her hair to get closer to this ideal: "To be listened to," she says. As an Arab woman, she has always been accustomed to the underrepresentation, and in some cases glaring absence, of faces and bodies that look like hers, broadcasting the news, acting in the most popular television shows and films, stealing the spotlight in magazines, and even playing roles in cartoons. But that doesn't mean she has been impervious to its effects. "I had to travel the world to meet all the role models I wanted," she says. "I hope my future children won't have to fight so hard."

In 2018, the CSA, Conseil Supérieur de l'Audiovisuel, France's broadcasting regulatory body, published its annual report on diversity and representation, announcing just how far France lags behind. If there were slight improvements in the rate of nonwhite individuals represented on screen (20 percent), it was a result of American series (the rate drops to 14 percent for French productions).[59] None of this would come as a surprise to the actors impacted by the exclusionary system.

In her book *Noire n'est pas mon métier* (*Black Isn't My Job*), an impassioned critique of the lack of representation in French cinema cowritten with contributions from fifteen other Afro-French performers, actress Aïssa Maïga describes with sobering detail an unbalanced system if you are black, Arab, or Asian. "It's the former colonial world in its entirety that is rejected."[60] So while the very fabric of French society is mixed, it is a very idealized white, and consequently uneven, view of the population that persists on-screen. The erasure of the black body manifests itself as much in its absence as in the types of roles they're offered, the majority of which reduce them to caricature and stereotype—the domestic worker; the prostitute; the accented immigrant. Some three hundred films and a plethora of new shows are produced each year in France, and yet the ease with which casting directors overlook minorities points to a system that, like the country it belongs to, isn't prepared to be part of a movement for needed change. "Those who see themselves rarely, if ever, on screens and stages are begging to exist in the deafening silence of a wonderfully mixed-race society," writes actress Nadège Beausson-Diagne in the book. "Otherwise, how can our children develop their identities?"[61]

Because the message these absences drive home is that if women and minorities are invisible in the fictional world, do they even matter in the real world?

There seemed to be some hope with the *Black Panther* phenomenon, a film whose impact reverberated in France, demonstrating the hunger for stories that give pride of place to the underrepresented. Young people everywhere could see superheroes that resembled them in leading roles, many for the very first time. That continued stateside with the breakout success of *Crazy Rich Asians*, which generated a stream of think pieces about the personal symbolism of seeing everyday moments on-screen. In an opinion piece for *The New Yorker*, writer Hua Hsu commented that what moved him was seeing "friends eating at the night market, an elder slowly studying the face of a newcomer, the pained but sympathetic expression of a native speaker, trying to decipher another's rusty Mandarin." Perhaps that's the end point of representation, he wondered. "You simply want the opportunity to be as heroic or funny or petty or goofy or boring as everyone else."[62]

In France, however, the film's release was delayed and virtually sans fanfare. For Grace Ly, an author and cohost of the *Kiffe ta Race* podcast, it's because France wasn't ready for it. "We're not even able to call anti-Asian racism, racism. It's sub-racism, ordinary racism, bad humor. It's jokes about Nem and Cantonese rice. It's not a film like *Crazy Rich Asians* that's going to change anything in France anyway," she wrote on her blog *La Petite Banane*.[63] So who or what will? People like her. Activists. Media consumers who look elsewhere to shape their worldview and support the creators focusing on inclusivity for the right reasons.

Media bias is a worldwide problem, but progress seems particularly slow in France. "While similar struggles exist in the US and the UK, the issues are out in the open; there are media outlets actively trying to do better," says culture journalist Jennifer Padjemi, who also hosts the podcast *Miroir Miroir*, which discusses issues of representation head-on. "France is always behind on these questions for the simple reason that maintaining the archetype is a way to continue dismissing certain individuals (always the same ones, it seems) and to prevent them from reversing the power structure." Addressing the issues of representation in France means pointing the finger at white, male, hetero, able-bodied privilege—the usual decision-makers.

And for women like Muriel Tallandier (page 214), Julie Mathieu (page 221), both in publishing, and journalist/LGBTQ activist Alice Coffin, the invisibility or heavily sexualized representations of lesbian women do nothing but reinforce the feeling that they've been sidelined from society. "The basis of lesbophobia is invisibility. Representing them isn't just about portraying their sexuality, it's a political act," Coffin told podcaster Lauren Bastide (page 35) in a live discussion at the Carreau du Temple. An act that is particularly crucial given the fiery, ongoing debate about the access to PMA (medically assisted procreation like IVF), which, at the time of writing, is still illegal in France for lesbian and single (uncoupled heterosexual) women who want children. The media coverage around the issue, including both the backing by the French bioethics body and the opposition, is dominated by men. Why? Journalists aren't doing their jobs. "The first thing they do is interview someone against PMA (a man) and someone for it, usually someone in politics or a representative from LGBT associations, but it's almost always a gay man," said Marie Kirschen, founder of the lesbian review *Well Well Well*, during an interview on Padjemi's podcast *Miroir Miroir*. And this cycle has grave consequences. "It's much easier to refuse a group of people their rights when we don't see them."[64]

Where are France's homegrown answers to Ellen DeGeneres, Samira Wiley, or Laverne Cox, popular culture icons in the media community? They don't exist. In the grievous absence of such figures in the local LGBT community, women look to uplifting foreign role models making themselves accessible online. It's incontestable that more needs to be done if the films, television programs, newscasts, and written media don't resemble France. There are some bright spots—the international

"Social media has allowed us to express ourselves and even better, to be heard. It's how movements have begun in representation. Communities are building, mixing, becoming slightly more mainstream, and entering into common visual language. Now it's either traditional media finally gets that it's time for them to do better in a big way, or we keep choosing to create our own networks and platforms."

—ADELINE RAPON, JEWELER

success of Héloïse Letissier, the gender-fluid performer better known as Christine and the Queens; the overdue dialogue around fat-phobia inspired by Gabrielle Deydier's powerful 2017 bestseller *On ne nait pas grosse* (*You're Not Born Fat*); the rising Afropop star Aya Nakamura; and the important work by documentary filmmaker Amandine Gay on race and adoption that is transcending French borders. But more needs to be done.

Thankfully, some women aren't willing to wait around for the old guard to change. More and more voices are emerging outside of traditional media that champion fluid notions of femininity and beauty, giving underrepresented young women a chance to connect with their "tribe."

One is Waïa, a 100 percent digital platform that celebrates black beauty in all of its diversity with millennial-focused content that includes stories from voices often omitted from traditional media. It's a hub for fashion and beauty that its five founders say is geared toward women bred on Anglo and Afro-European culture. The few Francophone magazines targeting black women that do exist, they write on their website, are meant for older audiences and detached from their preoccupying concerns—intersectionality and body positivity.

Adeline Rapon, a jeweler and popular figure on Instagram, has used her platform to discuss her mixed race, the decision to stop shaving her underarms for the benefit of others, and embracing her natural hair after many years of chemically relaxing it to fit in. When Waïa asked her to pose for a series of sepia-tinged photographs highlighting female body taboos, from menstruation to body hair and masturbation, she knew it was an opportunity to show commitment to her beliefs in front of a new audience. "It's in the same kind of softness I aim for on my own platform, all while speaking out against the violence women impose on themselves day after day."

It's also Instagram that Sophie Fontanel, author and fashion personality, has harnessed as her primary tool to chronicle in radical candidness everything from her sex life (or intentional lack thereof during her calculated twelve-year bout of celibacy, documented in the book *The Art of Sleeping Alone*) and stylistic choices (she's always identified with both sexes) to her fraught decision to stop coloring her hair to look younger and embrace her natural self, which meant growing out her lengths until she had a full head of iridescent silver hair. "It's social pressure that brings women to color their hair," she's said. That and the narrative that women's value and appeal have an expiration date, an idea she continues to reject online, in her column for *L'Obs* and in her books. As a result, she's been an alternative role model for women and men, and not only those approaching her age.

And thanks to podcasts like *La Poudre* (page 35), *Quouïr*, *Quoi de Meuf*, *Miroir Miroir*, and *Kiffe ta Race* (page 47), important discussions about race, sexuality, representation, feminism, identity, gender, and discrimination—*la vie!*—are finally being had with people who've traditionally been silenced.

Inroads are needed in representation, but change can also come from consumers, Internet users, readers—the average citizen. Jennifer Padjemi's suggestion? Start with social media. "People can be part of the solution," she says. If you're doing it right, you're following, reading, and listening to a variety of people that don't look and live like you.

Making Voices Heard

In 2018, women represented only 15.3% of the 1,000 most talked or written about personalities of the year.

WHERE ARE ALL the female sources and voices in media? Evidently, muscling their way, ever so slowly, through the old boys' club that still controls who is heard, when, for how long, and in what circumstance. In 2018, women represented only 15.3 percent of the one thousand most talked and/or written about personalities of the year in the French press, the second-lowest rate in six years (down from 16.9 percent in 2017, not a figure to get excited about either, let's be honest).[65] Only about 19 percent of experts interviewed by the media are women,[66] and in response, women have been expected to believe the go-to defense that there is simply a dearth of women experts to solicit. Whether malicious or simply lazy, it's an unacceptable, unethical journalistic practice. So two women launched Les Expertes, the first free online database for French and Francophone experts across professional sectors. Looking to interview an illustrator? An expert in gender studies or biotechnology? There's a place to find her.

But it's going to take a lot more than a database. It requires diversifying the student bodies in journalism and art schools as well as the editorial and managerial staff at news and media networks; it requires emphasizing the primacy of making space for a multitude of voices; it requires men giving up their seat or speaking up when they see that women haven't been included. Because what does this invisibility do over time? Teach the lesson that women's voices and opinions are less valuable. That they, as people in the world, are less valuable.

the
Storytellers

Extending access to smart news

ARIANE BERNARD

FORMER HEAD OF DIGITAL AT *LE PARISIEN*

ARIANE BERNARD TRAVELED 116,000 MILES internationally between 2017 and 2018, most of them between Paris and New York, her two anchors in the world. The logistics of the journey had become such second nature that she had mastered the precise chronological sequence of events, down to the minute, to find herself back in her Hell's Kitchen apartment in record time, just as she left it a month prior. She admits to feeling some level of pride in this. If she's going to be torn to a degree by two homes, two lives, she'd best create efficiencies to optimize the time spent in both.

I first met Bernard when she was the chief digital officer for *Le Parisien*, at a birthday dinner for our mutual friend, an editor at the *New York Times* and Bernard's former colleague for part of the fourteen years she worked for the *Times*. What I observed about her from those first few hours together was that she was a woman of great erudition and sharp wit, an insightful storyteller who's both confident and approachable. To be sure, all of this made her a clear asset for the media world. But those were among the same qualities I found most fascinating about her on a personal level, alongside her formidable language skills (Was she French? Was she American? Both? It was unclear), which only added a layer of intrigue.

"If you knew nothing about Ariane and spoke with her for an hour, you wouldn't be surprised to learn she's been in high-powered leadership positions," said my friend Jake, who also met her for the first time that evening. "She's a woman who has held big jobs but would rather talk about theater, travel, and culture." The ultimate Parisian— more interested in speaking about life than work; a woman who understands and can navigate the corporate apparatus but feels unbound by it. That value came through during our subsequent conversations, where we discussed everything from the tensions of a dual life to overcoming the discomfort in demanding a seat at the table.

You went to university in America and began your career there. How did that shape or alter your sense of Parisianness? If I try to analyze the seventeen-year-old who decided to go to school 3,500 miles from home, I think it was more about a desire to do something totally different rather than be someone totally different. I never felt I wanted to evolve from who I was, precisely because I always felt I was already very different from everybody I knew. But going to school in the US gave me a more hopeful outlook than what I was born or raised with. The desire to work from *yes, if* rather than *no, because*, which is a common default position of the French. Looking back, I can absolutely see the hybrid outcome of so much time spent away from France. I've been surprised to realize that default assumptions of my adult self are quite American, and I'd say I'm an American adult who had a French childhood. On the other hand, there are a number of personality traits and beliefs that I can identify as very French and likely will forever. Chief among them, the way I consider the relationship between the citizen and the state. In my mind, the matters of a society with a welfare state that spreads the costs and risks of the most unjust and unfair circumstances of birth (health, wealth, and how it otherwise affects access to education) are essential.

You've mentioned that it might have been easier to never have known what it feels like to live two lives. What is inherently troubling in your arrangement? There is always a piece missing. There are also tensions of being a self that's almost-but-not-quite organic to the place. And there is a specific cost that I bear there because this disquiet is invisible to everyone but me: being fully bilingual with no accent to distinguish me in either language and having the privilege of whiteness in these Christian countries, I am a welcome daughter of both. Both countries assume me to be their own, fully. They don't adjust or correct themselves to ease the way I navigate life. My French teams truly had no idea of the daily disconnect that I experienced working there and couldn't possibly understand how hard the adjustment had been. My American friends couldn't possibly know that I still open incredulous, sometimes uncomprehending, immigrant eyes on random pieces of America. So, unlike a foreign guest who is understood to be adjusting, who can be forgiven for her blunders or awkwardness, I don't receive this special treatment in either place. To be clear, I am not asking for special treatment; I am incredibly lucky to make both countries my home. But where neither country really perceives my "other" self, the burden of adjustment is both lonely and secretly borne.

Having spent the majority of your career working in the US, what have been the biggest differences and assets of both work cultures? In many ways, I've found myself to be ill-equipped for the task of working with a French team. The biggest difference is how each group approaches individual and collective risk. It's not that the French and American workers don't see the same risk, but their reaction to it is very different. The French consider that "the group" (their company, society as a whole) has a responsibility to minimize risk before anything gets done. Americans would certainly like for that to happen but don't require it to start. There's a great difference between fear and risk. Risk is and fear affects. But when you're not used to encountering risk, the exercise of separating out risk from fear becomes challenging, and I think it's hard for French workers.

And how does Paris shape the experience of being a woman in a senior leadership position? There are both privileges and constraints to being a woman in Paris. Social and aesthetic codes, even in the workplace, aren't meant to be broken without explanation. The challenge exists in New York, but the gentility and elegance of Paris makes it even harder to be negligent, to be a loudmouth, to say I, ME. To ask for what you want and deserve. To do that "ugly," disruptive thing you need to do for your seat at the table. The judgmentalness of the French is a self-fulfilling prophecy—you don't dare speak if you don't sound right, but then you won't be heard. You won't move forward.

The first step in going for your own goals is to accept that you're an individual that is as worthy and entitled as another. But Paris is so strong and beautiful that she seems to say, Well, yes, you are an individual, but I am Paris—I set the rules. So when you add that to all the other ways you feel inadequate and are at odds with or disrupt the rules, the fact that Paris is beautiful is probably more significant.

How do you overcome this? I keep in mind that my moral reason for grabbing a seat for myself at the table is that I'm so close to that goal or project I really want, which will give me the chance to be a friend to my ideas, to ensure that I can execute something I believe in. If I care about society's access to intelligent news that matters, I should not care what I look like when achieving this.

The question is not whether it's pretty to raise your hand or step up for a role, it's about what you can achieve and how you fix other problems and injustices once you get that spot at the table. All the ways in which I may have a slight edge mean that I can extend a hand to help those who don't, for whatever reason.

You transitioned from reporting and editing the news to managing the business of news. How does this allow you to continue working toward your goal of ensuring access to information? Initially, I thought I wanted to be a reporter because I liked the news. As I continued down that path, however, I began to see there were many other functions that participated in making news available in society. I was lucky that I got into this field as digital news truly overtook the traditional means of distribution, and this meant that systems of news distribution also evolved drastically. I have always been both a lover of the arts and also of systems and the building of systems. Yet again, I'm very thankful to my American education, that I was encouraged to "be hyphenated" in my interests and pursuits. The French education system sees education as a series of narrowing options and specialty selections (and the discarding of alternatives). What I understood about working in digital at the *Times*—where I was in charge of the product management of publishing tools and distribution systems—was that this was just as much about supporting the mission of making news available as what a reporter in the field does. In entirely different ways, of course, but each are essential. At *Le Parisien*, I led teams across all aspects of the digital business (engineering, design, data, and innovation, etc.) to ensure we had great, user-focused news sites that spoke to our audiences and smart tools for our reporters and editors.

And where might the next turn lead you? This is something I think about often—how to nurture the ideas I hold dear. If I believe that the diversity and health of the news ecosystem [are] important, am I present in the places where the destinies of this ecosystem are being shaped? I spend a lot of time at conferences. I am part of various product and strategic-partnership publisher working groups of Google and Facebook because, irrespective of how folks in the industry may feel about these two large members of our ecosystem, I will never remove myself from the conversation as long as the conversation can take place. But a place I know nothing about is the legislative framework of my industry. I'd love to broaden these horizons and hopefully contribute my own perspective and real-world experience to shaping future decisions, wherever I may need to be to do so.

Her Paris

THE FIRST PLACE (BESIDES HOME) YOU LIKE TO GO AFTER ONE OF YOUR MANY TRIPS?

It might be the Tuileries Gardens (shown above), or it might simply be the Marks & Spencer at CDG Terminal 2E, where I invariably do a quick shopping run when I get off the plane!

YOUR FOREVER HAPPY PLACE?

The Parc Monceau, for which I hold a deep affection. There is a picture of four-year-old Ariane holding her father's hand in the alleys of the park in the fall at dusk, on a day that I'll never forget.

A NEIGHBORHOOD THAT HOLDS SPECIAL MEANING?

The 9th arrondissement, where I spent a good chunk of my childhood. My parents have lived on the same block for thirty-one years, at two different addresses!

Putting women back into the heart of the city's story

HEIDI EVANS

CREATOR OF THE WOMEN OF PARIS TOURS

LONDON-BORN HEIDI EVANS came to Paris armed only with a love for the French language, a sense of adventure, and an amorphous idea of her future. While considering her options, she began working as a tour guide for various companies, covering the best-of-Paris landmarks, immersing herself in history, and connecting with curious travelers. Quickly, she recognized her gift for guiding and storytelling. But she also reached another conclusion, one that would lead her down the path of entrepreneurship: the majority of walking tours gloss over the role of historic women in shaping the city. In fact, women are framed as historical footnotes in a Paris narrative dominated by great, valiant men.

As disheartening as the realization was, it came with an opportunity. In 2016, Evans launched Women of Paris tours and the first of several thematic walks dedicated to women's history and their defining influence in art, theater, science, culture, politics, and everyday life. After joining her Sugar & Spice tour to learn about the struggles and achievements of women writers in Paris, we sat down to talk about the importance of balancing the story, her favorite historical figures, and taking *les femmes de Paris* several steps further.

At what point did you realize there was a lack of storytelling around the historic women of Paris in tourism? It was about two months into my arrival in France, and I was leading free tours of the city. My aunt came to visit and joined one of my tours and remarked at the end that it was interesting how little I talked about women. From that point on, I couldn't get the idea out of my head.

And then you couldn't help but see all the ways in which women are relegated to the background. Where else did you personally encounter this? Even as I was learning more about the work displayed in the Musée d'Orsay, for example, I discovered female Impressionists for the first time and was shocked that in all of my liberal arts education—which touched on the leading artists, writers, and thinkers of Europe—I hadn't learned about any of them. The travelers I was giving tours to, even those with a very basic working knowledge of art history, knew Monet, Degas, and Van Gogh, but couldn't name a female painter.

Why has it been so important for you to tell these stories and educate travelers? First, because I realized there are travelers actively seeking out this information. Many of my clients tell me they found me by Googling *feminist tour Paris* or *women's tour Paris*. And also because it's important to set the record straight. The narrative you tend to get in most introductory tours to Paris highlights *the great men* that influenced the city and secondary are *the bad, rebellious women*. They're almost always awfully reputed—Marie Antoinette, Catherine de Medici, both vilified by the French. And yet you have a figure like Simone Veil, who is beloved, and she only really earned a mention when she was buried in the Panthéon in 2018.

But this is problematic for you not only because the stories are framed incorrectly but also because women's contributions in science, politics, medicine, and the arts are largely glossed over. Exactly—tours are meant to be an informal education. They're an accessible way for people to learn about a city. It's extremely important to get the story right.

Why do you think the tourism industry has left the story so one-sided? The city's landmarks are connected to a patriarchal past. If you're giving tourists a list of marquee places they should absolutely see while they're visiting, very few pay tribute to or display work by women. The Louvre, for example, arguably the world's most famous museum, houses only a handful of paintings by women. The house and gardens of Rodin are an example of an entire museum devoted to a male artist. There are some works by Camille Claudel, his student and lover and sculptor in her own right, and she has her own museum, but it's rather unknown and located in the suburbs, where few tourists venture. Le Musée de la Vie Romantique, a museum connected to the life of George Sand, is a bit off the beaten track. So it's one-sided because the city, which can be described as a museum itself, is a reflection of the past, and sadly Paris's past was one in which women were largely invisible. I think it's particularly interesting to see given that I come from London, where one of the biggest tourist draws is the queen. The women who have helped to shape the United Kingdom are, for the most part, not hated; they are adored, like Queen Victoria and Elizabeth I—more than the men, I would even argue.

Here in Paris, you could argue the city itself is female. And we have the Iron Lady Eiffel. In the French psyche, the woman embodies this—the seductive iron lady, the sexiness of the Eiffel Tower. Certainly, a lot of historians describe her (the city) as a muse inspiring the male artists and writers who came here. So she's more of a passive inspirer than an active creator.

Some believe that to remember the women of today, we must first properly honor the women of the past. Do you think that you're helping to correct a wrong? I do think that we still look to the past to see how we can act in the future, to inspire us. We need to see those women for all the incredible things they contributed and the role they played in the city in order to project ourselves. Perhaps in some way, I'm trying to be a driver of change. What message does it send, for example, that so few women writers are taught in the French curriculum?

You mean at the baccalaureate level? Yes, I discovered this when I was preparing the first Women of Paris tour. There have been petitions almost annually to get women writers added to the baccalaureate curriculum (where specific texts are imposed) because they were completely absent. Finally, in 2017, great success—they added one woman (Madame de La Fayette) alongside the many required readings by male authors like Flaubert, de Balzac, and Hugo. And this is something I talk about on the women writers tour—the fact that women's writing was not considered important until the late twentieth century. There were Colette and a few others, but their writing was largely considered frivolous "chick lit." It's why the Espace des Femmes, one of the places I love to bring visitors, is so important. It's a bookstore, publisher, and gallery space dedicated to the work of women writers.

Among the many women whose work and lives you discuss on the tour, who speaks to you personally? Right now I would probably say Mata Hari, the Dutch courtesan and exotic dancer. I'd already heard of her because she actually does get a little love on other tours, particularly around the Eiffel Tower, because she was convicted of being a spy for the Germans during World War I. The tower was used to listen in on enemy transmissions. But that's all you often hear. What I find interesting about her, though, is why and how she ended up involved in such a situation in the first place. She married a wealthy but abusive man whom she later divorced. Her son died, and she lost custody of her daughter. She was left with nothing. She moved to Paris to reinvent herself and danced to survive. As a courtesan, she was rubbing shoulders with high-ranking military officials who saw her skills at seduction as something to exploit. I find it interesting to imagine how she might have fared in a post-#MeToo world.

On your tour, you mention the shockingly low number of women in the Académie Française, France's language authority (only nine members in 385 years, five currently active). What else might surprise people about the role of women in the arts or the way their contributions are recognized? What always shocks people is that there are around six thousand streets in Paris: four thousand named after men, only three hundred named after women. Then there's the fact that Simone Veil was only the fifth woman to be interred in the Panthéon (and one of them was only buried there because her husband was) and generally how delayed France was in women's rights legislation. But the big one is how all too often great women are defined by the great men in their lives. For example, George Sand is often known better for her connection with Chopin than for her writing, despite the fact that she is the second-bestselling French novelist (after Hugo). Simone de Beauvoir is often referenced in relation to Sartre (and there is a place attributed to both of them in the 6th arrondissement); and few people realize that the Shakespeare and Company bookstore is not, in fact, the original. That was another shop owned by American expatriate Sylvia Beach and located on rue de l'Odéon, which became a hugely important meeting place for writers, like Hemingway and Joyce (whose book *Ulysses* she published in 1922). And yet the plaque outside the original address makes no mention of Shakespeare and Company, only Joyce. Beach played a big role in shaping the arts in early twentieth-century Paris, but she's largely been forgotten in the popular narrative. She was too important not to include in my tours.

How has running these tours changed your own perception of the Parisienne? I see the Parisienne as any woman who considers Paris her home. And that's one thing I love about the city—it can adopt you. There are so many Parisiennes [who] weren't born here and weren't even born in France. And now I consider myself one of them.

Her Paris

FAVORITE WOMAN-RUN BUSINESS?

Two, actually! Muscovado, a café run by two sisters serving excellent breakfast, brunch, and lunch and hosting the occasional pop-up night; and Combat, a cocktail bar with a female-forward spirit (see page 233).

A STREET YOU LOVE?

The rue Sainte-Marthe in the 10th arrondissement, a narrow street lined with colorful houses, galleries, and bars.

SOMEPLACE YOU GO AFTER WORK TO RELAX OR CATCH UP WITH FRIENDS?

Martin (shown above), which feels like an extension of home. I always run into people I know, which is wonderful. The beer is cheap, the wine is good, and the produce comes from owner Loïc Martin's garden outside of Paris.

« Écrire c'est tenter de savoir ce qu'on écrirait si on écrivait »

L'essence de la littérature, c'est d'échapper à toute détermination essentielle, à toute affirmation qui la stabilise ou même la réalise; elle n'est jamais déjà là, elle est toujours à retrouver ou à réinventer.

Upending our beliefs about female identity and desire

LEÏLA SLIMANI

GONCOURT PRIZE–WINNING AUTHOR

WHEN THE RARE OCCASION presents itself to slip inside the confines of an artist's workspace, I am tempted to breathe in every corner and memorize every book, wall hanging, and tidy magazine stack, to try to lock in the sensation, as though it may leave some kind of indelible mark. It happens to me before I could even articulate what I was feeling, the day I go to meet award-winning author Leïla Slimani in her home office. Wearing a Keith Haring T-shirt, flared jeans, and minty green sneakers, she ushers me in swiftly, motioning for me to take the plush sofa, not the desk chair. Her mess of curls is tight and golden at their ends, and she smiles warmly, her back against the long desk strewn with handwritten notes and magazines. Facedown next to her computer is a copy of *Joseph Anton: A Memoir* by Salman Rushdie. "Research," she says. To my left, a framed portrait of Slimani from 2016 when she received the Goncourt Prize, France's highest literary honor, for her wrenching second novel, *The Perfect Nanny* (*Chanson Douce*); a smattering of family photos, her son's crayon drawings, magazine clippings, and letters from her publisher. To my right, a wall of books spanning generations of luminaries like Oscar Wilde, Simone de Beauvoir, Sophie Calle, and Simone Veil, her personal heroine.

This is her world, her creative space, where Louise, Myriam, Adèle, and countless other characters, complex and often troubled, come to life. It's in this meditative cocoon where she encloses herself from the time her kids go to school until they come home at four thirty p.m. and where she returns after the bon apps, the baths, the good nights, and the mealtimes with her husband, until midnight on most days. In one room, she's birthed stories that have reached millions.

Before I ever read Slimani's work, I knew her superficially as the next great voice in the canon of literary sophisticates that had long been marked by the contributions of men. As of 2016, she was one of twelve women and only the second Moroccan to have been awarded the prize, first granted in 1903, and the success of the book instantly propelled her into the limelight and captured the attention of the country's political and intellectual elite. Shortly after taking office, President Macron appointed her to be his personal representative of Francophone affairs, representing France and promoting the French language internationally. She went from a relative unknown to the embodiment of French culture.

Born in the administrative and political capital of Rabat, Morocco, Slimani was reared in a life she considered peaceful, family oriented, and protected but heavily conformist and disconnected from the kind of culture she craved. Still, she had literature, a vivid imagination, and a French education that primed her for a future in France. At eighteen, she arrived in Paris to study and stepped into another dimension, where life was solitary and individualistic but with seductive cultural offerings that fed her soul. "There was the possibility to do anything, to be anonymous, to reinvent yourself without anyone knowing your past," she explains, a longing she didn't realize she had until she observed the ease with which she could start over.

After graduate school, she worked as a journalist for the weekly newspaper *Jeune Afrique*, traveling regularly to Morocco and Tunisia on assignments, and had her first child before ever trying her hand as a novelist. At various points in her Paris life, there was loneliness, a struggle to make connections, and the fear of losing herself to fit in. "I've almost forgotten what it was like then, but I know I was afraid that people would be suspicious of me. I assumed I needed to speak better French than anyone else, be more polite and more discreet to prove I was *good*. As a woman from North Africa, I had to."

No matter what she did or how she excelled, her work and newfound celebrity invited disappointment. "For some, I wasn't North African anymore. I had lost those attributes because I didn't display any religion or any affiliation; I'd been whitewashed, in a way. And for many North Africans, I'm not a model at all because I'm not a *good* North African—devout, modest, obedient." What matters, she insists, are those who perceive her as an independent individual. "I hope that the girls who look like me and are scared of taking the risk to be free and independent will see my work and say it's worth it."

---

opposite A wondrous wall of books in Leïla Slimani's home office.

At its simplest, her work is about everyday life and everyday people. But once inside, the everyday emerges as a vehicle to offer incisive commentary on the broader, altogether darker sides of life and society—motherhood, love, sexuality, pleasure, mental health, identity, and tradition, which she treats with refreshing candor, even if it unsettles. In her prizewinning first novel, *Adèle* (*dans le jardin de l'ogre*), her protagonist's unshakable ennui—as a nihilistic newspaper journalist, wife, and mother in Paris—and insatiable sexual addiction, which she tries to conceal from her husband, send her plummeting into the depths of self-isolation. Though most of her readers may not personally identify with Adèle's chronic sexual compulsions, the question of satisfaction and living out one's unmasked self is eminently relatable. The sharpness of her prose, in all of her work, is accessible but never detracts from its power. It occupies a comfortable space in the stylistic spectrum between oversimplified and unnecessarily florid with carefully considered words that carry a sucker punch that haunts long after you've last glanced at them. But that's also why some readers couldn't get past *The Perfect Nanny*'s now-legendary opening line—*The baby is dead*. She asks her readers to feel something, often incredibly distressing, and to lean into it with abandon. "I want people to feel a human connection to these characters," she tells me. "I want them to feel shaken up and uncomfortable. I want their stories to prompt them to think about their own lives, to look differently at a friend or someone they meet, and judge less."

By inflecting the everyday with the bleak and sinister, she reminds us that behind even the most outwardly composed lives are people, humans, negotiating their desires, struggling to navigate social and professional dynamics, and sometimes flailing in despair. What earned Slimani an instant audience, of both supporters and critics, was more than her linear storytelling acumen but the way the stories subverted all expectations. For one, Paris as a backdrop for her narratives is packed in equal measure with the beautiful and the beastly, an honest reflection of the city that is nonetheless jarring.

"Paris is the most beautiful and interesting city in the world. It's one big theatrical stage . . . and still, it maintains its darkness and mystery. It's because it isn't only beautiful that it's extraordinary." According to what someone is going through in their lives, she continues, they are in contact either with that beauty or with sadness, violence, misery, and depravity, sometimes all of it at once, which make it a real place, not of fantasy but of life's spectrum of emotions and circumstances.

And then there are the subjects themselves—the relationship and role-playing between mother and nanny, between working mothers and society; the question of

"I'm proud to represent the French language as a tool for liberty. To be able to say to everyone who wants to speak it that they are free to do so in the way that they want, to modify it, transfigure it, to creolize it— the language is not sacred."

female desire. Why didn't she write about what was closer to home, she was asked incessantly, her birthright? Why was she so provocative? Part of what makes her a bold literary figure is that she is making a successful living writing about something beyond her own experience. She dares to write about that which she has been told she has no right.

"Every writer has something to say. I was raised in a very bourgeois milieu, and literature was a way for me to say what I couldn't say in real life. It's a space to talk about violence, sexuality, brutality," Slimani explains, adding that the ideas emerge from a single spark and often require her own education. The psychology and misfortune around hypersexuality in *Adèle*, for one, were loosely inspired by the Dominique Strauss-Kahn affair in 2011, while the infanticide in *The Perfect Nanny* draws its parallels in the 2012 murder of the Krim children in New York City by their nanny. She dives into worlds she must research like an actor taking on a role and letting themselves be consumed by it. "I didn't make a conscious choice between writing about my Moroccan identity and something else. National identity as a theme is already so dominant in everyday life, I wanted to escape it. Maybe it would have been the easiest and most obvious, but it didn't interest me."

While her own identity and personal experience with her maternal country leave her uninspired, she remains fascinated by the women, often anonymous, that she grew up with in Morocco and how they weather adversity. She thinks of her Algerian mother, who took refuge in Morocco, her aunt who left Algeria because of threats to decapitate her if she didn't wear the veil, and she thinks of the young girls, about fourteen years old, that she saw at the local train station in Casablanca—girls who'd been raped and impregnated and forced to leave home in shame. "These anonymous women devastated me then and continue to haunt me, as do the injustices they've suffered," she says passionately. "They turned me into a feminist."

If these anonymous women were catalysts, it was the work of women like Virginia Woolf or Gisèle Halimi that gave her the intellectual tools to conceptualize the

fight for women's and human rights. "My goal is to say what I have to say in the best way possible. It's up to readers whether they understand or want to take an interest or not. I'm fighting for women to have access to reading and writing because it's a fundamental injustice. Today, millions of little girls don't have access to school and will never learn to read or write." Slimani, raised with the help of a nanny who couldn't do either, observed the humiliation her caretaker felt by her illiteracy. She won the Goncourt Prize, but her grandmother couldn't read or write either. The oppression of women all over the world is intolerable and her ultimate reason to fight.

When she writes, then, it's not merely for the love of storytelling; it's for the power she wields. "I realize the privilege and the immense weapon I have, the only thing I know how to use—words."

---

above One of Slimani's other works, an ode to her hero Simone Veil.

Leïla Slimani's body of work spans fiction and nonfiction, essays, and commentary on human rights and current events. Her first nonfiction work, *Sexe et mensonges: La Vie sexuelle au Maroc (Sex and Lies: Sexual Life in Morocco)* explores sexuality in Morocco through first-person accounts.

Her Paris

FAVORITE WOMAN-RUN BUSINESS?

The BNF (Bibliothèque Nationale Française) on rue de Richelieu, whose director is a woman. It's one of the most beautiful libraries in the world with an inconceivable selection of books. The director is a guardian of humanity's greatest treasures.

YOUR PREFERRED NEIGHBORHOOD?

Pigalle, my neighborhood. Its history fascinates me. Each street reminds me of something— a film, a novel, a song, or a moment. It's inhabited and haunted by people from the past and present, and it's my family's neighborhood. I know all the café and restaurant owners. It takes so long to find your "village" in Paris . . . This is mine.

YOUR LITERARY HAPPY PLACE?

The Musée d'Orsay (shown above) is an extraordinary place for literary inspiration. Their bookstore is wonderful—you must go.

Anthologizing the classics for readers of all ages

SARAH SAUQUET

TEACHER, AUTHOR, AND CREATOR OF UN TEXTE UN JOUR

FROM THE TIME SHE READ Proust's *In Search of Lost Time*, Sarah Sauquet knew she was meant to teach. For more than a decade, she has taught literature to fifteen-year-olds at the Lycée Charles de Foucauld in the 18th arrondissement, passing on her infectious love for the classics. But getting a digital-first generation to take an interest in three-hundred-page tomes was a challenge. To capture their attention in a format they'd be receptive to, she launched Un Texte Un Jour (followed later by its English version, A Text A Day), a mobile app offering daily excerpts from nearly four hundred texts, along with quizzes, author biographies, and semantic anecdotes. Quickly, it became the most downloaded literary app in the App Store and has elevated Sauquet to something of a literary guardian, a role she happily assumes.

Book in hand, Sauquet joined me for tea at Café Marly, where we discussed the healing properties of books, her lifelong fascination with the arts, and the state of education in France today.

Did you grow up in a family of readers? I was an avid reader in a family of athletes! [*laughs*] Everyone enjoyed reading, but I found particular comfort in books. They opened up the world to me, made me curious. I realized early on that there was no greater emotional salve for me than a good book or an outing at the movies.

The arts in general guided your childhood, then. Who were some of the women who inspired you? Romy Schneider, Vivien Leigh, and Marie Trintignant. As a cinephile, I discovered these actresses at different moments of my life, and they each blew me away with their personalities. Janis Joplin, who has followed me throughout my life, connects me to a visceral, somewhat indescribable state of wildness through the burning power of her voice, to an America dotted with motels and a certain mythology I'd like to feel within reach. And then there's Hélène [Gordon] Lazareff, the founder of *Elle* magazine, and Régine Deforges, an editor, playwright, and novelist, who strived to distribute erotic literature in France (which is rarely read despite being talked about so often). She worked to bring out stories that had been circulating illicitly and to help new voices emerge. I devoured her series, *The Blue Bicycle*, when I was a teenager.

As an adult, are there books you turn to again and again? Many, and for different reasons. But Tatiana de Rosnay's *Sarah's Key* has a special place in my library, and not only because the protagonist is named Sarah. It's an incredibly important and necessary book that discusses the Vel d'Hiv roundup, a shameful period in France's history that we mustn't forget. And Sarah is a deeply moving and resilient character, reminding us that no path in life is simple, that we have the right to make mistakes and start again. Complicated life trajectories speak to me, and this book will always answer the questions I'm asking myself.

With such a fascination for the written word, you could have pursued any number of paths. Why was education the right direction for you? I wanted a career with meaning, and there are so few that allow you to be truly useful. Teaching is incredibly rewarding, as is the connection I have with my students. I find myself regularly surprised by the mark I leave on them. I wanted them to understand that literature, classic or contemporary, shouldn't be an escape but rather something that can propose solutions to almost any problem. It's okay that they don't read in the way that I did at their age; they have other skills. They are still receptive to the sincerity in my teaching and appreciate that I treat them as adults—this is actually something that has struck me over the years. I only give them books to read that I actually enjoyed, that I've put my stamp of approval on, and so going into it, they know I will be honest in my analysis. We've all gained something from that dynamic. And of course teaching part-time also allows me the flexibility to write (I have published several books) and take care of myself; I have a chronic illness, so time to rest is crucial.

Un Texte Un Jour is a clever, mobile, and far less overwhelming way to incite people to read the classics. What was the spark? It was actually my mother, an engineer! She had already been creating apps for her work and proposed the idea of

"There are fifty free libraries in Paris. I love the idea that access to culture is free."

creating a sort of digital literary anthology a year after I had offered everyone in my family their own paper-based literary anthology (as you can see, this is my way of connecting with the world). We built the app together, and in 2012, it was released. At the time, there were hardly any literary apps on the market, so we were instantly visible. Later, we came out with Un Poème Un Jour and then the English app, A Text A Day. We have six different apps available now.

What were your expectations? It was really created as a pedagogic tool. I used it with my students, and I wanted other teachers to find it useful in their classrooms. But what was unexpected was learning that the first app was predominantly downloaded and used by the general public, users between the ages of twenty-five and fifty. Proof that it's never too late to learn!

Your apps include the work of men and women, French and foreign. The French curriculum, however, has notoriously leaned male: It wasn't until 2017 that one of Madame de La Fayette's books, for example, was added to the curriculum for final-year students preparing for their literary baccalaureate exam. How do you select the works you teach? It's true that in the final year of the literary track in high school, the curriculum didn't include any work by a woman writer until a petition was passed and *La Princesse de Montpensier* was added. In tenth and eleventh grade, the teacher is free to choose what they want to teach. And I have a nuanced opinion when it comes to literature. Before concerning myself with the gender of the author, I choose based on the quality of the text. For example, Victor Hugo is a much greater novelist than George Sand; I find Ronsard's poetry more beautiful than Louise Labé's, and I prefer Marcel Proust over Marguerite Duras, so I will not choose the women writers for reasons of parity. However, each year I do choose women writers, often more contemporary (like Tatiana de Rosnay and Daphne du Maurier) for my students to study. I just don't make it a hobbyhorse. I think there are plenty of ways to demonstrate feminist values in education, from uplifting and shining the light on female students to offering them role models. Having them read women writers isn't the only solution.

Aside from methods of teaching and learning that have evolved since you've been in education, the level of dissatisfaction among teachers has risen considerably; strikes in the public system are common. What are the pain points? There is a lack of teachers and professors and a lack of financial resources to create a profession that appeals to the potential teachers of tomorrow. Then there's the fact that the relationship between the work and the effort is no longer the same—there are far too many students per class, sometimes as many as thirty-six, and not enough autonomy for teachers to build the classes and the coursework they want. Many teachers and professors will tell you that they are in the profession for the contact with the students, but it's very hard to nurture that relationship and help them grow with that many students and limited time.

Overall, the feeling is that a lot is asked of teachers (and of schools in general) in France when it comes to the personal evolution of a student. It's not up to the school to resolve everything; there must be agency with the parents and students themselves.

And it certainly doesn't ease that feeling to learn that President Macron plans to cut 2,600 public teaching positions in middle schools and high schools for the 2019–2020 academic year. Does that change your perception of the profession? Like many of my colleagues, I feel that this reform is problematic. Teachers will be asked to work longer hours even though a full-time position is already extremely intense and requires blocks of rest; the psychological and personal balance is vital to be able to carry a class, especially one that gets bigger and bigger. But since this announcement, there has been a lot of press coverage on the ills in the system, which I think is a good thing. People need to realize the extent of the problem. It makes me even more determined to teach because if nothing changes, younger teachers will become extremely rare. I hope this is the beginning of serious discussions on overhauling an eroding system.

Her Paris

FAVORITE WOMAN-RUN BUSINESS?

It's not run by a woman, per se, but *full* of women! The Marguerite Durand municipal library, the first in France exclusively dedicated to books on women's history, feminism, and gender.

A PLACE THAT INSPIRES YOU?

L'Opéra Palais Garnier (shown above). It always gives me the impression I'm in a Zola or Balzac novel!

WHERE YOU GO TO READ OR WRITE?

Café Marly. It's got everything: the view, Parisian classicism, and the exact image that I have of Paris when I close my eyes. I've had many special dinners here, but I also come just to read.

*Putting the spotlight on sub-Saharan
contemporary African art*

NATHALIE MILTAT

FOUNDER AND CREATOR OF THE APPARTEMENT

NATHALIE MILTAT IS RELUCTANT to call her space an art gallery in any conventional sense or even refer to herself as a gallerist, but when she opens up a section of her loft for an exhibition of contemporary works by sub-Saharan African artists, she acts as an important ambassador of culture.

Since 2011, the Appartement, as she calls her hybrid gallery–performance space in a nineteenth-century Eiffel-style building in the 10th arrondissement, has welcomed guest curators to design a season of exhibitions that can live within the context of a domestic space. With the success of each season came the desire to reinforce her support of emerging African talent. In 2014, she established the Orisha award, Europe's first prize for contemporary African art, and followed in 2016 with the creation of Orafrica, a nonprofit organization committed to promoting art and sub-Saharan culture through artistic and cultural initiatives.

We spoke from the Appartement about her journey from Benin to Paris, the issue of art restitution, and the necessity to give contemporary African art a permanent home in the local community.

You were born in Benin, lived in Cameroon, and moved to Paris in your late teens for school. How do you think those experiences shaped your sense of self? I was nine when we moved to Cameroon, where my father had already been living, but never did I feel torn between the various chapters of my life. To this day, I consider myself lucky to have lived in places with such rich cultures. Landing in Cameroon from Benin was already a significant experience in itself—I didn't have the same accent; it was difficult; some classmates mocked me. But in Paris, you have to keep in mind that language isn't the only entry point. I was seventeen when I arrived,

and I already had a foundation in French culture before even stepping foot here. The French living in Cameroon played pétanque, drank pastis, brought over their films (Louis de Funès was well known!). I can't dissociate any of those experiences from who I am today.

What was the spark for your studies in art—a fascination at home or something learned once in France? In Cameroon, I didn't have access to any museums, but my father had paintings in the house, and he loved sculpture. They were beautiful things, detached from any kind of cultural pursuit, but they were around me. It was much later, after dropping out of law school (a path my father had imagined for me), that I decided to see where art would lead me. I went to L'École du Louvre, and I discovered an entirely new world. I was fascinated by history as told through objects and archaeological materials, so I began with general art history and then specialized in contemporary art with a focus on sub-Saharan works. It was a time of much discovery for me because so many of the pieces I was seeing were only available here, not in Africa (and now several African nations, including Benin, are demanding the restitution of their artworks).

Do you agree with the idea of returning artifacts and artworks (those removed without consent) to their countries of origin? If we consider that these cultural works are part of a heritage and are important to ensuring the continuity of a certain culture, these works help us understand our past and what we're made of. In this case, it makes sense for them to be returned.

The Musée du Quai Branly would certainly be empty if everything was returned! Maybe that isn't such a bad thing. I'd say it's time to open little Quai Branly museums all over the world. I think it's important that Africans connect with their heritage and culture, to understand themselves anew.

You are among the few to highlight sub-Saharan art in Paris and have rightfully been noticed for the work you're doing to uplift these artists. How does that feel? There are more and more African artists represented in contemporary galleries today (like Galerie Anne de Villepoix, La Galerie Jérôme Poggi), which shows that African art has a value. And I'm happy to be part of putting the spotlight

opposite Inside the Appartement: One of the sculptures Nathalie Miltat inherited from her father.

on their work. What I have trouble with is that the works are shown sporadically—there's a push and then nothing. I would love for it to become part of the city's artistic programming, always in the minds of art lovers.

You earned quite a lot of attention in Paris with your first big project, Noire Galerie. Did you hope it would fill the gap in the art scene? When I left L'École du Louvre, I cofounded Noire Galerie to create a window into contemporary African art. In school, what I saw was a lack of coursework around the topic; the first large-scale contemporary art exhibition (non-occidental) had only taken place in 1989 (Les Magiciens de la Terre). There were so few dedicated spaces to this kind of art at the time, and our gallery was about finding the artists and creating visibility for them. We wanted it to be a nomadic gallery, with events held in unexpected places.

But I understand it only lasted a few years. Why stop while you were ahead? In the end, it wasn't the right format. But it did lead to me creating the Orisha Award in 2014 to continue the work around ensuring visibility for artists. I give it out every two years and mark the occasion with an award ceremony, which is a way of saying, *Yes, this exists! Yes, there's a prize for contemporary African art!* The recipients receive support in preparing an exhibition in Paris that takes place one year later, and a whole lot of press and communication to go with it. Many of the artists I've featured and awarded have told me that it's because of the prize that they're able to work. That's incredible.

And this hybrid space—which is also your home—is where it all happens. That's right; there's only this room where I display the works. When I run exhibitions, it's open from Tuesday to Saturday. Between exhibitions, there's virtually nothing here. These are breathing moments I need; I enjoy the emptiness.

What's next? Some of the artists have asked for my help in acquiring materials, and I realized there's a real need to create access to the tools for them to create. I'm thinking about creating a resource center in Africa so that they can access tools and coursework on art theory, participate in artistic residencies, and then come to Paris to work. As for the Appartement—we'll see!

---

opposite View from Nathalie Miltat's Appartement in the 10th arrondissement.

Her Paris

FAVORITE WOMAN-RUN BUSINESS?

I can't name only one! Le Baratin in Belleville, one of my favorite restaurants. I love Raquel Carena's cooking, both traditional and inventive. I'm also a fan of a concept store called Nelly Wandji, founded by a young Franco-Cameroonian, where you can get a glimpse of the richness of contemporary African craftsmanship.

YOUR PREFERRED NEIGHBORHOOD?

Where I live, the 10th arrondissement. It's still a very cosmopolitan neighborhood with a vast mix of cultures. I'm lucky enough to be right on the border of the 19th, the 11th, and the Marais, which is wonderful.

YOUR HAPPY PLACE?

The Louvre, which I have seen evolve and transform from my years as a student. It's so easy for me to lose myself, strolling the different rooms and halls of the museum, even after all this time.

Celebrating freedom in food and heritage

POONAM CHAWLA

CULTURAL GUIDE, AUTHOR, AND TRANSLATOR

BEFORE I EVEN STEPPED OUT of the elevator, I knew I had come to the right place. An intoxicating smell of spices, garlic, and onion wafted out from the apartment door, left slightly ajar. I tapped lightly and stepped inside, announcing my presence with my usual *allô?* "I'm in the kitchen; come right in," I was instructed.

There, I found Poonam Chawla, slight with a shoulder-length bob and a long, button-up dress, shuffling back and forth from the stove to the small prep table, where she was plating chicken kebabs and spooning generous amounts of spiced red lentil daal into bowls. "This is where I give my classes," she said of her spacious-for-Paris kitchen, which overlooks a leafy courtyard garden. Countertops were stocked to the brim with homemade condiments, herbs, and spices, including her own blend of chai masala.

"I made a recipe video this morning for my website about broccoli stalk–and-potato curry. I'll have you try that too. Broccoli is a nouveau riche vegetable; in India we use cauliflower." I was already learning something.

I helped her bring our lunch spread to the dining room table where we sat for two hours discussing the vagaries of life, her career as a translator, cultural guide, and author, and the healing power of food.

We tend to assume that America holds the monopoly on opportunity in the immigrant imagination, but France, and Paris in particular, has its own appeal as the land of possibility. Early on, this was clear to Chawla, who began learning French when she was sixteen. At the Jawaharlal Nehru University in New Delhi, she specialized in French linguistics and entertained the idea of a career in tourism. That's also where she met a man and married for love at twenty-four years old, against the wishes of her parents. "He was from a different caste. He wasn't a doctor; he was a travel agent. They blessed the wedding but didn't support it."

By the time she was twenty-six, her first son, Nikhil, was born and the marriage was already in sharp decline. "He was controlling and macho and emotionally unstable. It wasn't what I expected." After the birth of Pushan, her second son, she occupied the role of primary caretaker and stable breadwinner, working two jobs while her husband floundered. During the week, she was a translator for the Indian Railways, and on weekends, a tour guide in the city. "Tourism connected me to so many people, including the French," she recalled. That was the beginning of what would become a new life. "I got a job offer to work in translation from Bayonne, in the French Basque Country. I secured a visa, brought the kids with me, and told my husband to try to find a way over."

While the work was good and steady, the social exclusion she experienced made the adjustment challenging, particularly for Chawla's sons. "There were only a few families like us—the Pays Basque was extremely white. My boys faced racist remarks at school, and I felt like I was living in an aloof manner. It was hard to make friends. I even took out my nose ring for a time to try to blend in." What's more, her husband never joined them, turning the prospect of divorce from *maybe one day* (when it's socially accepted) to *where do I sign?*

After nine years in Bayonne and a finalized divorce, she picked up her family of three and moved to New Jersey, where her brother had been living for years. But she quickly found herself facing similar discrimination, a feeling exacerbated in the aftermath of 9/11. "There was a sharp rise in racism against 'brown' people that was deeply concerning. A photographer even refused to take passport photos for me! My boys felt French but [were] treated as Indians; we were all lost," she said, shaking her head. They stayed as long as they could before the lack of sufficient work and looming sense of despair ushered them out, back to France. Only this time, she settled them in Paris, where she's lived, a few blocks from the Place du Trocadéro in the 16th arrondissement, since 2003.

It was here that she found opportunity and created a home. It was here that she discovered Little India, the city's Indian and Sri Lankan quarter in the 10th and 18th arrondissements, with nearly one hundred specialized shops, from beauty parlors and fashion stores to spice markets and restaurants. And it's here that she began leading tours of the neighborhood, guiding tourists, journalists, embassy workers, and employees of French companies like Chanel and SNCF

---

opposite A corner shop in Little India, Poonam Chawla's favorite culinary neighborhood in Paris.

through its history and landmarks. Her dark eyes shimmer with pride when she tells me she became the connector—to shopkeepers, to be sure, and to her own heritage. "Paris completed me."

Then, in 2008, after years of mounting pain and muscle contractions in her leg that made walking increasingly difficult, she was diagnosed with dystonia, a neurological movement disorder that is considered a cousin to Parkinson's. "What I have is very rare. There's no biomarker, no cure, or even any treatment. The panel of doctors I've seen all tell me to just relax and breathe. Live your life, they say," she explains, her eyes despondent. "That's very complicated when you can't walk outdoors with any ease."

She scaled back the tours in Paris and limited the excursions she had been organizing to India for French travelers. Throughout our lunch, she never once lamented her hardships but recounted them as facts of life that build the layers of her character. Though visibly troubled by her disorder and its interference in her life, she doesn't feel frail or damaged. She has cooking—her greatest salve—to thank for that.

"Since I had to stay home more, I concentrated on cooking. I offer cooking classes on northern Indian cuisine, which I love, and document my recipes on my website," she said, filling my glass with chai masala iced tea. "I've even published two books in France with Pushan, who is now a photographer." Her sons have more than benefited from her experimentation and storytelling through food. "It always smells like her cooking when I come in," Pushan told me. "Curry leaves sizzling on the pan, the warmth of homemade chapatis, the smell of rice pulao and her mango cakes." The scent of home.

On occasion, when she feels strong, she delights in the ability to run tours of her favorite pocket of town. "I've been told to meditate, but I can't. Instead, I meditate through food," she said with a soft smile. "When I'm cooking or at the markets, everything else is forgotten. My pain disappears."

Her Paris

YOUR FAVORITE WOMAN-OWNED BUSINESS?

My physiotherapist and coach, Vanessa Alglave-Tefridj! I see her two to three times per month for massages, sports coaching, and deep breathing. I enjoy talking to her (and she really loves my food). I would also mention Stella Centre de Beauté Indien, named after the owner, where I occasionnally get my hair cut. I also recommend the salon for eyebrow threading and henna.

YOUR FAVORITE NEIGHBORHOOD?

In my two homes, near the Place du Trocadéro in the 16th arrondissement and Little India.

A MUST-VISIT IN THE INDIAN QUARTER?

VT Cash & Carry (shown above)—it's where I go for my Indian spices, vegetables, mangoes . . . all the groceries. I'd be lost without them!

the "Taste" makers

*Driving the conversation around the taste
and ethics of quality coffee*

MIHAELA IORDACHE

HEAD COFFEE ROASTER AT BELLEVILLE BRÛLERIE

AS VOCATIONS, CLASSICAL GUITAR and coffee roasting aren't the most obvious of bedfellows, but Mihaela Iordache, head roaster at one of the city's leading coffee companies, Belleville Brûlerie, insists her two great passions in life have more in common than one might think.

On the humid late-spring morning we meet for breakfast at Broken Biscuits, she is wearing loose-fitted silk pants, a dark linen T-shirt, and burgundy sandals. She keeps her hair swept back in a ponytail, unbothered by the few wispy curls that stick to her temples in the heat. She motions to a woman paying for her coffee in yoga pants and a concert tee and remarks, "I love how relaxed she is. There'd be none of this informality at home. You get dressed up when you go out in Romania, no matter where." She looks back to me with a smile of relief. "My mother would hate what I'm wearing too." Paris is freedom.

There was nothing preordained in Iordache's career in coffee. The daughter of a priest and a pharmacist, a pairing whose only obvious connection was their rigor of training, she grew up in Bucharest within the strict parameters of Christianity and classical music. From the age of nine until only six years ago, her training as a classical guitarist dictated her everyday life.

When she decided to leave home, it was initially to find herself outside of the boundaries of family and country, wherever that quest might have taken her. Her musical gift led her to Paris, where she had the opportunity to train under the guidance of the prominent Parisian classical guitarist Judicaël Perroy. But the hours were grueling, and after a time, music became a burden, without the sense of fulfillment it was meant to have. "You work alone all year, eight hours a day, toward one performance . . . You don't take breaks, and your brain gives out on your focus

after a while. I got to the point where I wanted any escape." She finished her degree but quit music professionally before she could see where it would take her.

That's when *le café*—the place and the product—inserted itself into her life as if by divine intervention. She was living near Pigalle and stopped into KB Café, one of the earliest craft coffee shops in the area, almost daily. When she started drinking coffee, a beverage she admits she disliked vehemently up until that first visit (and even went so far as to call a waste of money), it was because it was the cheapest thing on the menu. "I was going mostly to use their Wi-Fi to search for jobs and an apartment," she says with a laugh. "It was back when Tim Teyssier, who now owns O Coffeeshop, was working there. Every time I went in, I watched him work and listened to him talk so passionately about something that I had looked down upon with such arrogance for so long. That got me curious," she says. Then she started showing up with a notebook and sitting for hours, asking questions, heeding advice. He recommended she try a coffee cupping, a professional coffee tasting, with Belleville Brûlerie, and off she went.

That Saturday-morning cupping was a turning point. She brought the first coffee to her nose and inhaled deeply. "It was a Guatemalan that smelled like chocolate nut cake. People think I exaggerate when I say this, but it instantly took me back to being five years old in my grandmother's kitchen. She used to make a cake that smelled just like that at the holidays. And suddenly, I felt at home, which I don't experience often," she recalls. Overcome with emotion, she put the glass down and told herself, this is what she was going to do. "I think I fell in love with coffee like you fall in love with a person."

From there, she contacted every coffee shop in Paris looking for work, expressing her interest in learning. She knew she'd need to be trained, but the disciplined musician in her knew the learning curve wouldn't be a problem. Still, no one responded. Determined, she kept pushing until Ten Belles, another leading coffee shop, agreed to take her on. "But I wasn't allowed near the machine. I was doing service and dishes," she says regretfully. "Coffee had a bit of a bro culture then. But I put in my time."

People in the coffee industry who remember Iordache's earliest days love to remind her how serious she was—how she *lived* and *breathed* coffee and spoke of nothing else. "I don't have six speeds when I'm curious. I either care or I don't; that's the way I am," she admits. And so she threw herself into coffee full throttle— teaching guitar in the mornings for extra cash, working at Ten Belles from midday to evening, and paying Teyssier to train her in the evenings for several months. On weekends, she attended cuppings at Belleville and made sure the founders, David Flynn and Thomas Lehoux, understood her potential.

When she only had five months of experience on the machine, she tried her luck at the Barista Championship in Lyon and ended up making the finals. That's when Flynn and Lehoux offered to complete her training properly. She managed Ten Belles for one more year before joining the Brûlerie and working her way up to head roaster.

What fascinated her early on about coffee and coffee roasting was the precision and perpetual balance it requires, the ways in which the craft is, at its core, similar to music. "I roast on a fifteen-kilogram gas drum roaster in Belleville's headquarters. When we moved into the space, I had to rethink the profile for every coffee so that the taste would remain the same," she explains. Coffee, like the wood guitar she used to play, is an organic, living matter. When the weather fluctuates throughout the day, when the room temperature changes, and when the seasons evolve, she must adjust her setup, just as she adjusted her guitar to account for environmental shifts. "It's like a dance between the roaster, the green coffee, its age, the context, the gas setup of that day, my nose, palate, and ability to focus," she says in a mouthful. "This is the intuitive part of my job that I find most difficult to talk about but that I can trace back to everything I learned in music."

If she's come into her own in an industry whose importance in Paris has grown exponentially in the last six to eight years, in part thanks to the efforts of her employers, she thinks it's because she can believe in the mission. "The goal is to democratize good coffee, and that's something I can get behind. But also because it's happening in an ethical, transparent way."

We capped the conversation with a discussion that I first began having with her at the time of writing *The New Paris*, when she was still a barista: Why is good coffee valuable in Paris? I wondered if her opinion had evolved. What hadn't changed was her belief that, from a self-serving point of view, it offers an exploration of taste; it's about pleasing the senses. But beyond that, she insists now that it's truly an entry into understanding the way the world works. "I learned much more about the world by working in coffee than doing anything else. It's a product of colonialism; it's about economics. There are some seventy hands that are involved in getting those beans from farm to destination. The price that the majority of coffee consumers see, in supermarkets especially, is a reflection of an injustice."

She sees her contribution to Paris, to France, and to an entire industry as more than the production of a product worthy of recognition. She wants to be part of the

"I've always been surrounded by men who gave me space at the table. But I also seized the space. I wouldn't have it any other way."

dialogue around the ethics of coffee, one that both addresses the whole complex chain of production and encourages consumers to become better attuned to what they put in their bodies. "Coffee can lead to understanding that every choice you make has an impact on the planet, just like fashion and food. You, the consumer, have power by knowing what you're buying and demanding better. Everything is interconnected; we are interconnected." And she has seen the dial move on a small scale. "People feel helpless if they think that making an impact can only be achieved with big changes. It's about doing, not preaching." And if coffee can be part of that, *encore mieux*.

Four years into her role, she's only now realizing that she occupies a position that people are paying attention to. She will be heard if she shares her opinion. More and more she's asked to organize events around women in coffee, not only because she's a woman but because she is seen as someone with greater access and experience. "I've been so focused on the work; this is all so new to me," she says modestly. "Roasting has been like music—very solitary. I like the idea of connecting with people around coffee more. It would do me good!"

Her Paris

FAVORITE WOMAN-RUN BUSINESS?

I love going to Broken Biscuits, co-owned by Christine O'Sullivan, who is modest, hardworking, kind, and tremendously talented. I'm also in awe of what Carina Soto has helped build with her group Quixotic Projects (Candelaria, Le Mary Celeste, Hero, Les Grands Verres)—she has a great palate and an emotional understanding of what she tastes.

SOLO RITUAL?

Heading to the Buttes-Chaumont Park (shown above) before ten a.m., when there are only runners and gardeners—it's very calm. It's also one of the only parks to remind me of Bucharest.

SOMEPLACE YOU LIKE TO GO ON WEEKENDS?

It's not entirely disconnected from my work, but I love the jazz nights on Saturdays at La Fontaine de Belleville (owned by Belleville Brûlerie)—good music and a place to connect with friends.

Innovating in food and fighting to keep publishing alive

MURIEL TALLANDIER

PUBLISHER AND COFOUNDER OF FOU DE PÂTISSERIE BOUTIQUE

EVERY WORK MORNING BEGINS the same for Muriel Tallandier. The alarm goes off before seven a.m., but she lets herself sink back into bed for twenty minutes of contemplation—about the night before, the day ahead, life lived, and life to come. Her wife, Julie Mathieu (see page 221), makes breakfast and they take the time to eat with their daughter before it's off to school. They alternate drop-off and pickup duty, sacred moments they'd never give up no matter how much work might be piling up at the office. Then she heads to Pressmaker, the independent publishing company she launched in 2012.

I was introduced to Tallandier by Mathieu at the opening of their first pastry boutique, Fou de Pâtisserie. Mathieu had told me enough about her to have formed an image in my mind—an expectation, perhaps—but I couldn't have visualized the woman I met. With a confiding voice and an air of self-assuredness, I saw a driven, good-humored entrepreneur who beamed with gratitude for having a business she can run with her wife, with whom she shares a wonderful passion for food and culture. She was impossibly cool, which is the vaguest thing I could say about her, and yet it captured her essence. It still does.

From there, we would cross paths at pastry events, with and without Mathieu. We'd exchange messages on Instagram about the books we were reading and the restaurants we were vetting, until one day, she asked me to lunch with her and Mathieu because they believed my voice would be an asset to their magazine.

I preface her portrait this way because whenever I was in Tallandier's company, she'd always take more interest in my story than in sharing her own. She believed in my abilities more than I did. I'd collect tiny fragments from her life story, but it wasn't until I asked her to be part of this book that a fuller picture came together.

CHOCOLATS

*

CAKES

*

GLACES & SORBETS

*

VIENNOISERIES

*

CONFITURES

*

PÂTES À TARTINER

*

MADELEINES

*

FINANCIERS

*

PÂTES DE FRUITS

*

CARAMELS

*

GUIMAUVES

And that image, at least what I have taken from it, is that Tallandier is a woman of insatiable curiosity, warmth, boundless dedication to friends and family, and with a vision that has allowed her to run and build businesses that give her the freedom to live a life on her terms.

Like the generations of Tallandiers before her, Muriel was born in Saint-Denis to parents in academia. She grew up all over France, following her father wherever his assignments as a high school principal led their family. It wasn't until she started studying applied arts at the prestigious École Estienne in the early nineties that she made a long-awaited return to Paris. "I've always been the black sheep of the family— my brothers became professors in biochemistry and physics, and I'm in business!" She chuckles, leaning back into the worn leather armchair in her office. As a kid, she fantasized about two vastly different careers—becoming a surgeon or working for the press. "I'd read every magazine and newspaper I could get my hands on growing up. I devoured the *Elle* that my mother got delivered at home, despite everything in it feeling out of reach," she explains. "And I so badly wanted to be back in Paris. For me, editors and publishers were the ultimate symbols of Parisian life, and I wanted in."

She also wanted to be part of everything else Paris represented at the time. It was the city of freedom and fete, of stars and intellectuals commingling at legendary nightclubs. In Lille, where she was living just before her return to the capital, everyone knew who her father was and therefore knew who *she* was. She felt trapped by small-city dynamics, particularly given the trying, coming-of-age emotions she struggled to overcome there. "I was nineteen, and I had just come out to my parents. I liked the idea of being anonymous in the big city," she begins. "Plus, everything was produced in Paris. Everything I was watching and reading was made in Paris. I felt like I wasn't really living until I was there."

She describes her transition back into Parisian life as being akin to Alice falling through a rabbit hole and into another world in *Alice's Adventures in Wonderland*, only in her case, it was crossing the Périph. Those formative years in her twenties were spent with a socially mixed gay crowd, hailing everywhere from the 16th to the *banlieue* (suburbs)—a refreshing departure, she says, from the stratified system common to much of Parisian life, "where you're easily reduced to the schools you attended, the family you're from, and the neighborhood you live in." If she flourished in such an environment, it's because she forged ahead as though the system simply didn't apply to her.

Despite the media's preoccupying importance in her daily life, her career kicked off in the music industry: first at Polygram (which was eventually acquired by

"We need to destroy the fantasy of the mother-father binary, of Prince Charming, and invent our own narratives. I think that's possible in Paris."

Universal), then as marketing director at Sony Music, before finally leading the charge of a music program at TF1, the French media and television group. The program fizzled quickly, but the company saw her as an asset and offered her a role in the area she had always hoped she'd end up: publishing.

"I was in charge of everything TF1 that *wasn't* television, and one of the big projects was developing the magazines for popular shows. I liked it so much I established TF1 Publishing, creating a whole unit of books, magazines, and printed products." When she left after several years, it was to launch the first of several publishing businesses of her own.

At thirty, she met Mathieu in a nightclub. They fell in love, moved in together shortly thereafter, and have supported each other through ambitious ventures ever since—Mathieu's pursuit of (and eventual withdrawal from) politics and Tallandier's growing collection of magazines for kids and young adults under her first publishing arm.

"We both loved travel and especially the idea of working hard to fund time off to travel more, to give ourselves the best life we could. As an entrepreneur, my schedule was more flexible for that," she says. "Once I gave birth to our daughter, Gabrielle, we reorganized our lives to have time together, in and out of Paris."

Shortly after Tallandier launched Pressmaker, her second and current publishing house, Mathieu joined the business. "I taught her everything she needed to know about the industry, but she was a naturally good writer and manager. Such forbearance. I call her *la force tranquille*," she says with a laugh. "And I'm, well, the opposite. *Pas tranquille.*" They complement each other both at home and at work, and that's clear to the talented roster of writers and designers they've worked with to bring to life their signature publication, *Fou de Pâtisserie*, and its sister title, *Fou de Cuisine*.

From the start, their goal has been to make the work of *grands chefs* and emerging talents accessible through profiles, interviews, recipes, and baking secrets that pastry lovers couldn't get anywhere else. The natural extension was to re-create that experience in real life. Together, and over the course of several years of running the magazine, they earned the trust of the country's most talented pastry chefs, bakers, and chocolatiers who greeted the idea of a pastry concept store favorably, handing over control of their image to Tallandier, Mathieu, and their team of well-trained pastry pushers. Today, they run three boutiques and a pastry corner in the gourmet grocer Maison Plisson and have published a tome featuring eighty-five recipes from forty top pastry chefs. "I want to create things that are beautiful but *populaire*—accessible. Too often, these heritage products have been reserved for an elite. We wanted to create an equal playing field."

She gently rebuffs the suggestion that she and Julie are visionaries in the industry. "First of all, Julie's the real star of the boutique. I'm the woman in the shadows. I try to break down barriers and make our vision possible," she says, smirking. "What I will say is that it's about diversifying. It might be the only way for the press to survive."

And she doesn't consider these projects *too* ambitious. There's no such thing as over-the-top or off-limits for Tallandier. "I don't want to say nothing's impossible, because that's so hokey, but I don't look at things in life or work as unattainable," she tells me. She finds a solution, lifts away obstacles. That philosophy applies to motherhood too. "We knew we wanted children, but we also knew that it wasn't necessarily going to be easy. It still isn't authorized in France for lesbian couples or single women to have access to IVF, but we found a gynecologist in Paris who was willing to . . . bend the rules."

Now the obstacle she's facing is one much larger than her and has demanded the efforts of an entire collective of publishers and government officials who are committed to finding a solution to the troubled fate of publishing in France. She's made it her personal mission to save what can be saved, beginning with distribution. As one of twelve trustees on the board of France's leading media distributor, which handles 75 percent of all titles, including national newspapers and Tallandier's own publications, and is on the verge of bankruptcy, she has been tasked with helping to turn things around.

"France remains one of the countries in the world with the richest and most diverse offerings in media, and it's precious," she insists. "I'm one of those people who believe that it's by acting on behalf of the group, the collective, that I'm most useful. That's how I find meaning."

Her Paris

FAVORITE WOMAN-RUN BUSINESS?

I can't name only one! Maison Plisson run by Delphine Plisson, a woman I adore and who has an eye for exceptional French culinary products. Adeline Grattard's Café Lai'Tcha, whose Southeast Asian menu is a voyage in itself, and Emmanuelle Zysman's namesake jewelry boutique on the rue des Martyrs. I feel like her shop is where you sense the true spirit of Paris. She's a true artist.

YOUR PREFERRED NEIGHBORHOOD?

The 10th, of course! It's the self-proclaimed stronghold of the new food scene, the most creative, the most audacious, the most *gourmand*. It's trendy but *populaire*, there's an unparalleled cultural offering, and there are downright magical spots to hang out—Canal Saint-Martin, around République, Faubourg-Saint-Denis, La Cour des Petites-Écuries. It's only missing some greenery.

SOMEPLACE YOU LIKE TO TAKE YOUR DAUGHTER?

La Villette for the exhibitions and activities, and the Centre Pompidou (shown above). We'll spend a half day, go for lunch, see an exhibit, check out one of the numerous street performers in front of the museum, get some ice cream.

Championing the craft of French pastry

JULIE MATHIEU

EDITOR IN CHIEF AND CO-OWNER OF
FOU DE PÂTISSERIE MAGAZINE AND BOUTIQUE

IT SEEMED LIKE KISMET that I met Julie Mathieu when I did. It was 2015, and I had arrived at Charles Compagnon's restaurant Le 52 to interview him for my first book. He led me into his office, and there was Mathieu with Claire Pichon, her executive editor of *Fou de Cuisine*, one of the two magazines she oversees, beginning their day shadowing Charles for a story of their own. I ended up staying for lunch and getting to know both women, talking to them about my work, the food scene, their magazine, and, naturally, how fond we all were of Charles's restaurants. I distinctly remember leaving that day with the impression that I had been in the company of veteran food journalists, deeply embedded in the past, present, and future of dining movements. And in a way, I was—both magazines draw from a deep reservoir of knowledge about not only the city's but the country's gastronomic landscape and the people and techniques shaping it. But I was surprised to learn that they'd been doing it professionally only as long as I had.

When we sit down in the 10th arrondissement office she shares with her wife and business partner, Muriel Tallandier (see page 214), in front of a library nook stacked to the brim with the best cookbooks to have been published in France and Europe in recent years, the first thing she tells me is that she's a late bloomer. It wasn't shared with any shame or regret, simply presented as fact. And that's an important, self-appointed qualifier when you know that France is a country that urges its citizens to have identified the precise career path they intend to follow when they're barely out of puberty. She didn't get into full-time writing, editing, and managing until more than a decade after she had been with Tallandier; after becoming a mother and realizing that the life that she wanted with her family wasn't compatible with the career she had pursued in politics. Regardless of which came first, the dwindling interest in the work or the desire to see more of the world with her daughter with greater flexibility, she was in her forties when the realization hit.

Conversation has always been easy with Mathieu. We've talked about our cats—the painful loss and the joyful adoption of them—and our love for travel and food. Her life revolves around the people making the best dishes and recipes in the country and those who aspire to do the same. But that's largely all I knew. "Come round, I'll tell you my story," she said with a wide grin.

Mathieu was born in the 12th arrondissement, raised in Vincennes until she was six, and then she moved to the southeastern suburb of Charenton-le-Pont. After her parents' separation, her father was mostly absent and she and her brother were raised by her mother, a nurse, who assumed all the roles—father, mother, disciplinarian, educator, friend, confidant. She spent her childhood playing with her brother and her adolescence playing team sports—rugby, volleyball, water polo, hockey, whatever she could get involved with. Though they didn't speak about her preferences or sexuality at that age, Mathieu's convinced her mother knew. "For my third birthday, my grandmother sent me a dress that I promptly threw in the trash. That doesn't have to mean anything, but for me, it did. And my mother knew that."

With her mother working around the clock to support them, Mathieu took refuge in academics and the family she was able to create outside of the home. She wasn't focused on what she was going to do professionally. With these friends, they talked about politics, movies, and love, and it was during this time that she says she had her civic awakening. "I wanted to be part of something that mattered," she says, but that would have to be on the other side of the Périphérique, in Paris. She dreamed of attending the Sorbonne to study history and living out some version of the fantasy she had created in her mind of Paris as the one true epicenter of intellectualism. For her mother's generation, a woman was meant to start a family, or if she worked, it was as a secretary or a nurse. High-level studies for women were a sign of personal emancipation. "Like Simone de Beauvoir, independent and liberated from her social condition through education, I thought, that's what I want. When I'm older, I'll live in Paris and study and be free," she says.

When her "new life," as she calls it, finally did begin in Paris, she was living in a shoebox apartment in Montmartre but spent all of her time in the cafés, like the Café de Flore, associated with the illustrious thinkers that came before her. "It was part of my social ascension. I wanted to live well," she explains. "I never wanted to be rich; I wanted a *good* life."

"A Parisian woman does things for herself, not anyone else. And life doesn't have to be put on pause because she has children."

She threw herself into academia, going so far as to begin a PhD, and funded her life working at Gaumont cinemas for five years. She liked the independence it bestowed. "I lived in a historic neighborhood. I lived life fully, went out until five a.m. most nights, and was in a relationship with my first serious girlfriend."

Mathieu formally came out to her mother when she was eighteen years old. Though she was embraced, like Tallandier, it came with the platitude that she hadn't "chosen" the easiest path. "My mother's best friend was gay and was never an example of stability. I think she worried that that was necessarily the future for me," she says. As for coming out as a lesbian woman then versus what she observes of the experience today, she's not sure much has changed. Lesbians are still largely invisible in media and yet relatively accepted. "In the collective unconscious, two women together is considered beautiful. Heterosexual men find it attractive, and women don't seem to mind. But gay men together? That's another story; that 'offends' because it challenges a straight man's virility," she reasons. "I never hid my sexuality—not at home, not at school, not at work. My mother gave me her blessing, but I didn't need approval from anyone." Nor did she feel any shame. For a time, she affirmed her masculinity with Doc Martens, blazers, and ultra-short hair, clichés in their own right, she says, but part of a necessary phase. The codes of the Parisienne were never far from view—her beauty, her style, and the way she carried herself—but she felt blissfully detached from them. In many ways, she came into her own much the way her wife did.

When she met Tallandier at thirty-one, she found herself not only someone she wanted to share her life with but someone who believed in her changing ambitions—and supported them. She had dropped the PhD and went for a master's in political science, with the goal of working for Arnaud Montebourg, then a deputy at the National Assembly (and later, minister of economics under François Hollande). "In 2002, it was the first time the National Front, the far-right political party, had made it to the second round in the presidential elections. It sent shock waves all over France and turned me and Muriel into active, card-carrying socialists," she tells me. She went on to work with Montebourg as a parliamentary attaché for two years and fought alongside him to reform the socialist party ("*Tant pis*, it didn't work," she adds casually). "I almost ran for a deputy position at the National Assembly, but it would've meant sacrificing my personal life, and by that point, I wasn't prepared to do it." A few other roles followed, in crisis management for elected officials and in headhunting for politicians, before she ultimately made the decision to step back entirely to work with Tallandier.

"It was like starting from the beginning again, but we wanted to work together and have more time as a family. Tallandier taught me everything about publishing, and I just jumped in," she explains of the career that she's become most associated with today. They created *Fou de Pâtisserie* magazine together, two gastronomes at heart, just as pastry was emerging as a focus of great fascination in books and on television shows, the chefs themselves assuming the status of celebrity. "The goal was to make the work of leading chefs accessible to as many people as possible. That wasn't being done in any other magazine—there was an obvious gap to fill," she says of their inspiration. The first issue was released in 2013, and Mathieu stepped in as permanent editor in chief shortly thereafter. Within a few issues, she and her editorial staff became veritable ambassadors of French pastry and the magazine a primary source for intel on the industry's rising talents, like Nicolas Haelewyn of Karamel or Myriam Sabet (see page 227) of Maison Aleph.

If you can find Pierre Hermé's Ispahan croissants and chocolates from Dijon-based chocolatier and Meilleur Ouvrier de France Fabrice Gillotte alongside éclairs by Carl Marletti in the Fou de Pâtisserie boutiques on any day of the week, it's thanks to Mathieu. She's the guardian of their stories; they trust her to make them shine. "We all want the same thing," she says. "To preserve the incredible craftsmanship we have in this country and make it available."

Her daughter, now nine, is being raised to understand and value the importance of passion in one's work. It's not a guarantee, but she has two significant reminders at home of the twists and turns a career can take. She's also learning the influence one's environment can make on her life. When Mathieu and Tallandier decided to build a family, they moved out of western Paris—too white, too affluent, too conservative—and into the 10th for the life that would be good for them as a unit.

"We know where we come from. We wanted her to be confronted with real life, the real Paris that isn't homogenous," she says in her soft, but assured voice. "Our neighborhood might be changing, but no one here cares about our family structure. We're just us."

Her Paris

FAVORITE WOMAN-RUN BUSINESS?

The Galerie Miranda, owned and run by Miranda Salt. She displays fine photography by international artists who have little visibility in Europe. It all makes a statement.

SOMEPLACE YOU LIKE TO TAKE YOUR DAUGHTER?

The Centre Pompidou, for its vibrant neighborhood, fascinating exhibits, workshops for kids, rooftop with incredible views of the city that I never tire of seeing, and openness to the outside world.

YOUR HAPPY PLACE?

Anywhere on my bike! I can listen to music, my face in the wind, with the feeling of being free, on vacation.

above Some of the exquisite pastries from Julie Mathieu's boutique, Fou de Pâtisserie.

Bringing the flavors of the Levant to the pastry scene

MYRIAM SABET

FOUNDER AND OWNER OF MAISON ALEPH

TO THE UNTRAINED EYE, the Marais's historic Jewish and gay quarters, with their falafel shops, independent boutiques, and LGBTQ-friendly bars, have gone the way of the city's most well-heeled enclaves: overshadowed by chain stores and luxury houses. But when Myriam Sabet's Levantine pastry shop, Maison Aleph, moved in, she helped to revive the artisanal flavor that local residents had been clamoring for. And she did it with something unique.

On one of the rare moments of quiet at her beloved shop on rue de la Verrerie, I chatted with Sabet about her radical career shift, her vision of Levantine pastry, and finding support from industry veterans.

You spent the majority of your career as a financial trader before changing course altogether. What did you like about it and then what changed? I liked the adrenaline and all the highs, which were intense. The trades were big, and there was a lot of pressure. I could tolerate the pace because I was a workhorse and happy with the lifestyle the job afforded me: nine weeks of vacation, for starters. And if I stayed twelve years, it was for the challenge. I was one of few women, and I was succeeding at trades with clients that my peers didn't think were possible.

It wasn't until I had my first child that I realized my priorities were off. The women I worked with would backstab to get ahead, and I was never very good at the politics of the job. Once I became a parent, I didn't want to waste my time on that stuff anymore. And even the idea of the challenge that had motivated me before proved meaningless. My husband was the voice of reason; he told me to leave if I was unhappy. He supported and understood my decision to leave the security of the job, even when others didn't.

It would be five years before you opened your bakery, Maison Aleph. What was the path to getting there? I didn't waste any time; I enrolled in the intensive CAP (professional pâtisserie training) program at the École de Boulangerie et de Pâtisserie de Paris and acquired all the formal skills I needed. I interned at a neighborhood bakery and Ladurée, to have experiences on both ends of the spectrum, and it was during this time that the concept was maturing in my head. I wanted it to be a new but still very Parisian brand, balanced in flavors and design. It took me two years alone to find the name, though. It happened when my mother was with me; all good things happen when she's in town, I swear. I'm a big believer in things happening when they're meant to.

It takes time to land the perfect name! What were you going for? Aleph is the first letter in many alphabets, in Hebrew and Arabic; it's the first page, the beginning of a new story. It's a nod to Aleppo, of course. And symbolic of early sweet pleasures of childhood.

What you're bringing to the industry is something familiar and yet unfamiliar. Parisians know Levantine pastries as cloyingly sticky-sweet confections served at the end of a filling meal, but you've put a whole new spin on the idiom. I may be born Syrian, but I don't like geographic limits, so I intentionally wanted these pastries to highlight the region, which includes Lebanon, Jordan, Syria, Israel, and parts of Turkey. Usually, the heaviness and excess of these pastries, which are soaked in sugar syrup, are what people remember about them. They're associated with discomfort. But I have memories of better varieties. I mix French pastry technique with textures and flavors from the region to offer something different (like the Kadaïf angel hair "nests" made with clarified butter, filled with flavored creams or candied fruit, or baklava revisited).

Did you feel like you were entering an entirely new world on your own, or did you find support? I found that there was a tremendous amount of mutual support in the entrepreneurial pastry space and even found mentors among some of the city's Meilleur Ouvrier de France; they generously offered their help to me. They said they were touched by my arrival in the industry. All I needed to do was ask for help—there's a lesson there, for everyone.

---

previous spread, left to right Myriam Sabet's temple of Levantine pastries in the Marais; Kadaïf angel hair "nests" at Maison Aleph, made with clarified butter and filled with flavored creams or candied fruit.

Her Paris

FAVORITE WOMAN-RUN BUSINESS?

Maison Plisson, the gourmet market and café. It's extraordinary what Delphine Plisson created in a city dense with specialty grocers. She makes the impossible possible, even if it's difficult along the way. And she keeps her cool with the challenge of running it all.

WHERE YOU GO AS A FAMILY?

The Marché d'Aligre (shown above) on Sundays—it's our precious family time. I've been going there with my husband for the sixteen years we've been together. We do our food shopping from the local producers and then sit and relax with a coffee.

PREFERRED NEIGHBORHOOD?

The Marais! And not just because my business is here. I love it for its diversity, its energy, and the spirit of novelty that can be felt in the northern part of the neighborhood, approaching Place de la République.

MARGOT LECARPENTIER

MIXOLOGIST AND COFOUNDER OF COMBAT

MARGOT LECARPENTIER MAY HAVE discovered cocktails in New York, but it was in Paris that the intrepid entrepreneur ultimately decided to swap her previous life as legal counsel for music labels for the booming bar scene. In 2017, she opened Combat, an award-winning cocktail bar whose name is symbolic in more ways than one: Combat was the former name for the neighborhood, between the place du Colonel Fabien and Belleville. But as I learned from our chat before opening hours at the bar, which could easily pass for a French café, it also denotes her fight as a woman and as an entrepreneur to bring the concept to life.

What was the moment you knew that your future would be in leading the next wave of cocktail bars in the city? It was gradual. I had just returned to Paris from my stints at Sony Music and Domino Records in New York, and I was looking for work in the midst of a crisis for the music industry. Turns out, my solid experiences didn't matter; I didn't have the right contacts or friends in high places. Needless to say, I was disillusioned, so I said screw it. Experimental Cocktail Club was looking for help, and I started the very next day behind the bar. It was a real turning point for me because I realized there was a real *métier* I could pursue. They trained me to become a mixologist, and I invested myself completely. No one tried to block me from getting ahead. I was able to move up quickly, and they gave me their blessing when, after three years, I left to prepare to open my own place with my friend Elena Schmitt.

As you were working your way up, were there moments you felt like you had to fight for your spot at the table? Starting out in the bar scene wasn't a struggle. Or maybe I was too naive to recognize the sexism, but I just kept on. I've always been a

"The Parisienne is someone who can make it in the ferocious city but isn't about to make themselves miserable just to belong."

fighter and a bit daring. But then I started to come up against a number of different obstacles. What I discovered was a glass ceiling on the road to entrepreneurship that had everything to do with being a woman.

In what way? As soon as you demand respect, you're met with paternalism, this kind of passive misogyny that some men might not even recognize in themselves, but it's insidious. I encountered it when I was applying for business loans at the bank (one man asked why I wasn't opening a tea salon, instead—no joke), when I was doing the administrative work to set up the business, and when I was dealing with contractors and other professionals (lawyers, architects, all men). At first I thought it was a reaction to my age, but that was naive. It was because I was a woman. They took a posture of superiority. It wasn't immediately palpable, but it does its damage. It did, however, awaken the unabashed feminist in me.

How do you handle these obstacles, as you call them, now? Generally, I try to avoid complaining about them—there's always something. Instead, I try to focus on talking to other women about how I've gotten to where I am in my perspectives, how I wasn't always treated fairly, how I made excuses for the bad behavior of others. If I can help with a feminist awakening in other women, I'm doing something right. "When you think something isn't normal, ask yourself if we'd say or do it to a man" is what I like to remind women. It gives them a jolt every time.

As soon as you have a community of any kind, the word communautarisme gets thrown around. How has your decision to hire only women been received? Some ask questions, but I've stopped explaining myself. If you have two résumés, one from a man and one from a woman, and the guy's is better, it's because he had more opportunities. I don't feel guilty about hiring women.

---

opposite Combat, Margot Lecarpentier's craft cocktail bar on rue de Belleville, a welcoming hangout and safe space for women.

Has the women-first message impacted your business? Some nights, there's only women in the bar. We have a strong LGBT clientele—it's important for them to feel safe here, that they can be themselves and get comfortable. We have so many regulars, which I love. Too often, it's poorly regarded for a woman to be a regular of a bar, especially on her own. At Experimental Cocktail Club, when a woman came in alone, the guys would say, "We know what she's looking for!" There's none of that kind of judgment here.

You were welcomed by the community and recognized by the industry (Le Fooding Best Bar d'Auteur award in 2018) in your first year of business. How do you envision the future of Combat? I'd like us to become much more than a cocktail bar. It's already happening, actually. We support feminist projects. We collaborate with organizations and creative women who share the same values and need a place for their work. We want to be firmly established in the cocktail landscape, known for quality and consistency. We had so much luck when we opened to be embraced by the press, be recognized by the industry, and be asked to collaborate with bars abroad. But that can't get the best of us, we have to make sure we're creating the best experience possible day in and day out. I will be so proud if we're still as well liked and recognized for what we do in five years' time.

Her Paris

FAVORITE WOMAN-RUN BUSINESS?

Mamiche! It's an excellent bakery run by laid-back women. If I can get myself up and out in the morning, I'll cycle up to the 9th arrondissement for their babka (shown above).

WHAT DO YOU DO WHEN YOU'RE NOT BEHIND THE BAR?

Go out to eat (probably more than I should!). I basically organize my free time and my cycling routes around what I'm going to eat. That might be Aux Deux Amis, Le Chateaubriand (I know the staff and often go have wine with them), La Cave à Michel, or Double Dragon. And three times a week I play badminton at a community club (Club Populaire et Sportif du 10ème).

YOUR HAPPY PLACE?

The bridges of Paris. With music in my headphones, no matter where I look, the view is always beautiful.

Redefining the food scene, one cookie at a time

MOKO HIRAYAMA

BAKER AND CO-OWNER OF MOKONUTS

IT ALWAYS SMELLS OF FRESHLY ROASTED COFFEE and toasted sourdough in the morning where Moko Hirayama works. And that's entirely by design. A fresh cup is waiting for her once she arrives at the restaurant-café-bakery-destination extraordinaire that she opened with her chef husband, Omar Koreitem, at eight forty-five a.m. after dropping off her daughters at school. She's there just in time for the morning regulars. Some come in with their stacks of newspapers and their notebooks, others with their computers or a friend eager to try her cake of the day and observe Hirayama and Koreitem prepare for what is invariably another fully booked lunch service.

Walking into Mokonuts, a name that might affectionately nod to Hirayama's unbridled energy but is actually a nickname bestowed to her by a former colleague, is like stepping into a family kitchen: it's calm at times, frenetic at others, and you're bound to get in the way at some point, but Hirayama will always be kind about it.

The lunch menu, which inspires some diners to reserve weeks in advance, is a mélange of flavors and inspirations from their joint backgrounds—French, Lebanese, American, Japanese—and changes daily. Hirayama insists that their cooking isn't so easy to categorize, though people have certainly tried. "People remind me of my background more than I even think of it," she says. "The French really try to label what we do here, just like they try to do with me. But categories aren't so simple."

Nor are they important to the loyal customers, who instantly understood that they were trying to offer something different without any neatly defined concept. Those people are still regulars today. And for those who aren't regulars when they arrive, they invariably leave aspiring to return, charmed to death by the experience and the food, both refreshingly simple and refined. There's a particular specialness in the pocket-size space she and Omar have laid claim to. It could be the elevated cooking in a casual environment or the languid pace of the meal that forces you to focus on your dish and your dining companions. It could be Hirayama grinning behind the counter, joking with clients as she slices up a seasonal pie, or the chatter from the kitchen. "Let's do something with this today," Koreitem will say, pointing to a spice or obscure ingredient. In a time with overwrought choice and rushing about, Mokonuts is where life slows to a near halt in a way we typically only allow ourselves on vacation. Option-anxiety disappears. It's special for all the reasons above and all the intangible ways it brings joy.

A former metal workshop with mosaic tile floors, Mokonuts is virtually an extension of the couple's home. And in that spirit, nothing is meant to be ornate or stuffy. They wanted the space to be minimalist and transparent to keep the attention on the ingredients, which are piled up in crates and labeled clearly in plastic boxes in the open kitchen. Their favorite cookbooks sit on the shelf above one banquette and their selection of natural wines and preserves on the wall above the other. For so many of us, including the out-of-towners who make a point of returning on each trip to Paris, it's a reassuring place, where Hirayama knows our names, our favorite tables, and our cookie preferences, and remembers the meaningful moments from past exchanges. It's the corner café par excellence that isn't necessarily around the corner.

Like the dozens of times I had been there before—for a morning coffee with labneh on toast, a two-hour-long lunch, or a much-earned cookie break in the afternoon—Hirayama is wearing her usual Crocs, formfitting jeans, and linen apron over a faded graphic tee when I go to chat with her at the end of the lunch service one autumn day. Her hair was in low-hanging pigtails that swept her shoulders gently as she shuffled out from behind the counter to serve a plate of her cookies and a cup of hibiscus tea to a lingering customer. She cranes her neck toward the door as I enter and greets me wildly. "Lindsey! *Ça vaaa?*" she sings. "Take a seat, I'll be right with you. Café?" Yep, *comme d'hab*, I tell her in our usual Franglish back-and-forth. Koreitem is cutting vegetables and readying the kitchen for a private dinner he'll be hosting that evening. Hirayama slips behind the counter to dry her hands, pours me a cup of coffee, and hastily removes her

opposite Moko Hirayama's legendary chunky chocolate chip cookies, sprinkled with sea salt.

apron. "I gotta pick up Aly and Mia—be right back. Don't move!" she says, setting the cup down before me.

In a flash, the door swings open and two bubbly sisters—eight and five—race into their second home, throwing down their backpacks to jump and greet Koreitem. As we talk, they play games and color, interrupting every so often with requests and sibling rivalries to resolve. "Are we leaving yet?" Aly asks after a while. "Not until you help me with my dough!" says Hirayama, breaking off a chunk for her to roll out on a corner of the counter. Moko turns back to me and says in a hushed voice, "Most moms in the neighborhood have their kids with a babysitter after school; they detach so quickly. But I think my presence is important for them right now." The whole work-motherhood balance or imbalance is a dynamic she may handle differently than others, she admits, but she sees the value in sharing as many moments together as possible. "If they see us here, at the restaurant, they understand why we can't be available in the same way as other parents. Then they can identify with this place. They even say, 'We're part of the nuts family!' It's part of them too."

Hirayama was born in Kōbe, Japan, but grew up between San Francisco and Tokyo, developing a vivacious personality that falls somewhere between the two cultures. Her parents gave her the freedom to choose her future and, she says, unusual latitude from her birth country's strict expectations on life and comportment. "It isn't just me who's atypical. My parents didn't run a very traditionally Japanese household. They were far more liberal, less conformist," she explains. When she was graduating high school, her parents moved back to the US, but Moko stayed put. "I decided to try out college in Japan. But I was bored. My parents thought I was nuts for having chosen a female college in the first place—it wasn't right for me at all. So there I was, seventeen and living alone, and bored—I'm telling you, Moko nuts!" she jokes. Electing to attend university in Japan was one of many impulsive decisions in her life. So back she went to her second home, this time to New York City, where she went to NYU for a degree in urban studies and found herself enthralled by the challenge.

When she finished her degree, she attempted to kick off her career in Tokyo, where her parents had yet again set up residence. That atypical personality would prove to be a roadblock she could never quite surpass. "I was rejected right on the spot from several jobs during the interview because I didn't fit in: my skirt was too short, my suit color was too light, my heels were too high. There was a whole dress code I didn't even know about. And the hiring managers told me that my father

"It's good to be different—that's something our kids need to keep hearing."

should have warned me—can you believe that?" *Don't come back to Japan; you won't survive here!* her father advised.

Once again back in New York, she became a labor negotiator for the New York City Department of Parks and Recreation, where she met Koreitem, the only other foreigner working in the service. She went on to become a finance lawyer, working long hours as Koreitem attended night cooking school to pursue his dreams of becoming a cook.

When her firm failed to secure her green card, they sent her to their London office and Koreitem followed shortly thereafter, finding a job as a line cook at Gordon Ramsay's Savoy Grill. The rhythm was intense. "I had no life. The days and the workload never ended. I was fed up and burning out." But not without a glimmer of hope. Ladurée, the Parisian pastry temple, had just opened an outpost in Harrods, and Hirayama, intrigued by baking, called the lab, asking to visit and see how the products were made. "It was a bit impulsive, but I wanted to learn!" she says with a laugh, rolling out more dough. For a year and a half, she'd begin her mornings at Ladurée, assisting with finishings and decorations before heading into work.

But for both of them, London offered a miserable life. Hirayama was depressed, lost in her professional hamster wheel. Once it felt insurmountable, they both resigned from their jobs and moved to Paris. She said it simply made sense: "It's where the best food is anyway!"

While Koreitem quickly got swallowed up into the restaurant world, cooking at Michelin-starred restaurants, Hirayama wanted to learn to bake more seriously. She skipped over pastry school or any official training programs and was schooled by Fabrice le Bourdat, the former owner of the much-loved bakery Blé Sucré. "He gave me a chance—every morning at three thirty a.m.!" She stayed six months, learning the kind of techniques that would impress big-name chefs and restaurants. Restaurant Senderens later provided her working papers but a discouraging work environment. "I was given no support as a chef, but they saw I worked hard, and they took advantage of that. They'd ask for me to propose ideas but never let me execute them." When she knocked on the door of Adeline Grattard, *Chef's Table: France* star and chef at the one Michelin-starred restaurant Yam'Tcha, she found a constructive place to learn. "I had changed my life and was questioning whether it was all a huge mistake, but then Adeline showed me what I could be doing. She let me do the pastry I wanted to do," says Hirayama of her untraditional style, which plays up herbs, spices, and fruit and eschews embellishment. Then she got pregnant and was back to square one.

She returned to the kinds of desserts she used to make with her mother, comforting but toned-down American treats that she says bring her peace. Cookies became an obsession, and she experimented with recipes until she landed on these perfect mounds of joy—crispy on the outside, soft on the inside, in flavors like rye-cranberry chocolate chunk; tahini, miso-sesame, multigrain, and dark chocolate; and peanut butter and milk chocolate. They were instant hits, and Hirayama began supplying them to other cafés until she and Koreitem opened the doors to Mokonuts at the end of 2015. Now she's responsible for everything, from sourdough and pita bread to halvah cake, labneh cheesecake, and mind-blowing babka (and plays barista, sommelier, and waitress during lunch!), but the cookies inspired her unparalleled cult following.

They're beckoning from the counter when I go back in at the end of breakfast on another morning. And when they're not there, the cookies can usually be found lined neatly on cookie sheets stocked on shelves underneath the oven. "I'm going to need to start rationing them!" Moko says with a smile. That's partly because of the (much-deserved) praise they've earned from bestselling authors and bakers such as Dorie Greenspan, Melissa Clark, and David Lebovitz, a fact that never ceases to amaze her. After all, she's a self-taught baker who transformed an escape from an intense job into her full-time career, equally as intense but far more rewarding.

"It's incredible that this business has brought us so many encounters," she says, adding that the attention they get sparks a happy-strange feeling. And the attention shows no signs of slowing, even with a format that some say is restrictive— Hirayama and Koreitem close for dinner service and on weekends to spend time with their girls. Could they be earning more by working more? Sure. Would that come at a risk for the family? She thinks so. "I like to think we're doing something different in all aspects, across categories. And sending the message that *it's okay* to create your own rules."

---

opposite Inside Mokonuts, the 11th arrondissement café-bakery Moko Hirayama opened with her husband, Omar Koreitem.

Her Paris

FAVORITE WOMAN-RUN BUSINESS?

Chef Adeline Grattard's Yam'Tcha—she's the most humane chef I've ever worked with and also the city's most productive mom. She really takes care of her staff. I have tremendous respect for her.

PREFERRED NEIGHBORHOOD?

The border of the 11th and 12th arrondissements, where we live and work. It's unpretentious, easygoing, full of people with mixed backgrounds, different age groups, and it's multilingual. Our kids will never feel like they're out of place speaking multiple languages here.

WHAT DO YOU DO FOR YOU?

I have such limited time for myself but on the rare occasion that I do, I run at the Parc de Vincennes. It's freeing!

on motherhood

"MAYBE MORE OF US would have children if it weren't seen as such an exercise in sacrifice. If we weren't told that we were going to lose every bit of the self we had finally grown to love. I want to be a mother and a writer, and a whole slew of other things, with no thought given to the order of those identities."[67] I read this passage in an opinion piece published in the *New York Times* countless times until I realized that what struck me so intensely about it was that the author was unwittingly describing a desire to be, if not French, then at the very least Parisian.

If I've learned anything from nearly fourteen years of living in Paris and observing how my friends, friends of friends, colleagues, neighbors, and even favorite shop owners approach motherhood, it's that children—the having, the rearing, or the eschewing altogether—are merely the extra comma in a long list of how these women define themselves.

In the French perspective, the ability to reproduce and raise children is not a woman's greatest accomplishment in life. They're not good and virtuous because they have devoted themselves to child-rearing as a higher calling, but because they've chosen to embrace mothering in the traditional sense as one piece in a bigger vision of life that includes but is not limited to: a career, friendships, advocacy, traveling, and learning. And this fits into a whole set of cultural beliefs— like the fact that parents aren't meant to be at the service of their children, it's unhealthy for mothers and their kids to spend every waking second together, and children are meant to cultivate their own lives just like their parents, as documented by Pamela Druckerman in her essential parenting reference *Bringing Up Bébé*—that allow women to navigate their lives without the same preoccupying anxieties so common to the American experience.

Which is likely why it wasn't until I prompted the women I spoke to that many of them even acknowledged their choice to have or not have children and addressed their feelings about motherhood. It isn't an obsessional topic because it doesn't have to be one.

Victoire de Taillac (page 102) shook her head in amusement when I asked her how her three children fit into her personal story, since she hadn't mentioned them in our two-hour discussion. "It's not very French to define oneself by motherhood," she told me emphatically. "It's an important part of my life. But my kids are never the focal point of a conversation. We have a life outside of them. When I lived in the US, I saw how American mothers pushed themselves, often to extremes, to be extraordinary. They embody motherhood at the risk of losing themselves." Architect Aline Asmar d'Amman (page 70) jokes that her work is her vacation; parenting is the hard work. "I don't feel guilty about that. When I'm with my sons, I'm fully with them, but what I built on my own [with my firm Culture in Architecture] is something special that is equally as important to me," she says. "Every woman finds her way when she becomes a mother."

To be sure, it's easier and less anxiety-inducing to enter the world of parenting when the system is set up to make sure you succeed and return to work quickly and smoothly—if that's what you want.

From an American perspective, working mothers in Paris have it made: there is paid maternity leave, partially subsidized childcare (crèches—state-run day-care centers—with costs on a sliding scale according to family income; nannies or nanny-share programs; free preschool as of age three made mandatory by President Macron in 2019), tax credits, and a range of government assistance for the most in need. And that's in addition to nationalized health care. To be clear, it isn't a perfect system—spots in the crèches are in short supply and high in demand, and the cost of a nanny may equal or exceed the amount of one parent's monthly salary. Still, the variety of options available allow women to return to work if they so choose.[68] And there's little to no shame in taking advantage of them either. For the women I spoke to, the support available was the entire reason behind their ability to continue creating, building businesses, and exploring the future of their careers.

Leïla Slimani (page 181) openly acknowledges the conditions that allow her to create. "I'm lucky," she says, referring to her nanny. "I wouldn't be able to do this work without her." Long before Valérie Lafarge-Sarkozy, a prominent corporate lawyer, had her first child thirty years ago, she knew she'd never give up her career. The women before her had fought too hard to obtain the right for women to work, free from needing the permission of their husbands, for her to squander the gift. "My generation benefited from the changes brought about by women like Simone Veil. When I got married, I lost my mother at the same time and chose a career path that would allow me to earn enough money to remain independent," she tells me. "It's always harder than it would be for a man, but it isn't impossible." By the time Valérie had her second child, she had made partner in her firm and couldn't afford to take the same amount of time off. "I was back at work after five days and was criticized by other women for having left my son so quickly—I didn't feel guilty. I didn't have a choice!" Now she positions herself as a mentor for young women in the office, making herself available for questions related to navigating work *and* motherhood.

That the road to motherhood isn't always pleasant isn't kept secret here either. "The 'bad mom'—the one who doesn't like being pregnant, doesn't breastfeed, and wants to get right back to work—goes over easier in France," says Lauren Bastide (page 35) emphatically. "I immediately wanted to go back to the woman I was before. I love my kids, but I find my fulfillment in my work and in my encounters." That's largely what Benedicte Reitzel-Nielsen, a Danish NGO director and cofounder of the online travel community #SeeMyParis (page 298) says she values about having given birth to her three children in Paris. "The problem with Americans and Scandinavians is the extent to which they glorify pregnancy and motherhood," says Reitzel-Nielsen, who has lived in the US, Denmark, and France and experienced the differences in behavior firsthand. While she admits the services and benefits in Denmark and Sweden are plentiful and designed to encourage both men and women to have the flexibility to spend time with their newborns, the early expectations on mothers can foster an unhealthy mind-set. "There's a pressure to breastfeed for six to twelve months, regardless of your ability or desire. And you're scorned if you don't. They put tremendous pressure on women to sacrifice themselves, to feign happiness even during parts of the journey that aren't pleasant."

What women like Rebecca Amsellem (page 55) and Christelle Delarue (page 117) *would* like to adopt from Sweden, however, is their model of gender-neutral parental leave. While France has tried to implement a parental leave that is equivalent for both parents—either reducing one's professional activity or stopping work entirely for the three years after the birth of a child (unpaid)—it's an option that fewer and fewer women in France opt for given that men, on average, earn more and can't take such a considerable absence without creating a financial imbalance in the family (on top of the social and cultural pressure that persists for men not to leave work to take care of children). Sweden, on the other hand, allows both parents 480 days of *paid* leave during their child's first eight years. The first thirteen months are paid at 80 percent of their salary (and there is paid leave for the unemployed). As of 2016, fathers are obliged to use their allocation of ninety days of leave to encourage more equitable parenting.[69]

PMA is where France really falls behind though: medically assisted procreation. As the law stands today, lesbian couples and single women are not authorized to access treatment, such as in vitro fertilization, to assist in becoming pregnant and must go abroad—to Spain, the UK, the Netherlands, Portugal, or most of the Scandinavian countries[70, 71]—to pay for such services. In 2018, the country's highest bioethics came out in favor of assisted reproduction for *all* women who want children (surrogacy, however, was still ruled unethical), which was the first step in what many women hoped would mean the swift passage of a bill, as promised by both President Macron and Marlène Schiappa, the junior minister for gender equality, making it legal. However, the vote has been delayed numerous times, leading activists to believe it's yet another example of government inertia and indifference to the rights of women (no decision had been made on the issue at the time of writing).

Meanwhile, the heated debates around PMA, which initially began after gay marriage passed in 2013, continue unabated. "Individuals situated in the conservative bourgeoisie, who are among the intellectual, political, or economic elites, always mobilize to maintain the unequal status quo and resist change,"[72] writes Pauline Delage in her book *Droits des femmes, tout peut disparaître* (*The Rights of Women Can Disappear*), and they dominate the opposition. The reality is that France remains a conservative country, despite the diminished role of the Catholic church. Still, the media have their own hand in fomenting destructive debate by giving majority airtime to bishops and representatives from religious organizations, not the women whose rights are being disputed. "It's maddening—we're far less religious a country than Spain, and that's where many women go for assistance," says Julie Mathieu (page 221), whose wife, Muriel Tallandier (page 214), was able to find a doctor in Paris willing to perform IVF in secret. It all plays into the issue of representation—if lesbians are invisible, it's easier to deny them their rights.

On balance, there's not a nation on Earth that gets motherhood, and the myriad discussions around it, right. There's no utopian approach to it at all, the women in these pages argue, but simply a way for the choice—to be or not to be a parent—to be less fraught, more humane. And that begins by respecting a woman's right to decide.

"Because this ideal of the attractive but not whorish white woman, in a good marriage but not self-effacing, with a nice job but not so successful she outshines her man, slim but not neurotic over food, forever young without being disfigured by the surgeon's knife, a radiant mother not overwhelmed by diapers and homework, who manages her home beautifully without becoming a slave to housework, who knows a thing or two but less than a man, this happy white woman who is constantly shoved under our noses, this woman we are all supposed to work hard to resemble—never mind that she seems to be running herself ragged for not much reward—I for one have never met her, not anywhere. My hunch is that she doesn't exist."

—VIRGINIE DESPENTES IN *KING KONG THEORY*

the
Visionaries

Reimagining the city of tomorrow

ALICE CABARET

URBAN STRATEGIST AND FOUNDER OF THE STREET SOCIETY

WHAT WILL THE PARIS OF TOMORROW look like? If urban strategist Alice Cabaret has a say, it will be a dynamic, accessible, inclusive city made possible through building reconversion and the rehabilitation of unique urban spaces. After years of working on regeneration projects in Johannesburg, she returned to Paris to launch The Street Society, her collaborative agency based in Paris, which promotes innovation in the fields of sustainable property development and urban transformation.

She took me to Les Grands Voisins in the 14th arrondissement (see "Her Paris" on page 261 for more on that space) to talk about her proudest accomplishments, the evolving city, and the improvements that she hopes will foster lasting change in the capital.

You're one of few truly born-and-bred Parisians. Have you always lived in the same place? Always in the 9th arrondissement! Born there, went to day care there, did all my schooling there, and now I'm back after my university years and five years in Johannesburg. I think it's so interesting to live an entire stage of your life in the same neighborhood. I've seen it evolve, and that really nurtures my interest in the city.

The 9th in particular is often used as an example of egregious gentrification. How do you feel about the neighborhood's change? I'm neither aligned with those who want to overhaul it nor those who are vehemently against gentrification. I think the reality is somewhere in the middle. The city needs to evolve, without adhering to any idealistic vision of a certain *kind* of Paris. When I was seventeen,

I used to walk up to the place de Clichy, where my boyfriend lived, and it was incredibly dangerous. I'm not complaining that some spaces were renovated. The fact that the areas around Pigalle known for prostitution were transformed into bars is linked to the economic evolution of prostitution—places close because of the Internet, and these spaces become vacant or used for other purposes. It's not always a clashing of the classes. A solution against complete gentrification of the neighborhood would be more ephemeral businesses with affordable rents to help jump-start the careers of young entrepreneurs.

Those are among the things you'd consider on the projects you work on today as an urban strategist. What led you into the field? I actually discovered it through studying geography. Ever since I was a kid, I've always loved walking the streets of Paris, often alone. It's always been the people of the city that interested me—people in certain places, how they confer a certain identity on a neighborhood, how one neighborhood transitions into another. During my *classes préparatoires*, I had an incredible geography professor who talked about the ways in which cities were designed. And that was the spark. I went on to do a master's in urban strategy at Sciences Po University and trained as an urban strategist.

Were you inspired by anyone in particular from the field? Very early on, I read Jane Jacobs and identified with her organic, incredibly human-centered approach to cities. She introduced ground-breaking ideas in terms of urbanism, with an approach deeply rooted in her community-based beliefs. She fought to give a voice to local residents on the evolution of their neighborhood and inspired creative responses for the urgent advancement of social, economic, and environmental justice. In my practice, I apply some of her methods: common sense (sometimes the simplest solution is best—small changes can have a big impact), site observation (I visit the sites I am working on at different times of the day, the week, the year, if I can, and take notes about how people behave), and focus on the human experience (the importance of perceptions and emotions in the urban experience).

You spent five years living and working in Johannesburg. How did that experience inform your work? It's the complete inverse of Paris. It's a city that's far more dynamic in terms of professional opportunities, and there are no age barriers. You can make a real impact. The alternative culture is incredible—you feel freer to

"What defines the Parisienne is her intellect, her culture, her inner critic, her cynicism, her intellectual panache. She has a certain something that goes far beyond cliché."

express yourself through fashion and music. In Paris, we're far more critical, and that can block creativity. I was lucky to meet people who gave me opportunities very quickly, even though I was young, and I'll forever be grateful. I try to do the same now, in Paris, with the people I collaborate with, regardless of age and diploma. In Johannesburg, no one knew Sciences Po. That was incredibly freeing. The importance that one's school and pedigree continues to have is unjust for the people who simply don't have access to these networks.

Your brother was at the Bataclan the night of the attacks on November 13, 2015, and survived. I understand the trauma precipitated your return to Paris. Did the tragedy change your vision of the city? Absolutely. I started thinking about security in the context of urbanism, which was also deeply tied to my experience in Johannesburg, which is a city built on safety principles. Criminality dictates urban spaces—there are walls and barbed-wire fences and gated communities. After the attacks in Paris, when soldiers patrolled the streets and public squares had been modified or blocked off as a security measure, you could see the direct consequences of terrorism on public spaces. On projects, we now have to take into account a whole new set of security constraints, and that evidently has an impact on how the city evolves. I don't want to see Paris become dictated by security measures. It's why I created the collective [S]CITY in 2016 with researchers and fellow urbanists to study the link between cognitive science and architecture and urbanism. We study the way the brain functions, how it processes perceptions and emotions within the city, all in order to create the most suitable urban environment.

How do you think the city has changed for women in the last decade? Parisian women are freer here than in so many other places. For one, we can get around. In some cities, that's extremely limited for women. What persists, though, is harassment. I have yet to meet one woman who hasn't been bothered or harassed by men in the streets or on public transportation—I've faced it countless times myself. It makes me extremely angry as it has an impact on our ability as women to feel free and confident in public spaces as we navigate the city.

The question of the safety of women in public spaces is linked to the accessibility and safety of all urban users—children, disabled, homeless, or elderly people. Urban design plays a major role in making streets safer for all, with efficient lighting, or mixed and lively spaces. Playgrounds, transport, and green spaces should be designed to empower women from a very young age. Feeling accepted and empowered as women in the city can also be increased by targeted interventions: feminist street art, street signage representing women, streets or infrastructure being named after inspiring women. But there is only so much that urbanism can solve: We need strong policies and citizen awareness around these issues as well. In the last few years, the city has implemented campaigns to address and condemn street harassment, which is a start, but there's a lot more to be done.

Among the city's urban pain points, what stands out as the most critical? The real issue is accessibility, of housing and businesses, for disabled people. The government doesn't work toward developing systems adapted to their needs. There's the legal requirement and then how to take that even further. In my projects, I make sure to think about this, to consider how women and children of all abilities might feel in a given space, to create environments that are accessible to all facets of the population, 24/7.

And in terms of urban planning, what needs to change? Decisions need to be made by people with far more diverse backgrounds. If we involve different perspectives from the beginning of a project, that's when things get interesting. But we need to be willing to risk clashing—our vision of things against others. And being okay with the fact that risk takes time.

Are there cities that are doing this better? That's a good question—perhaps. But in Paris, we need to shake things up. Decisions are often made by older people with a certain diploma. Usually old white men.

You seem like you're quite capable of shaking things up, diving in headfirst and speaking up to defend your vision. I just tell myself: *We have one life, so either you create your own destiny or other people are going to create it for you.* I don't like

---

opposite Les Grands Voisins, a former abandoned hospital transformed into a hybrid space with housing, ateliers, workspaces, events, and more. Alice Cabaret wants to see more spaces like it across the city.

injustice; you can't wait around and be the victim. You have to charge forward, and sometimes that means taking risks, butting heads. Risk isn't very French. The types of urban development that are really interesting at the moment are in cities like Marseille and Nantes. Some people think that the heritage Paris carries is too heavy, and this creates a barrier to innovation. But I think that we have to base ourselves on what the past gives us to go even further. The educational system doesn't encourage experimentation, and unlike in the US, risk isn't valued. We're taught that from childhood. That has an impact on what we create here, and there are brilliant minds that leave because of it.

How do you see yourself contributing to the city's future? Strategists are never the lead because we're only one link in a network of people, investors, decision-makers. But I want to pursue projects that bring the most beneficial change to Paris. The question of the accessibility of public space, especially public transport, is urgent: More than three hundred metro stations are not accessible (to disabled individuals, people with strollers or luggage, etc.). There are obvious technical challenges to this problem, but it needs to be turned into a high priority. All of the projects we work on include design solutions to make them fully accessible.

Among the projects you've been involved with, in and out of Paris, what are you most proud of? The Maboneng Precinct is very close to my heart—a creative and inclusive neighborhood in Johannesburg. I joined the development team at the very beginning of the project and helped turn the abandoned industrial neighborhood into a vibrant destination alongside architects, street artists, entrepreneurs, landscapers, and residents.

And in Paris, we're part of the team with the architect Dominique Perrault transforming the underused Gare des Invalides into a museum dedicated to French craftsmanship, a food hall, and an experimental space for kids. It's an exciting time for us and for Paris.

Her Paris

FAVORITE WOMAN-RUN BUSINESS?

Denise Acabo's chocolate and candy shop, A l'Étoile d'Or. She knows everything about confections, and you can see the sparkle of passion in her eyes. I hope to have the same at her age! She owns her looks, always with the pigtails and the kilt. I love it all.

SOMEPLACE YOU GO TO DISCONNECT?

The Palais-Royal and its gardens (shown above). It's my favorite place in the entire world. It's a question of scale from a cognitive science point of view; its width is perfect. You can even see the expression on someone's face from the other side of the garden. There are no cars, the architecture is incredible, and you feel the weight of history. It feels like home there.

A SPOT YOU LOVE TO TAKE OUT-OF-TOWNERS?

Definitely Les Grands Voisins in the 14th arrondissement, an example of urban regeneration. In a former abandoned hospital, it is now a hybrid space with housing, ateliers, workspaces, events, cafés, and more.

*Pioneering studies on the impact of new technology
and digital culture on everyday life*

RAHAF HARFOUSH

DIGITAL ANTHROPOLOGIST AND BESTSELLING AUTHOR

SYRIA WAS HOME for only the first six years of Rahaf Harfoush's life, but those early memories are as vivid today as if they were from yesterday. She remembers the pungent scent of za'atar wafting out from the *man'oushe* stands she'd pass on her way to school. She closes her eyes and sees summers at her grandfather's orchard, swimming in frigid water, climbing trees, and picking apricots with the family to make jam. The smell of wet earth in the early morning is almost within reach, from a time when she'd sneak outside to keep her grandfather company as he watered his plants. She can picture herself sprawled out in the grass, gazing up at the night sky, and running wild with her cousins, sparklers in hand, as they celebrated Eid.

Any combination of those scents, sounds, or sights instantly transports her back to the days long before Syria was a place to escape from. "Seeing that part of Syria destroyed by the revolution has been heartbreaking," she tells me from her sofa as Pixel, her long-haired Chihuahua, gently licks her hand. "Pieces of my childhood only exist in my memories now."

For a host of complex geopolitical reasons, her parents sensed that their futures would be limited if they stayed in Syria. So they left, quickly. The family landed in Toronto during a snowstorm with meager savings and only three suitcases for the five of them, leaving behind respected careers and an extended family they knew they'd never be able to return to see again. The struggle that followed was expected—her mother, an esteemed architect in Syria, felt lost without her career and community. Harfoush and her sisters were thrown into another language they hadn't realized even existed.

Over time, they moved from an apartment into a town house in the suburbs of Toronto, and Harfoush watched her father, an engineer, build a business in

informatics out of the basement. Gradually, the Canadian equivalent to the American Dream kicked in, and life improved. "I saw how much my parents sacrificed for us to live better, and that made a huge impact on me. I promised never to squander the chances they gave us." She describes her upbringing in great detail—how she excelled in academics and took advantage of every opportunity the state offered, like French Immersion, a free program offered within some public schools across the country. France wasn't even a blip on her life radar, but looking back, she sees that encouraging her to broaden her global skill set was one of the best gifts her parents gave her. That and simply being part of a system that so heavily emphasized the value of multiculturalism, readying her for a global life. "No country is perfect, but Canada gave me everything with open arms. Affordable education and socialized health care make the difference when you're starting out," she says. "They allow you to ascend."

That Toronto was their landing spot was lucky, Harfoush insists. *Luck* resurfaces often in conversation with her, and yet I'd argue that her good fortune and professional success later in life have come not merely from chance but from instinctively knowing how to seize opportunities. Even from our earliest getting-to-know-you conversations six years ago, I understood that all of her piercing wisdom—that for which she has become known, among friends and clients, and been paid to bestow on the world—stemmed from a trail of decisions leading to Paris.

And it all began with what could have easily been a passing, adolescent curiosity in the early-stage Internet. Like many from her generation, she became active in a host of AOL chat rooms and saw the potential to build community far and wide. "I realized I was part of something far bigger than my suburban home," she recalls. While she was in college studying business, strategy, and communication, she got into blogging—reading them and writing one of her own (called *A Sense of Something Coming*, a nod to her favorite poem by Rainer Maria Rilke)—reading about the web, following Facebook's arrival into her generation's lives, and then writing articles about technology for websites for extra cash. "I was fascinated by the ways in which technology was not only changing the way people were connecting but how they were creating."

What happened next can be described as a series of important encounters that helped shape the woman Harfoush has become. The father of one of her college friends turned out to be Don Tapscott, the visionary technologist, author, and business consultant, whom she had the chance to meet and talk to about technology. He became her first employer. She joined his think tank, then called

"Paris is complementary to my creativity. I feel at peace here. People often find the city to be ornate and fussy, but that's on the surface. When you peel back the layers, what you find is a dedication to simplicity that I find eminently appealing."

New Paradigm, to research one of his books and manage a syndicated research program that looked into the ways that millennials were using technology. "He took me under his wing, showed me that a career in this field was possible, showed me how to write a book, showed me how to market myself . . . He's still an incredible mentor to me," she remembers. After a stint as a research analyst to learn about data, she started her first consulting company and ended up back on another research project for Tapscott that would change everything.

It was 2008. She had interviewed Chris Hughes, one of the cofounders of Facebook, for Tapscott's book *Growing Up Digital* and learned about his work as the head of internal organizing for the Obama campaign. "He was in charge of all the social networks and tools the team was using to mobilize people. I was paying a lot of attention to the campaign and wanted to be part of it," she tells me. She reconnected with him and within no time, she was packing her bags for Chicago, dipping into her savings to cover six months of volunteering on the digital team. That hands-on experience harnessing the power of new technology led to her first book, *Yes We Did! An Insider's Look at How Social Media Built the Obama Brand*.

More luck ahead—back in Toronto, Harfoush was invited to speak about her book at the Rotman School of Management in what she thought would be an intimate discussion. "It ended up being a five-hundred-person event, and in the audience were two of the people who would go on to sign me to their speaker's bureau," she says, still struck by the fortuity of it all. She started getting paid to speak around the world about technology, media, big data, and their implications on society. One such place was at the World Economic Forum in Geneva. "I was pulled aside after that talk and offered a job on the spot. I said yes. I'm telling you, there *is* luck involved!"

Perhaps, but also a steady stream of support from powerful women who have been generous and open with their experiences and have offered Harfoush invaluable advice about networking and building a business. "I basically modeled my expectations on the life of one of my mentors, Mary Jane Braide, who runs a design and branding firm in Toronto. She was the first person to show me that I could build a life that was aligned to my own way of working," she says. With that in mind, she left the World Economic Forum after several years as associate director of the Technology Pioneer Program, working to identify disruptive start-ups that were improving the state of the world, to go back to consulting, writing, and speaking, this time from Paris. "It had always been a dream. From seeing the city in *Sabrina* with Audrey Hepburn to the semester I spent at HEC, the beauty of the city called to my soul. It wasn't a fleeting or insignificant feeling," she recalls. What she calls the puzzle pieces of her identity, those that didn't quite fit anywhere else, slipped naturally into place when she moved.

As a Parisienne for the last eight years, she has fastidiously documented the evolutions of digital culture on human behavior in and out of the workplace— the impact of big data, the emergence and influence of artificial intelligence on business, the debate around net neutrality, and the cult of productivity—in bestselling books,[73] in speaking engagements, and for organizations that solicit her expertise. She is a reference, a genuine thought leader in a sea of self-proclaimed thought leaders, who deeply understands the stakes of technology and can hold forth with supreme confidence about the precise ways it's rewriting the rules of culture and power.

She likes to think of herself as a bridge, a rep for the Paris ecosystem as she travels the world, and a source for outside expertise she can bring home to enhance the global vision of local start-ups and businesses. "I bring that bit of *other*—a clash of ideas that can spur innovation," she says, smiling.

Looking back at her path from Damascus to Paris, Harfoush knows how everything could have been different under slightly different circumstances; with different parents; with a different education. Contributing to the world through her research, visionary ideas, and mentorship is one way for her to express her gratitude for good fortune. "Syria will always be my birth mother; Canada is my adopted mother—she gave me everything, the tools," she says emphatically. "But Paris is home. This is where I build."

Her Paris

FAVORITE WOMAN-RUN BUSINESS?

I love Holybelly, co-owned by Sarah Mouchot. She's a genius in the kitchen, and it's the best place in the city for a delicious, Western-style breakfast with coffee. Their legendary savory stack is one of my favorite rewards for hitting a project milestone.

WHERE DO YOU GO OR WHAT DO YOU DO WHEN YOU'RE STRUGGLING WITH WORK?

I wander around my neighborhood, the 2nd arrondissement (shown above), but leave my phone at home. Walking through the streets reminds me of all the other creatives in this city's past who were struggling with setbacks. It connects me to the city's creative legacy, and I always feel inspired and refreshed to get back to work. It feels like the city has my back, like it's saying, *I've nurtured all sorts of people here for hundreds of years. They've found their answers and so will you.*

SOMETHING YOU DO FOR YOU?

I love practicing mixed martial arts, particularly Krav Maga, at Maccabi Paris. Krav taught me to turn the fire inside me into fuel. The aggressive physicality of it helps calm the chaos of my brain.

Revolutionizing the way we see the world

SANDRA REY

FOUNDER AND CEO OF GLOWEE

WHAT IF THE CITY OF LIGHT became the city of bioluminescence? That ambitious goal drives Sandra Rey's award-winning start-up Glowee, the company she founded in 2014, which designs and develops biological lighting sources from the same chemical reaction that makes fish glow underwater (bioluminescence is the production and emission of light by a living organism). While there is a lot still to accomplish, Rey has already attracted plenty of attention. She was named an "Innovator Under 35" by *MIT Technology Review* magazine in 2016, and Glowee's bioluminescence technology has found its way into installations for companies such as LVMH, Air France, and Adidas.

We spoke over breakfast at Hexagone Café in the 14th arrondissement about building a company from the ground up, overcoming barriers, and what Glowee has the power to transform—give or take a few pesky regulations.

How did your studies in industrial design lead you to work in bioluminescence?
Design is a bridge between multiple disciplines. The designer isn't necessarily an expert but can put themselves in the shoes of the marketer, the engineers, and the clients to understand what the needs are and create the link. I specialized in system design with a master's thesis in the overhaul of the French medical system, which required solutions in terms of product, interface, and process optimization. I always interned in forward-thinking industries: I worked in innovation and design at Microsoft, in an AI start-up called Sensory, and then I worked for a trend-forecasting agency called Peclers Paris. My role there was to create concepts according to social trends they identified. The transition to something slightly more scientific was actually a natural extension. But this particular idea actually emerged

out of a group competition in my last year of my graduate studies at the Strate École de Design de Sèvres. It was a student project, not entrepreneurial in focus. My team and I won the competition in 2013, and a lot came after, including Glowee. But we all had to learn how to turn it into more than just a smart idea.

Did bioluminescence exist as a design focus in France when you launched the company? Not at all. Bioluminescence had been a known phenomenon for nearly thirty years, and today, it's a genetic marking tool. We know that animals, including around 80 percent of marine life, can emit light. But we needed to create the link between a need, an existing technology, and what seemed like an obvious solution, even if it wouldn't be easy to produce. Bioluminescence exists either in the genome of the species, as with fireflies, or on a bacterial level. It's the bacterial bioluminescence that interests us because it has the advantage of it being multiplied.

While it's certainly getting easier, it's often been a challenge for entrepreneurs to launch and operate start-ups in France. Given the current administration's emphasis on driving innovation, have you found adequate support to grow? France has been amazing in this way. Of course there are regulatory and administrative aspects of the business that can get complicated, but in terms of financing, it's a wonderful ecosystem—especially with research loans and grants from the BPI (Banque Publique d'Investissement). What also helps is the small Parisian ecosystem: we have relatively easy access to government ministers and can have open discussions about the issues we're facing as young entrepreneurs. The government understood that innovative start-ups were the economic force of tomorrow. The growth potential isn't necessarily in big corporations.

So in the end, part of your job is lobbying. Absolutely, because we're up against regulatory constraints. We work with modified microorganisms, and that falls into the category of GMM [genetically modified microorganisms], with regulations stricter than GMOs [genetically modified organisms]. Even though it's different from genetically modified food, it's complicated. In terms of fund-raising, everything we've brought in has allowed us to recruit a team of seventeen (and pay them!) and finance our research. But as of today [2018], we're still not profitable; our revenue comes from events. So we needed to raise more funds, and explore other options, like entering the wellness market with relaxation spaces called Glowzen Rooms.

"It's much easier to disrupt when you come from the outside."

Your technology has been used in installations for large companies, like LVMH, among others. Are corporate events an important business driver? When we first started, I thought we'd have a product in three months that would set us on the path to being able to illuminate outdoor spaces. But it requires enormous performance in terms of light intensity, and it would take time. After the first year, we had a product that could last stably for a few hours, and I realized three important things: We needed to monetize this R&D, get out of the lab and experiment with real-life constraints, and set short-term milestones to keep the teams motivated. That's ultimately why we started bringing the product into events—to explain its value. Anything we earn from these events goes right back into R&D, so they have been hugely important to our growth. The light source now has a duration of six days in its primary form (it is limitless in liquid form; however, its applications are restricted), and we divided our costs per unit by 100 by improving the ways in which we control it (we need less bacteria now for a better result).

Looking beyond the current parameters of your work, how could bioluminescence benefit the world? First, it's important to question how products themselves are made. We tend to think of how LED consumes little energy, but we don't think of how it's produced. Most lighting systems are made from LED produced in China from black metals drawn by destroying Chinese land. It's unbelievable pollution that no one talks about. Some metals are already disappearing after only several years of being mined. Next, the bottom of the ocean will be raided for its rare metals. Today, we can take biomimetic approaches and think of a production chain that pollutes less. With bioluminescence, we have a biological energy source that can grow endlessly and that produces a 100 percent organic raw material. It's sustainable energy.

Do you feel optimistic that this technology could change the world? I think it's a mix of optimism and naiveté. Some things seem so obvious to me that I say to myself there must come a time when they become obvious to everyone else. Maybe in fifty years, we'll realize the limits of bioluminescence. The only perfect solution lies within nature, and it will take billions in R&D to find it.

Would Paris illuminated by bioluminescence radically change the city? Definitely, but in a positive way. It's not about replacing a bulb with another. The issue is rethinking the way we illuminate overall. The way it's being done now is inconsistent with our way of life and our everyday concerns. But as city centers all over France become increasingly pedestrian, we can go about it in a different way. Of course it would be easier to implement the technology in new cities, starting from zero rather than replacing what exists. In Paris, changes would first hit street furniture, building façades, undergrounds, gardens, and then down the line see the removal of streetlights. Our focus is on how to redesign the urban landscape in its entirety.

To what extent has being female played a role in your trajectory? To be honest, I don't think I would have gotten here if I weren't a woman. There are so few of us in this industry, it's easier to get noticed. What I did face were reactions that I was too young to be doing this, and at one point, they were right. I was a young designer building a company in biotechnology without any real professional experience. I earned credibility by demonstrating what I could do, in building a team, in releasing products into the market, in getting noticed by MIT. It's easier to disrupt when you come from the outside. I see far fewer barriers than the experts, and that ignorance serves me well. I know where I stand and where I'm going.

Is gender balance within the company an important consideration for you? Right now we have 50/50 gender parity in the company, and I don't think I'd want it to be predominantly female. Men and women are complementary, and it's important to have a diversity of opinion.

Have there been women that have guided or inspired you throughout this journey? I tend to question everything, so I have trouble affixing myself to any one model or mentor, but I know when to ask for help. The key is surrounding myself with the right people.

Her Paris

FAVORITE WOMAN-RUN BUSINESS?

Mûre, a restaurant in the 2nd arrondissement with excellent produce and a predominantly female staff. It's a comfortable spot for breakfast, getting a bit of work done, having lunch, or just stopping by for tea.

THE DESIGN SPOT YOU'D RECOMMEND TO VISITORS?

L'Atelier des Lumières (shown above), a digital fine arts museum in a former foundry that is completely immersive. It's a fascinating artistic experience.

SOMEPLACE YOU'D GO WITH FRIENDS FOR AN APÉRITIF?

La Colonie in the 10th arrondissement, a sort of modern agora that's open all day and always changing. It's at once a bar and a cultural space, with art exhibits, debates, and concerts.

*Championing the tech and start-up ecosystem
at home and abroad*

KAT BORLONGAN

DIRECTOR OF LA FRENCH TECH

DÉBROUILLARDE—**CLEVERLY RESOURCEFUL** with the keen ability to figure things out; to face insurmountable problems and find solutions to them—could be an apt way to describe Kat Borlongan and explain her atypical career path. It's certainly one of the words that comes to mind by the time our nearly two-hour conversation reaches an end on a summer afternoon at the Station F tech incubator campus, where her office sits. But it only captures part of what makes the director of La French Tech, a government-led task force to boost the tech ecosystem in France, and her arrival into such a high-profile role so compelling. What's missing from that is an incredible adaptability and the vision she brings to the table as an outsider with a distinctly global outlook.

Born and raised in the Philippines, Borlongan finished high school in Japan, went to college at Sciences Po Bordeaux, did graduate work at McGill University in Montreal, and moved back to Paris, where she cofounded an innovation agency. But that path to Paris was circuitous and fraught with personal upheaval. In fact, that she took an interest in tech as a kid at all was largely the result of circumstance.

At thirty-five, her entrepreneurial father had become the CEO of a young bank, taking on a very visible, high-profile role that drew attention—not all of it very good. As improbable as it sounds, "My dad was kidnapped when I was fourteen," she says, quickly adding that he was returned within forty-eight hours when she saw my eyes widen. "But he got very tech-savvy after that. He became obsessed with the latest IoT hardware for security and surveillance—motion detectors, cameras, and sensors. Plus tracking devices on all of our vehicles. It's all basic now, but in the nineties, it was novel."

She and her siblings had tracking devices on them too. Her father could query their whereabouts via texts, and it would feed him their coordinates. "None of this felt like a huge deal. I went to an all-girls' Catholic school where we learned to code. The Philippines is a country with a rapid tech adoption curve and the highest per capita consumption of social networks to this day," she explains. What interested her in all of this wasn't merely the technology but the access to information, which presented itself as an avenue of study yet again through her father's misfortune. "In 1998, he was accused of economic sabotage. Even today, one of the biggest regrets of my uncle, who was handling my dad's case, was that they hadn't hired people to help manage information. There were so many falsehoods published and so much journalist censorship at the time," she describes, aware that her story had the making of fiction. At several points in her retelling, she pauses to insist that while unbelievable, it was absolutely, and unfortunately, true. "My father couldn't defend himself in the media. He found proof to support his case, and the papers refused to publish it. That's when I started discovering issues related to information access and that the Philippines had among the highest impunity rate for killing journalists."

Borlongan's newfound awareness in the importance of information and transparency led to her first job at Reporters without Borders in Canada, working on policy and safety issues with journalists in conflict zones. One of the unexpected but eminently useful skills she acquired from the trauma with her father was equanimity in crisis management. "I remember that the director at that time went on vacation, during which someone was detained in Iran and I was handling the case. This had come just after another incident with a detainee who had been killed. I was twenty-three and the only one who wasn't freaking out," she describes calmly.

It wasn't that the ordeal with her family made her impervious to stress but that her stress exists on a completely different register. "My tolerance is a lot different. I mean, in that job, you're exposed to people getting shot, people in serious danger—we're not talking about a start-up having trouble raising their series B funding," she says, putting her roles into perspective. "I would get calls in the middle of the night, 'Someone got shot, you need to relocate their family from Kabul and get them somewhere in Mumbai transitionally while we work out their visa to come to Canada,' and it all had to happen in twenty-four hours."

She held her own, quickly moving up to become the director of Reporters without Borders. What instills confidence in the people she works with, she presumes, is her ability to think outside of the box. "But that's mostly because I didn't know what the box was. I was twenty-four; I didn't know what I was supposed

"Not only have I been a woman in France, I've been a woman in different countries, and the way you experience that identity isn't exactly the same, nor are the discriminations. The truth is, in France I never know if I'm a woman or an immigrant first. What do people see? Which handicap comes first? Are people talking to me in a certain way because they think I'm young? Because I'm a woman? Because I'm an immigrant? It's hard to tell."

to do anyway. I just saw a problem and found a solution. And I learned to ask for help very quickly—I don't wait until it's too late."

That natural agility carried her through a role in communication with the UN's ICAO (International Civil Aviation Organization), ensuring that all forms of policy-making were transparent, and then back to Paris, where she stepped into the tech space through open data. "I spent months looking for work in [tech] policy, but I couldn't find anything that fit me and my eclectic background." So she created a niche of her own. Up until 2018, she co-ran Five by Five, a consulting agency she founded with open-data pioneer Chloé Bonnet that built or reinforced innovation teams within large organizations and start-ups. Simultaneously, she was named a marketing and product strategy expert at Google, directed the Open Data Institute in Paris, and served as an open data advisor to the French government, all of which anchored her to an ecosystem that was fast emerging as a European start-up hub.

And that's when Mounir Mahjoubi, the former secretary of state for digital affairs in the Macron administration, encouraged her to apply for the director position of La French Tech, a role that would have her speaking on behalf of France and working to ensure that the government is a better partner to start-ups in their growth. When she applied, landed the role, and accepted the challenge, it was partly for the symbolic nature of the opportunity itself. "I wanted to take the job because it was such a powerful sign to me that France had changed. Because the France that I moved to in 2003 for the first time would have never hired me as the director of a French institution."

Mahjoubi valued her seemingly incongruous experiences, her atypical skill set. And where that can often be a red flag in a country that values the familiar, the future of the French tech ecosystem needs someone unwed to the tried-and-true formula, someone who sits comfortably at the intersection of several worlds—business, government, start-ups, venture capital—and can speak to all of them. "I'm the CEO that comes in when nothing makes sense and it's never been done before and there's no manual for it," she says with a laugh.

What's she tasked with solving in this role of all-around fixer is an economical problem. While France's start-ups are raising as much if not more funding than any other European country, they haven't produced many global champions. In 2018, France raised a record 3.6 billion EUR and is becoming the fastest-growing country for European investment. And yet France has so far produced six unicorns, private companies with valuations of over $1 billion USD, compared to nine in Germany, eighteen in the United Kingdom, and 147 in the United States. "The issue isn't the founders or the ideas. We're simply experiencing challenges at the growth stage," she explains. "What I know from conversations with founders is that one of the major pain points is a lack of executive-level talent. People who have already taken a company from twenty to two hundred to two thousand—the French tech scene is young and simply hasn't grown enough of that kind of talent in France, attracted it from abroad, or had enough big exits[74] to reinject what we have back into the ecosystem."

As big as the job is and as daunting as the pressure is to shape the future of French tech, Borlongan sees herself as a backend asset, much like her mother was for her father—the woman behind the scenes with immeasurable influence. "My job isn't to do big, beautiful speeches or to inspire or to talk about the vision of the country. My job is to get things done," she tells me. And that includes ensuring that despite growing pains, Paris rises to be the start-up nation that President Macron has ambitiously declared it can and should become.

"The truth is," Borlongan begins, leaning in as though she's about to reveal an industry secret. "There isn't one future of tech; there are many, with competing narratives. You can go for the narrative of the US, and Silicon Valley and what tech has come to represent in a time of Cambridge Analytica; you can go for China and say that big markets are what matter; or you can go for France's vision—come and build companies that matter, and if you want to build the kind of start-up that solves people's problems then you'll have a home here and you'll be surrounded by people that care about those things." And with any luck, Borlongan will be waiting on the other side.

Her Paris

FAVORITE WOMAN-RUN BUSINESS?
Frichti, a homemade meal–delivery service and app run by one of the most dedicated founders I know, Julia Bijaoui. The company is totally an extension of her and her passion for food.

A SOLO RITUAL?
When I can, I'll go on a date with myself to a restaurant or a local bistro, like Tannat, which I love. Usually, it's someplace where I know the owners or servers and I'll set myself at the bar with my notebook or a book.

YOUR GO-TO OUTING ON WEEKENDS?
When it isn't food shopping at individual purveyors—the cheesemonger, the butcher, the baker—my husband and I usually go out wandering to take photos without any particular destination in mind.

---

above The café and meeting space at Station F, the incubator where La French Tech offices are located.

NIDA JANUSKIS

ASSOCIATE DEAN OF ADVANCEMENT FOR INSEAD BUSINESS SCHOOL

THOSE CLOSEST TO NIDA JANUSKIS say that knowing her is transformative. There's how richly she embraces life and the lives of others, but there's also the kinetic energy she gives off, fueling herself and uplifting those around her in the process. As the associate dean of advancement for INSEAD, consistently ranked among the top business schools in the world, and one of only three women to sit on the executive committee, she extends that energy and a preternatural ability to lead into paving a path to leadership positions for women and fostering a perspective shift within the institution itself. Because change won't come only from businesses, she told me during our conversation one afternoon in her 7th arrondissement apartment, it must begin with education.

You're a Lithuanian American living in Paris with a work travel schedule that has you traversing the world each month. Have you always been a global citizen? Not entirely. I was born into a Lithuanian family in Chicago, and the Lithuanian community was so strong (the largest diaspora outside of Lithuania!) that I didn't speak English until I started kindergarten. I went to Lithuanian Saturday school, I went to Lithuanian folk-dancing classes—it was my life. A big part of that was because my grandparents and parents immigrated to the US after World War II. Having been occupied by the Soviet Union, the diaspora felt it was their responsibility to preserve the language and culture. My grandparents always thought they'd return to the homeland one day, but that didn't happen. So I was very much a Lithuanian living in America. I'd never been there until 1993 (and eventually spent time working there) and yet to this day, I identify more as Lithuanian. That grip on tradition is something I brought with me to France.

"The best piece of advice another woman has ever given me? 'You belong here. Don't let your inner voice get in the way.'"

Having worked in both US and French environments (albeit with a global outlook), what strikes you as a key difference in the way women are evolving in business? I think the US does a very good job of celebrating women business leaders. In terms of role models, we look to the Mary Barras and the Indra Nooyis. However, the lens through which Americans look at some women can be both highly positive, elevating women leaders to celebrities, and extremely negative, scrutinizing them in ways no man would ever have to endure. I think that France and Europe are much more judicious; we don't subject our women leaders to that level of intense inspection, but this can also come at a cost, if we don't promote and position our women leaders. Think of the extraordinary women leaders we have here, like Anne Richards and Isabelle Kocher. We should celebrate them and others, not just for the benefit of other women, but also to show children and men that women can and should be serving in these leadership positions. As of right now, Isabelle Kocher is one of only two female CEOs on the CAC40 (the other is Anne Rigail, CEO of Air France).[75] The percentage of women in senior roles is slowly growing worldwide, and at the current pace we won't reach parity until 2060, so we have so much work to do. Visibility is key—kids, students, leaders of tomorrow need to know it's possible, and businesses need to try harder.

Knowing that the percentage of women in senior roles is growing so slowly worldwide certainly lends greater importance to your work within the institution as a champion for women. What is the end goal? We need to create an easier path into senior positions for women, wherever they might work. Business schools are one of the main pipelines for that, and at the moment, INSEAD is in the top three schools in the world graduating women per year. Still, there is a disconnect between the population and the number of women in leadership positions, and I want to change that. Our global reach is powerful—fifty-five thousand alumni in 174 countries. Our tagline is "We are the business school for the world," but I don't want this to be the business school for only half the world. Overall, equity in business leadership is not just a women's issue; it's a societal issue. We know that diversity, and gender diversity specifically, is good for business. But as a business school, we have a responsibility to be part of the change in making sure that diversity is visible, externally and internally. It can't just be about celebrating what happens outside our doors; we have to change ourselves.

How does the school's gender initiative drive this? The initiative is about increasing representation among our student body, faculty, and board; engaging men in our efforts; funding scholarships for female students; and leading cutting-edge, data-driven research. By creating a pipeline of future business leaders who are passionate and equipped to drive gender balance within their organizations, we can positively impact business and society. My hope is that one day, through our collective efforts, gender diversity will no longer be cause for debate.

What did it feel like to shift into such a high-profile leadership position, knowing you'd be playing a role in a cultural shift? Leadership on a global level requires a nimble, adaptive, proactive mind-set, and women, myself included, who are natural jugglers of variability, thrive in such a context. We can pivot very rapidly, and many of us have learned to do so in our everyday lives, in the choices we make between work and family. I came to Paris as a trailing spouse with three children and am now leading a department at INSEAD. That transition has meant striking a different type of balance, but what I'm trying to teach my team and my children is that work-life balance isn't any more of a woman's concern than a man's.

We often hear about the guilt wrapped in the decisions women with children make in going back to work and especially taking on leadership roles. Rarely does this come up in France. What was your experience? It can be challenging, but I don't feel shame or guilt, which is definitely something that feels built into the culture of mothering in the US. In France, there's the idea that your life as an individual doesn't stop just because you have kids, and the country created an environment for women to be able to go back into the workforce fairly easily and quickly. What I've faced, like so many women everywhere, are the assumptions people are quick to make about working women, even in 2019. When I first started at INSEAD, I would attend events with my male counterpart, and I was always the one asked how I was able to do it all—manage the demanding role and the travel schedule with the family. He told me that he'd *never* fielded that question (unsurprisingly, they don't even ask if he has kids!). The assumption is: woman, big

position, family, sacrifice. I'm making an impact, and I hope I'm a role model for my kids, that I'm giving them the confidence to know they can do whatever they want.

Is that the kind of role model you had at home growing up? My mother was absolutely an excellent role model for a future working woman. Despite coming to the US as an immigrant, she graduated two years early from university with a degree in French, starting her professional life as a high school French teacher. Later, she completely changed careers and was part of the first class of women police officers in Chicago. Eventually, she switched gears again, going into business and becoming a real estate entrepreneur. As kids, my siblings and I saw that there were no limits. She was and continues to be a strong matriarch, someone who adapted to her environment and pushed societal norms and boundaries. I like to think I'm setting the same example.

Her Paris

FAVORITE WOMAN-RUN BUSINESS?

Brand Bazar, a multibrand clothing boutique across from Le Bon Marché that I've been frequenting for years. They have fantastic salespeople who will guide you based on your body type; it's definitely my go-to.

WHERE DO YOU LIKE TO GO AS A FAMILY?

I love taking the kids to the Rodin Museum (shown opposite), especially the outdoor park with the lovely café. It feels like an escape from the city. Our other favorite is La Javelle, a *guinguette* on the riverbanks by the Parc André Citroën (shown above) with food trucks and live bands—it's fantastic. And we can often be found riding bikes along Les Berges de Seine, setting up a picnic or stopping for drinks at Rosa Bonheur sur Seine.

YOUR SOLO RITUAL?

CrossFit! While it's typically something I do by myself, I'll occasionally bring the kids. They can participate or not, but I want them to understand the importance of fitness.

*Working to close the funding gap for women
entrepreneurs around the world*

ANNE RAVANONA

FOUNDER AND CEO OF GLOBAL INVEST HER

THE SHORT VERSION of Anne Ravanona's journey from Dublin to Paris is that she was a precocious polyglot who found herself building and running the French arm of an Irish pharmaceutical labeling company straight out of college. Her keen business sense and ferocious tenacity led her on an auspicious twenty-year career generating multimillions in new business and overseeing operations and culture-change transformations for start-ups and Fortune 500 companies. In 2013, she left the corporate world to launch Global Invest Her, the first online platform and community exclusively dedicated to assist early-stage women entrepreneurs learn about funding and get investor-ready.

When we met, she shared the longer version of that journey and why she decided to commit her life to closing the funding gap.

You went from succeeding in positions of tremendous responsibility to venturing out on your own. What was the spark? I had been the associate director of global business development for The Oxford Group, a management training company, for four years, making a six-figure salary and loving it. During this time, my brother passed away in rather traumatic circumstances, and I went on leave. Shortly after I returned to the office, I had a serious accident and was out of work again for nearly eight months. That's a lot of time to think about whether I was doing what I really wanted. With so much time on my hands, I started blogging, learning new skills, and eventually, negotiated my exit from the company, which gave me my start-up money. I wanted to find a problem worth solving, but beyond knowing it would be international in scope and involve women and leadership, the rest was unclear. But then I heard a talk by a female entrepreneur in London and was surprised to learn that her biggest challenge was access to funding. It was like a light bulb immediately went off in my head: *You're telling me it's harder for women to raise money for their businesses?* I started researching the funding gap between what men and women raise, which the IFC (part of the World Bank Group) estimates to be about $300 billion worldwide. Only 2 percent of venture capital goes to women, down from 5 percent a few years ago. There was my problem to solve.

What can the funding gap be attributed to? Several things, but a lot of it comes down to unconscious bias in the minds of male investors stemming from the usual gender stereotypes—women can't be committed if they're going to get married and have children. They think women are a risky investment in part because there are so few women entrepreneurs who make it. Many investors are also naturally biased toward investing in the familiar—white male entrepreneurs with a similar background to them. It's a cycle that keeps repeating. The trouble is, this thinking is ingrained from such a young age, and therefore both men and women are likely to apply it without even realizing it. The reality is, research shows that female founders yield a higher return on investment than male founders on one-third less capital, because we manage the business better.

Is it also a question of women underselling themselves? Definitely. It's a double-edged sword—there's bias in the minds of the investors and bias with the female founders, themselves. They struggle to believe they could conceivably ask for the money they deserve. Women often underestimate their funding needs and projections by at least 50 percent while men tend to overestimate theirs.

This scenario sounds like what happens when women ask for raises at work or negotiate their starting salaries. Exactly. I want female founders to know that there *is* a process, it can be learned with tools and tricks, and we can boost their confidence in asking for what they need. And most importantly, that they're not alone; there's a community of women who have done it.

Before you launched the full Global Invest Her platform, with tool kits, funding road maps, and tailored mentoring programs, you began by interviewing more than one hundred women. Why? How did this inform your vision? Ever since I read a book on Joan of Arc when I was eight years old, I've been hungry for stories on women leaders. I saw the opportunity to capture some of my own, not only for their legacy but to provide practical resources for other women. I drilled down into their actual funding journey in a way that had never been done before. These are women who raised from $500,000 to $200 million, and it was important to extract the *how*: How did they do it? What were their challenges? Looking back to some of my early interviewees, I see I was spotting winners before they fully blossomed— some having gone on to raise $50 to $100 million or more. But the takeaway I got from nearly all of them was that they wished they had better known what investors wanted. So I developed my education platform inspired in part by their feedback with the goal of giving female founders the tools and the access to role model investors so they understand how to prepare with confidence.

Advocacy is clearly a big part of your work too—you're regularly traveling the world to lead talks. What are the key messages you try to drive home? I've spoken internationally to raise awareness to investors about the challenges female founders face, the biases that still exist, and the great investment opportunities they're missing—always anchored in data. But I also use those speaking engagements to encourage more women to become investors because that's the other piece of this puzzle. Too many women assume they can't be investors, but in fact, we can! We can do so with the power of our purse, even just by choosing to buy certain products and services led by female founders. We need more women investors at a consumer level and at a professional level, as business angels. Right now, only 8 percent of venture capitalists are women. That unconscious bias isn't going to disappear without education and more women involved.

Closing this gap sounds like it requires the work of an army of Anne Ravanonas! For the rest of my life, my mission is to help close this funding gap, but you're right, it takes more than me! We have to work on changing hearts and minds and that's a long-term business; it will take generations. We have to start somewhere. We have to make role models more visible, see more women investors and women founders who succeed, so that investors take note. My other focus in the years to come will be the creation of a new form of funding for female founders. Much like Muhammad Yunus developed microfinance loans as a way for women in developing countries and emerging markets to start their own businesses, I want to create a new method because the current funding system is broken. An old boys' club in Silicon Valley created the rules fifty years ago. It's time for new rules, knowing that women are 51 percent of the global population. We have power to wield.

Looking back on your career in Paris and considering how it has evolved as a start-up hub, do you think the city can be a meeting place for all these ideas to converge? I think Paris can absolutely be a leader in innovation of all kinds. From the time I started my company, the city has created Station F, and we have a president who has pushed reforms to encourage greater entrepreneurial activity, a slew of coworking spaces, 42 (Xavier Niel's nonprofit and tuition-free computer programming school focused on project-based learning), and more access to grants and resources. We have an international pool of researchers, engineers, and developers and incredible cultural life to feed young, intelligent minds. The changes to the ecosystem are drawing people back, and that's good for everyone. In France, about 30 percent of new start-ups are set up by women every year, which is higher than in some places.

Do you observe a difference in the way French entrepreneurs pitch their businesses? To succeed as an entrepreneur, you need stamina, vision, leadership, organization, and ambition. I think any successful female founder needs all of those traits, whether she's French or foreign. I do see that American female founders have more confidence, but that's because it's a cultural value woven into the system from childhood. As kids there, you're standing up in front of class giving presentations. There's a unique, pioneering spirit that gets infused into young girls and women and, therefore, female founders. The French women founders who succeed not only have that (learned) confidence but aren't afraid to pitch their businesses in English. They know that to grow their business, they must think global from the start. Confidence and ease in English are two big barriers to overcome.

You consider yourself a feminist and are raising your son and daughter with similar values. How do you convey to them what this fight is all about? [I teach them that] it's about equal opportunity for respect, for education, for opportunity in work. It's about not being sidelined for a promotion or being paid less. Many of the negative experiences during my career—sexual harassment, underpayment, being fired illegally because I got pregnant, being overlooked for promotions by male superiors who were intimidated by me—happened because I'm a woman. My kids understand that. I won't stand for it, and neither should they. That's why I want to be part of the change. That's why I will keep speaking, mentoring girls and women, and advising women-run start-ups. I'm grooming an army for revolution. It will be pacifist, but there needs to be one, and I know my kids will be part of it.

Her Paris

FAVORITE WOMAN-RUN BUSINESS?

MH Coiffure, specifically for Tan, one of the colorists. No one does my blonde better!
And of course, Station F (shown above), the world's largest start-up campus, directed by
Roxanne Varza.

YOUR HAPPY PLACE?

Besides the Joan of Arc statue, the Pont Neuf. When I was nineteen, my friend brought me
to the bridge for the first time and had me close my eyes while I exited the métro. I could
hear a musician playing "La Vie en Rose" on an accordion. It was totally cliché, but I was
blown away by the moment. I knew there was no other option for me—it had to be Paris.

AN OUTING *EN FAMILLE*?

I love the Cité des Sciences de l'Industrie, the largest science museum in Europe. They
always have engaging temporary exhibitions and interactive stations.

their
Paris

In this section, you'll discover five women and five itineraries for an ideal day (or simply, an enjoyable day off) in Paris. Then, dive into the collection of the places and spaces much loved by the women in this book, plus a few of my own favorites. For a complete guide, visit thenewparisbook.com.

SARAH ANDELMAN

She may have closed Colette after twenty years, but Sarah Andelman's influence in fashion, art, and design lives on through her new consultancy, Just an Idea. When she's not traveling to the US or Japan for work, she might be living out some variation of this day in the city she's still happy to call home.

8:00 TO 9:00 A.M. PICK-ME-UP AT WILD & THE MOON After I drop my son off at school, I'd swing by the Wild & the Moon café at the place du Marché Saint-Honoré for a golden latte, then over to Mar'co for a croissant (and a chat!).

11:00 A.M. MASSAGE WITH A VIEW On an ideal day, I might book myself a massage at Ladda Paris, a wonderful institute in the 10th arrondissement with one of the most incredible views of the city from the terrace balcony.

1:00 P.M. LUNCH For a quick lunch, Udon bistro Kunitoraya. I particularly love their chirashizushi. And for a *loooong* lunch, when I have the time, Yam'Tcha, Michelin-starred chef Adeline Grattard's award-winning restaurant, which is always delicious. Don't miss the tea pairing.

3:00 P.M. TEA AND CULTURE I'd break for matcha tea at Toraya (but during the summer, I get their frozen ice dessert, which is the most refreshing thing on earth), and then go for a little walk in the Tuileries. And since I'm there, I'd invariably stop to see an exhibit at the Jeu de Paume.

6:00 P.M. *APÉRO* AT THE RITZ At the classic Bar Hemingway, I'd have a cocktail prepared by their legendary barman, Colin Field.

8:30 P.M. DINNER AT VERJUS For a special occasion, I'll book the private room upstairs. I'm a big fan of Braden's cooking! He always serves up an inspiring meal.

LATE NIGHT. STROLL ALONG ÎLE SAINT-LOUIS For the beauty of Paris by night.

Illustrator-author

ELIANE CHEUNG

With her cookbook, À la table d'une famille chinoise: Recettes de mes parents, *author-illustrator Eliane Cheung brought readers and home cooks into her life as a third-culture kid reared among the pots, pans, and flavors of her parents' southern Chinese restaurants in Paris. Her ideal day in Paris looks much like her usual day—full of creative time, personal time, and memorable meals.*

7:30 TO 8:30 A.M. MORNING SWIM Almost every morning I get up early to swim. It's not only crucial for me to start the day (and be in a good mood), but it's my favorite moment. My usual spot is the Piscine Pontoise, but if it's closed for any reason, I'd alternate between pools on the left bank.

9:00 A.M. WORKING BREAKFAST After I have a quick coffee with my swim buddies, I tend to go somewhere calm where I can read or draw while I eat. Usually that's Hexagone Café for the granola and a coffee or Mokonuts for labneh on toast.

12:30 P.M. LUNCH AT SEPTIME Once a month or so, I like to treat myself to a solo lunch at Septime. It's my own little luxury. The cooking surprises me every single time, and the staff is always so attentive.

3:00 P.M. AFTERNOON AT THE MOVIES I love going to morning movies, but since my schedule is usually quite packed, I'll see a film in the afternoon. I'm a fan of small, art-house cinemas in the Latin Quarter, such as Le Champo, but I also love the Louxor and L'Escurial. And after, I stroll in the Luxembourg Gardens, where I've gone since I was a kid.

4:00/5:00 P.M. *GOÛTER* (SNACKTIME) AT LA GAMBETTE À PAIN This is one of my absolute favorite bakeries and a wonderful spot for a snack—*chouquettes*, pastries, and flan. Don't leave without trying the Pain Préféré (secret: baker-owner Jean-Paul Mathon trained star baker Christophe Vasseur, whose much-loved *pain des amis* at Du Pain et des Idées was inspired by the Pain Préféré).

8:30/9:00 P.M.—BOOK CLUB DINNER For book-club night with my friends, we'll meet at any number of iconic spots where we eat well and discuss what we're reading: Le Café des Musées, Bonvivant, or Lao Siam.

Cofounder of the #SeeMyParis travel community

BENEDICTE REITZEL-NIELSEN

When Benedicte Reitzel-Nielsen isn't working in the nonprofit sector, she's nurturing the online travel community she cofounded. The #SeeMyParis collective is an attempt to present an unidealized look at Paris that falls somewhere between the romantic and the real, with everyday moments captured in photo. You may even catch a shot or two from a day like the one she shares below.

9:00 A.M. TEA AND TARTINES AT MÛRE This little café has an excellent tea selection and serves delicious homemade marmalades. The spot is cozy, the staff is friendly, and almost all of their products are fair-trade, local, and organic.

11:00 A.M. MARKET STOP I love shopping on the rue du Nil, where there is a concentration of grocers. Terroirs d'Avenir carries a beautiful selection of fruits, vegetables, and cheese; there's a fishmonger and butcher in one and a bakery a few doors down. All shops sell only high-quality products that are carefully sourced from producers and are a feast for the eyes as well.

1:00 P.M. LUNCH BREAK I'll either cook at home with the products bought in the morning or I'll sneak out for lunch at one of my favorites: Élémentaire for a light meal; Blend if I'm bringing the kids because they have high-quality meat and bread for their burgers (and I love their sweet potato fries); or Coinstot Vino in the passage de Panoramas for a heartier meal with a glass of wine.

3:00 P.M. A PROPER WANDER With a neighborhood or market in mind, I'll walk around leisurely (something I rarely do on weekdays), noticing façades, alleys, and details I've overlooked. I'll press door buttons to see if they open, looking for hidden courtyards (often bumping into angry concierges instead). I may make stops along the way, but mostly I'm observing, taking mental notes of people and places.

6:00 P.M. UNTIL LATE *APÉRO* ALONG THE WATER La Seine is the best place for apéritif when warm summer evenings return. Everybody brings something to drink and snack on, and we watch the sun set.

Itinerant chef and cofounder of Tontine

CÉLINE PHAM

What does Céline Pham, France's most in-demand culinary nomad, do in the moments when she isn't a chef in residence, taking over restaurants, or running Tontine, a pop-up she set up with her brother Julien? Apprentice with bakers, cheesemongers, butchers, and florists and, of course, eat her way through Paris.

10:00 TO 11:00 A.M. *LES COURSES* **(ERRANDS!)** I'm lucky to live so close to all of my favorite places to source ingredients for my own meals or dinners I'm asked to cook. I'll either walk or cycle between them all, beginning with Taka & Vermo, a wonderful artisanal fromagerie where I'll pick up cheese, yogurt, milk, and eggs. I'll go through the Passage Brady for my spices and then head to Terroirs d'Avenir for produce, fish, and bread.

11:30 A.M. TO 1:15 P.M. COFFEE BREAK AND A WORKOUT One of my best friends is a yoga master and fitness coach and teaches spinning at Dynamo, where I go regularly. Just before Clotide's 12:15 p.m. class, I'll stop in for a coffee at Telescope, have a chat, and then head to the gym's Opéra location for an intense workout.

1:30/2:00 P.M. SNACK TIME Ravenous after spinning, I'll go straight to Kunitoraya for udon noodles. And since I'm in the neighborhood, I can't leave without going to Aki Boulanger for onigiris, soba salad, and eggplant *laqué* (which I may or may not save for later).

3:00 P.M. CULTURE STOP I'll go wherever there's something showing that I'm interested in or that I may have missed while I was stuck in the kitchen. And it may not be anywhere near where I was previously, but I'll travel for it, like the Galerie Nationale du Jeu de Paume, which I love.

6:00 TO 8:00 P.M. *APÉRO* **AT THE LOUXOR** Drinks on balcony of the Louxor cinema as the sun sets (spring and fall); movie optional!

9:00 P.M. LE RIGMAROLE A late dinner at this temple of masterful yakitori (also fresh pasta, tempura, and desserts).

LATE NIGHT. Time to pop in a movie I rented (yes, a few of those shops still exist) from JM Vidéo on avenue Parmentier to finish off the night.

Food photographer and cookbook author

EMILIE FRANZO

When she's not in the kitchen creating recipes for one of her cookbooks or in someone else's kitchen, documenting their cooking process, Emilie Franzo can usually be found traversing the city in search of the city's best places to eat, drink, shop, and hang out. Here's how she'd spend a day in Paris.

8:00/9:00 A.M. BREAKFAST AT TEN BELLES BREAD It's the perfect place to have a good coffee in the morning with excellent pastries and breads. It's run by Alice Quillet and Anna Trattles, two wonderful women I've had the opportunity to interview for my work before. Everything is homemade, from the sourdough starter to the bread itself. And I love being able to see the bakers work through the kitchen window, a bit like watching a performance.

11:00 A.M. STOP BY MAKE MY LEMONADE I'm a huge fan of Lisa Gachet's clothing line, so I'd stop into her shop to browse. Her collections are colorful, original, and designed for all types of women, including those who don't fit the mold of a size six.

1:00 P.M. LUNCH AT MOKONUTS Simply because it's one of my absolute favorite places to eat in Paris. I would cross town for Omar's labneh and dishes of the day and Moko's unforgettable cookies.

3:00 P.M. BOXING CLASS AT CHEZ SIMONE I love this hybrid space that mixes fitness classes such as yoga, pilates, dance, and boxing with a healthy canteen, pop-up events, and even a coworking space.

6:00 P.M. *APÉRO* AT BISOU Some of the most original cocktails can be found here, partly because there is no menu! The mixologists concoct drinks according to your tastes, interests, and flavor preferences, so every cocktail ends up unique.

8:30 P.M. DINNER AT DOUBLE DRAGON I'm a big fan of the Levha sisters, and this Asian canteen (their second restaurant) is the best place to discover the flavors and influences they loved growing up between the Philippines and Thailand. Inside, it's a real throwback, with neon lights and an eighties playlist, which is fun but the draw is really the food: mouthwatering fried tofu with XO sauce, spicy grilled corn, and more.

THEIR PARIS GUIDE ♡ LINDSEY'S PICKS

Coffee, Baked Goods & Sweets

A L'ETOILE D'OR
30 rue Pierre Fontaine, 75009

AKI BOULANGER
16 rue Saint-Anne, 75001

BELLEVILLE BRÛLERIE
14 rue Lally-Tollendal, 75019

BONESHAKER DOUGHNUTS
77 rue d'Aboukir, 75002

BOULANGERIE MAMICHE
45 rue Condorcet, 75009
32 rue de Château d'Eau 75010

BROKEN BISCUITS
13 avenue Parmentier, 75011

CAFÉ MÉRICOURT ♡
22 rue de la Folie Méricourt, 75011

CONFITURE PARISIENNE ♡
17 avenue Daumesnil, 75012

FOU DE PÂTISSERIE
45 rue Montorgueil, 75002
36 rue des Martyrs, 75009

HEXAGONE CAFÉ
121 rue du Château, 75014

LA CAFÉOTHÈQUE
52 rue de l'Hôtel-de-Ville, 75004

LA GAMBETTE À PAIN
86 avenue Gambetta, 75020

MAISON ALEPH
20 rue de la Verrerie, 75004

POILÂNE ♡
Multiple locations; poilane.com

RÉPUBLIQUE OF COFFEE
2 boulevard Saint-Martin, 75010

SECCO
31 rue de Varenne, 75007

TÉLESCOPE CAFÉ
5 rue Villédo, 75002

TEN BELLES BREAD
17–19 rue Breguet, 75011

TORAYA
10 rue Saint-Florentin, 75001

USED BOOK CAFÉ AT MERCI
111 boulevard Beaumarchais, 75003

Lunch & Dinner

BLEND HAMBURGER
Multiple locations; blendhamburger.com

BONVIVANT
7 rue des Écoles, 75005

CAFÉ DES MUSÉES
49 rue de Turenne, 75003

CAFÉ LAI' TCHA
7 rue du Jour, 75001

CAFÉ MARLY
93 rue de Rivoli, 75001

COINSTOT VINO
26 bis Passage des Panoramas, 75002

DOUBLE DRAGON
52 rue Saint-Maur, 75011

ÉLÉMENTAIRE
38 rue Léopold Bellan, 75002

HOLYBELLY
5 and 19 rue Lucien Sampaix, 75010

KUNITORAYA
1 rue Villédo, 75002

---

previous spread Chez Ajiri Aki: a beloved perch in the 11th arrondissement. *opposite* Illustrator Eliane Cheung creates sketchbooks filled to the brim with inspiration on places to go and food to try.

Cecina de Astorga (boeuf de Galice séché) (offert) ***

Carte Blanche (soir) (65€ x2)

THURSDAY
April 30

granola *** (8€!)
passion, kiwi, blanc, poire, banane, myrtilles, groseilles

pommes de terre fumées au bois de hêtre, crème crue ***

infusion fraîche fraises, fleurs de sureau *** (3,50€)

artichaut calico ***

gelée de mandarine

Coque (crue) (un peu goûté mais pas mauvais)

sabayon au Beaufort

asperges blanche du Poitou
oignons au vin blanc (cachés)

cochon Kinba ****

JOOD

Soupe d'orties et d'ail des ours ***

brioche toastée (miam)

Caillé de chèvre à la fleur

turbot ***

concombre brûlé
salicorne
fève
beurre blanc infusé au laurier
concombre brûlé

saumon
seiche
maquereau mariné

Thé vert **

Sauce soja

fleur de ?

coeur de sucrine
poirier

poulette du pays (de la Sarthe)
grenobloise (câpres citron noix)
granité à l'oseille

Menu Midi
Sashimi
(12 tranches de poisson)
14,50€

sorbet fraise

tuile au sarrasin, chantilly
caramel au beurre salé ****

SEPTIME

OYA

...umes mijotés ***

LA DAME DE PIC
20 rue du Louvre, 75001

LA MARINA
8 rue du Château Landon, 75010

LAO SIAM
49 rue de Belleville, 75019

LE BARATIN
3 rue Jouye-Rouve, 75020

LE CHATEAUBRIAND
129 avenue Parmentier, 75011

LE RIGMAROLE
10 rue du Grand Prieuré, 75011

LE SERVAN
32 rue Saint-Maur, 75011

LES GRANDS VERRES
13 avenue du Président Wilson, 75016

LIZA
14 rue de la Banque, 75002

MA COCOTTE
106 rue des Rosiers, 93400

MAR'CO
4 rue de la Sourdière, 75001

MARTIN
24 boulevard du Temple, 75011

MOKONUTS
5 rue Saint-Bernard, 75011

MÛRE
6 rue Saint-Marc, 75002

MUSCOVADO
1 rue Sedaine, 75011

PEONIES
81 rue du Faubourg-Saint-Denis, 75010

RACINES PARIS ♡
8 passage des Panoramas, 75002

SEPTIME
80 rue de Charonne, 75011

TANNAT
119 avenue Parmentier, 75011

TAVLINE
25 rue du Roi de Sicile, 75004

VERJUS
52 rue de Richelieu, 75001

(V)IVRE
3 rue de la Michodière, 75002
60 rue de Lancry, 75010

WILD & THE MOON
19 place du Marché Saint-Honoré, 75001

YAM'TCHA
121 rue Saint-Honoré, 75001

Bars, Cafés & Cocktails

AUX DEUX AMIS
45 rue Oberkampf, 75011

BAR HEMINGWAY (HÔTEL RITZ PARIS)
15 place Vendôme, 75001

BISOU
15 boulevard du Temple, 75003

CANDELARIA
52 rue de Saintonge, 75003

COMBAT
63 rue de Belleville, 75019

LA CAVE À MICHEL
6 rue Sainte-Marthe, 75010

LA COLONIE
128 rue Lafayette, 75010

LA FONTAINE DE BELLEVILLE
31–33 rue Juliette Dodu, 75010

LE MARY CELESTE
1 rue Commines, 75003

LE PAVILLON PUEBLA
39 avenue Simon Bolivar, 75019

LE PETIT FER À CHEVAL
30 rue Vieille du Temple, 75004

LE PICK CLOPS
16 rue Vieille du Temple, 75004

LE ROYAL MONCEAU
37 avenue Hoche, 75008

ROSA BONHEUR SUR SEINE
Port des Invalides, 75007

VERJUS BAR À VINS
47 rue de Montpensier, 75001

Bookstores

7L
7 rue de Lille, 75007

ARTAZART ♡
83 quai de Valmy, 75010

BERKELEY BOOKS OF PARIS
8 rue Casimir Delavigne, 75006

CHANTELIVRE
13 rue de Sèvres, 75006

ESPACE DES FEMMES
35 rue Jacob, 75006

ICI LIBRAIRIE ♡
25 boulevard Poissonnière, 75002

LA PROCURE
3 rue de Mézières, 75006

L'ECUME DES PAGES
174 boulevard Saint-Germain, 75006

SHAKESPEARE AND COMPANY
37 rue de la Bûcherie, 75005

VIOLETTE AND CO
102 rue de Charonne, 75011

Florists

DÉSIRÉE ♡
5 rue de la Folie Méricourt, 75011

RACINE
198 boulevard Voltaire, 75011

VERTUMNE
12 rue de la Sourdière, 75001

Cinemas

L'ESCURIAL
11 boulevard de Port-Royal, 75013

LE CHAMPO
51 rue des Écoles, 75005

LOUXOR
170 boulevard de Magenta, 75010

MK2 QUAI DE SEINE & QUAI DE LOIRE
14 quai de la Seine, 75019
7 quai de la Loire, 75019

Markets, Epiceries & Fromageries

BARTHÉLÉMY ♡
51 rue de Grenelle, 75007

MAISON PLISSON
93 boulevard Beaumarchais, 75003
35 place du Marché Saint-Honoré, 75001

MARCHÉ D'ALIGRE
place d'Aligre, 75012

PASSAGE BRADY
46 rue du Faubourg Saint-Denis, 75010

TAKA & VERMO
61 bis rue du Faubourg-Saint-Denis, 75010

TANG FRÈRES
48 avenue d'Ivry, 75013 (original location)

TERROIRS D'AVENIR
3, 6, 7, 8 rue du Nil, 75002

VT CASH & CARRY
11–13 rue Cail, 75010

Shopping

BRAND BAZAAR
33 rue de Sèvres, 75006

EMMANUELLE ZYSMAN
81 rue des Martyrs, 75018

FAUBOURG 43
43 rue du Faubourg-Saint-Martin, 75010

GALERIES LAFAYETTE
40 boulevard Haussmann, 75009

JAMINI ♡
10 rue Notre Dame de Lorette, 75009
10 rue du Château d'Eau, 75010

LE BON MARCHÉ
24 rue de Sèvres, 75007

L'OFFICINE UNIVERSELLE BULY
6 rue Bonaparte, 75006
45 rue de Saintonge, 75003

MAKE MY LEMONADE
61 quai de Valmy, 75010

MAMZ'ELLE SWING
35 bis rue du Roi de Sicile, 75004

MANSAYA
49 rue Léon Frot, 75011

MARCHÉ AUX PUCES
93400 Saint-Ouen

NELLY WANDJI
93 rue du Faubourg-Saint-Honoré, 75008

SÉZANE ♡
1 rue Saint-Fiacre, 75002

YUME STORE ♡
50 rue Jean-Pierre Timbaud, 75011

Wellness & Fitness

BAN SABAÏ
12 rue de Lesdiguières, 75004

BOXER INSIDE
81 boulevard Masséna, 75013

CALMA PARIS
15 rue Dauphine, 75006

CENTRE DE DANSE DU MARAIS
41 rue du Temple, 75004

CHEZ SIMONE
226 rue Saint-Denis, 75002

CLUB POPULAIRE ET SPORTIF (CPS 10)
www.cps10.fr

DYNAMO
Multiple locations; dynamo-cycling.com

LADDA
32 rue de Paradis, 75010

MACCABI PARIS
70 rue René Boulanger, 75010

MH COIFFURE
15 rue Boissy d'Anglas, 75008

MOLITOR
8 avenue de la Porte Molitor, 75016

PISCINE GEORGES HERMANT (MUNICIPAL POOL)
8–10 rue David d'Angers, 75019

PISCINE PONTOISE (MUNICIPAL POOL)
19 rue de Pontoise, 75005

REFORMATION PILATES ♡
175 rue du Temple, 75003

STELLA CENTRE DE BEAUTÉ INDIEN
27 rue Philippe de Girard, 75010

Art & Culture

APPARTEMENT
appartement-27bis.com

ARTS FACTORY
27 rue de Charonne, 75011

BIBLIOTHÈQUE DE LA SORBONNE
17 rue de la Sorbonne, 75005

BIBLIOTHÈQUE FRANÇOIS MITTERAND
Quai François Mauriac, 75013

BIBLIOTHÈQUE MARGUERITE DURAND
79 rue Nationale, 75013

CARREAU DU TEMPLE
2 rue Perrée, 75003

FOLIES BERGÈRES
32 rue Richer, 75009

FONDATION CARTIER
261 boulevard Raspail, 75014

GALERIE MIRANDA
21 rue du Château d'Eau, 75010

JEU DE PAUME
1 place de la Concorde, 75008

JM VIDEO
121 avenue Parmentier, 75011

L'ATELIER DES LUMIÈRES
38 rue Saint-Maur, 75011

LA CIGALE
120 boulevard de Rochechouart, 75018

L'OPÉRA PALAIS GARNIER
8 rue Scribe, 75009

**LE CITÉ DES SCIENCES
ET DE L'INDUSTRIE**
30 avenue Corentin-Cariou, 75019

LE LOUVRE
rue de Rivoli, 75001

MUSÉE DE LA VIE ROMANTIQUE ♡
16 rue Chaptal, 75009

MUSÉE D'ORSAY
1 rue de la Légion d'Honneur, 75007

MUSÉE DES ARTS DÉCORATIFS
107 rue de Rivoli, 75001

MUSÉE DES ARTS ET MÉTIERS
60 rue Réamur, 75003

MUSÉE DU QUAI BRANLY
37 quai Branly, 75007

MUSÉE JACQUEMART-ANDRÉ
158 boulevard Haussmann, 75008

MUSÉE RODIN
77 rue de Varenne, 75007

**PALAIS DE LA DÉCOUVERTE
(GRAND PALAIS)**
Avenue Franklin Delano Roosevelt, 75008

PALAIS DE TOKYO
13 avenue du Président Wilson, 75016

SLOW GALERIE ♡
5 rue Jean-Pierre Timbaud, 75011

THÉÂTRE DE POCHE-MONTPARNASSE
75 boulevard du Montparnasse, 75006

THÉÂTRE DU CHÂTELET
2 rue Edouard Colonne, 75001

Stroll

BOIS DE VINCENNES
46 route de la Pyramide, 75012

COUR DES PETITES ÉCURIES, 75010

DOMAINE NATIONAL DU PALAIS-ROYAL
8 rue Montpensier, 75001

LES BERGES DE SEINE
Right bank: from Pont Neuf to Pont de Sully;
Bassin de l'Arsenal
Left bank: from Pont de l'Alma to Pont Royal

THE BRIDGES OF PARIS
Pont Neuf
Pont des Arts
Pont Alexandre III

LUXEMBOURG GARDENS
Place Edmond Rostand, 75006

PARC ANDRÉ-CITROËN
2 rue Cauchy, 75015

PARC DES BUTTES-CHAUMONT
1 rue Botzaris, 75019

PARC MONCEAU
35 boulevard de Courcelles, 75008

PLACE DU TROCADÉRO, 75016

PORTE DE CHOISY, 75013

TUILERIES GARDENS
113 rue de Rivoli, 75001

Hybrid Spaces & Centers

GROUND CONTROL ♡
81 rue du Charolais, 75012

**GUINGUETTE LA JAVELLE (SPRING/
SUMMER)**
Port Javel Bas, 75015

LES CANAUX
6 quai de la Seine, 75019

LES GRANDS VOISINS
74 avenue Denfert-Rochereau, 75014

PALAIS DE LA FEMME
94 rue de Charonne, 75011

STATION F
55 boulevard Vincent Auriol, 75013

SUPER CAFÉ
16 rue de Fontarabie, 75020

ACKNOWLEDGMENTS

IT WAS AN EMOTIONAL AND EYE-OPENING JOURNEY to research and write this book, and I am forever grateful to each of the women who shared their precious time with me to make it happen. Thank you to my agent Judy Linden of Stonesong for believing in this project, right from our earliest conversations about it, and instantly understanding what I wanted to achieve. To Laura Dozier, my supportive and insightful editor, who saw what this could be and encouraged me every step of the way. You are a dream to work with! To Joann Pai, *ma meuf*, for joining me on this adventure. Your exceptional photography brought this vision to life! I'm so grateful for your dedication, your good humor, and your friendship. *Un grand merci* to Agathe Singer, also a Parisienne, whose illustrations amplify the book's message and make me smile each time I see them, and to designer Sarah Gifford, who knew how to dream up the book I imagined. To my best friend Lauren DeGeorge: I could not have gotten here without your wisdom, unwavering support, tough love, and guidance. You call me out when I need it, and you push me in the best ways to challenge myself. This is for you!

Thank you to the Tramuta family and my friends, near and far, old and new, for checking in, offering words of advice, and always letting me run ideas by you: Lisa Higgins, Sara Lieberman, Amy Feezor, Guy Griffin, Alice Cavanagh, Frank Barron, James Rose, Jane Bertch, Lauren Collins, Elle McClelland, Benoît Santiard, Bryan Pirolli, Jesse Morgan, Nichole Robertson, Amy Verner, Charli James, Jackie Kai Ellis, Roxy Matiz, Jon Bonné, Jeremy Schuster, Amy Thomas, David Santori, Jamie Varon, Elizabeth Mazz Hanna, Rebekah Peppler, Yasmine Khatib, Emily Petrone, Amber Cooper, Charissa Fay, Pat Fay, Cody Delistraty, Will Taylor, Marisa Lenger, Jake Cigainero, Anne Ditmeyer, Jennifer Han, Marisa Williams, Mary Winston Nicklin, and Sophie Peyrard.

A special shout-out to Erin Alweiss, Shelly Porges, Ariel Pasternak, Amy Serafin, Clémence Pène, Julie Bloom, and Katinka Sarkozy for generously introducing me to some of the women in these pages.

And to Cédric, Leo, and Charlie, *ma petite famille*: thank you for the talks, the hugs, the stress-relieving purrs, and the endless encouragement. I love you.

---

opposite C'est moi, strolling around the 2nd arrondissement with photographer Joann Pai, during the preparation of this book.

ENDNOTES

INTRODUCTION

1   Eliza Brooke, "How to Sell a Billion-Dollar Myth Like a French Girl," *Vox*, July 5, 2017, accessed January 3, 2018, https://www.vox.com/2017/7/5/15880176/how-to-french-girl-style-beauty.

2   Emmanuelle Retaillaud-Bajac, "Entre chic et chien : les séductions de la Parisienne, de Jean-Jacques Rousseau à Yves Saint-Laurent," *Genre, sexualité et sociétés*, no. 10 (Autumn 2013), http://gss.revues.org.

3   Anne Vermes, "Aristide et Marguerite Boucicaut, Fondateurs du Bon Marché: Ils ont Invente le Commerce Moderne," Capital, June 1, 2018, accessed December 5, 2018, https://www.capital.fr/votre-carriere/aristide-et-marguerite-boucicaut-fondateurs-du-bon-marche-ils-ont-invente-le-commerce-moderne-1290738.

4   Emmanuelle Retaillaud-Bajac, "Entre chic et chien: les séductions de la Parisienne, de Jean-Jacques Rousseau à Yves Saint-Laurent," *Genre, sexualité et sociétés*, no. 10 (Autumn 2013), http://gss.revues.org.

5   Chimamanda Ngozi Adichie, "The Danger of a Single Story," Ted.com, 2009, accessed February 6, 2019, https://www.ted.com/talks/chimamanda_adichie_the_danger_of_a_single_story/transcript?language=en.

6   A reference to the transformative period of civil unrest in France in May 1968. There were street fights, mass protests, and nationwide strikes that brought together university students, workers, intellectuals, and the next generation of feminists.

BEFORE YOU BEGIN: A CULTURAL PRIMER

7   Joan Wallach Scott, *The Politics of the Veil* (Princeton, NJ: Princeton University Press, 2007), 98.

8   Idem, 88.

9   Adrien Favell, *Philosophies of Integration* (Basingstoke, UK: Palgrave Macmillan, 2001), 42.

10 Joan Wallach Scott, *The Politics of the Veil* (Princeton, NJ: Princeton University Press, 2007), 11.

11 Rachel Donadio, "The Meaning of France's March Against Anti-Semitism," *The Atlantic*, March 29, 2018, accessed February 2, 2019, https://www.theatlantic.com/international/archive/2018/03/the-murder-of-mireille-knoll-in-france-might-be-the-last-straw-for-french-jews/556796.

12 Celestine Bohlen, "France Fears Becoming Too 'Anglo-Saxon' in its Treatment of Minorities," *New York Times*, September 19, 2016, accessed August 2, 2018, https://www.nytimes.com/2016/09/20/world/europe/france-minorities-assimilation.html.

13 Elizabeth Zerofsky, "Can a New Generation in the Banlieues Change French Politics?" *New York Times Magazine*, June 7, 2017, accessed May 22, 2019, https://www.nytimes.com/2017/06/07/magazine/can-a-new-generation-in-the-banlieues-change-french-politics.html.

14 With the exception of studies conducted by researchers and statisticians with anonymous participants, as the law allows (according to the CNIL, *Commission nationale de l'informatique et des libertés*).

opposite Retro vibes at the Pavillon Puebla in the Buttes-Chaumont park.

15   Zack Beauchamp, "Trevor Noah's Feud with France Over Race, Identity and Africa, Explained," *Vox*, July 19, 2018, accessed January 25, 2019, https://www.vox.com/policy-and-politics/2018/7/19/17590302/trevor-noah-france-french-ambassador-araud-world-cup.

16   Joan Wallach Scott, *The Politics of the Veil* (Princeton, NJ: Princeton University Press, 2007), 13.

17   Alana Lentin and Valerie Amiraux, "François Hollande's Misguided Move: Taking 'Race' out of the Constitution," *The Guardian*, February 12, 2013, accessed January 10, 2019, https://www.theguardian.com/commentisfree/2013/feb/12/francois-hollande-race-french-constitution.

18   Rokhaya Diallo, "France's Dangerous Move to Remove 'Race' from Its Constitution," *Washington Post*, July 13, 2018, accessed January 10, 2019.

19   See note 15.

20   Grégory Pierrot, "Fear of a Black France," *Africa Is a Country*, July 8, 2018, accessed August 10, 2018, https://africasacountry.com/2018/07/fear-of-a-black-france.

21   Crystal M. Fleming, *How to Be Less Stupid About Race: On Racism, White Supremacy, and the Racial Divide* (Boston: Beacon Press), 14.

22   Catherine Millet et al., "Nous défendons une liberté d'importuner, indispensable à la liberté sexuelle," *Le Monde*, January 9, 2018.

23   Serene J. Khader, *Decolonizing Universalism: A Transnational Feminist Ethic* (New York: Oxford University Press, 2019), 79.

24   Jane Kramer, "Against Nature," *The New Yorker*, July 25, 2011.

25   Rebecca Amsellem, *Les Glorieuses: Chroniques d'une Feministe* (Paris: Editions Hoebeke, 2018), 98.

The Activists

ELISA ROJAS

26   "Hausse du taux du chômage des personnes handicapées," Sénat.fr, January 11, 2018, https://www.senat.fr/questions/base/2017/qSEQ171102160.html.

27   Andrew Grim, "Sitting-In for Disability Rights: The Section 504 Protests of the 1970s," *Smithsonian*, July 8, 2015, accessed November 10, 2018, http://americanhistory.si.edu/blog/sitting-disability-rights-section-504-protests-1970s.

28   Romaric Godin, "Stéphane Peu: 'La loi ELAN est une régression totale pour les personnes handicapées,'" *Mediapart*, October 26, 2018, accessed November 9, 2018, https://www.mediapart.fr/journal/france/261018/stephane-peu-la-loi-elan-est-une-regression-totale-pour-les-personnes-handicapees?onglet=full.

29   "Observations préliminaires de la Rapporteuse spéciale sur les droits des personnes handicapées, Mme Catalina Devandas-Aguilar au cours de sa visite en France, du 3 au 13 octobre 2017," Nations Unies Droits de l'Homme, accessed June 16, 2019, https://www.ohchr.org/FR/NewsEvents/Pages/DisplayNews.aspx?NewsID=22245&LangID=F.

ROKHAYA DIALLO

30   Quinn Slobodian, "Trump, Populists and the Rise of Right-Wing Globalization," *New York Times*, October 22, 2018, accessed April 6, 2019, https://www.nytimes.com/2018/10/22/opinion/trump-far-right-populists-globalization.html.

31   "Enquête sur l'accès aux droits, Volume I: Relations Police / Population; le cas des contrôles d'identité," *Défenseur des Droits*, January 2017, accessed February 1, 2019, https://www.defenseurdesdroits.fr/sites/default/files/atoms/files/rapport-enquete_relations_police_population-20170111_1.pdf.

32   Rokhaya Diallo, "A student leader is the latest victim of France's obsession with the hijab," *The Guardian*, May 28, 2018, accessed December 28, 2018, https://www.theguardian.com/commentisfree/2018/may/28/union-leader-maryam-pougetoux-france-hijab.

CLÉMENCE ZAMORA CRUZ

33   "Trans Day of Remembrance 2018 Press Release: 369 reported murders of trans and gender-diverse people in the last year," TMM,

November 12, 2018, accessed April 5, 2019, https://transrespect.org/en/tmm-update-trans-day-of-remembrance-2018.

34 Zamora Cruz also noted that while there are more and more child psychiatrists specializing in transgender issues today, the wait time to getting an appointment can be up to a year. For a person and family in crisis, that's simply too long.

35 Figures according to the National Coalition for the Homeless, http://nationalhomeless.org/issues/lgbt.

36 Deborah Schembri, "Discrimination Against Transgender People in Europe," *Council of Europe Report from the Committee on Equality and Non-Discrimination*, April 2, 2015, https://www.refworld.org/pdfid/55b241e24.pdf.

37 Alexis Patri, "La Souffrances des Ados Trans en France," *Slate*, January 10, 2017, accessed January 26, 2019, http://www.slate.fr/story/133997/enfants-trans-integration-france.

38 Amar Toor, "Transgender people no longer required to undergo sterilization in France," *The Verge*, October 14, 2016, accessed January 26, 2019, https://www.theverge.com/2016/10/14/13283086/transgender-law-france-sterilization-gender-change.

39 See note 38.

The Creators

ELENA ROSSINI

40 Dr. Stacy L. Smith et al., "Inclusion in the Director's Chair: Gender, Age & Race of Directors Across 1,200 Top Films from 2007 to 2018," USC Annenberg Inclusion Initiative, January 2019, http://assets.uscannenberg.org/docs/inclusion-in-the-directors-chair-2019.pdf, 9–15.

INNA MODJA

41 Aboubacar Dicko, "Mali: l'excision, un business lucratif . . . pour les féticheurs aussi," *Jeune Afrique*, October 5, 2017, accessed April 5, 2019, https://www.jeuneafrique.com/480695/societe/mali-lexcision-un-business-lucratif-pour-les-feticheurs-aussi.

The Disruptors

ANNE HIDALGO

42 Climate 100: The World's Most Influential People in Climate Policy, *Apolitical*, 2019 Ranking, https://apolitical.co/lists/most-influential-climate-100.

43 Michael J. Coren, "Nine countries say they'll ban internal combustion engines. So far, it's just words," *Quartz*, August 7, 2018, accessed May 20, 2019, https://qz.com/1341155/nine-countries-say-they-will-ban-internal-combustion-engines-none-have-a-law-to-do-so.

44 Laura Bliss, "The Automotive Liberation of Paris," *CityLab*, January 19, 2018, accessed May 22, 2019, https://www.citylab.com/transportation/2018/01/the-automotive-liberation-of-paris/550718.

45 Solène Cordier and Isabelle Rey-Lefebvre, "Face à la mendicité des enfants roms, les 'échecs' et les 'belles réussites' de la Mairie de Paris," *Le Monde*, April 29, 2019.

46 Lauren Bastide, interview with Anne Hidalgo, *La Poudre*, November 1, 2018, https://www.nouvellesecoutes.fr/la-poudre.

47 Marianne Mairesse, "Anne Hidalgo, femme forteresse," *Marie Claire*, July 2018, 111.

48 Alexander M. Toledano, "Sharing Paris: The Use and Ownership of a Neighborhood, Its Streets and Public Spaces, 1950–2012" (PhD diss., University of California, Berkeley, 2012).

49 "Le Vrai du Faux: idées reçues sur la voiture à Paris," *Paris.fr*, September 7, 2017, https://www.paris.fr/actualites/a-paris-seuls-22-des-conducteurs-ont-reellement-besoin-d-un-vehicule-3876.

CHRISTELLE DELARUE

50 Ekaterina Walter, "The top 30 statistics you need to know when marketing to women," *The Next Web*, January 24, 2012, accessed April 9, 2019, https://thenextweb.com/socialmedia/2012/01/24/

the-top-30-stats-you-need-to-know-when-marketing-to-women.

51 The 3% Movement, https://www.3percentmovement.com/mission.

52 "Image des femmes dans la publicité télévisée: les décalages et stéréotypes persistent," Conseil Supérieur de l'Audiovisuel (CSA), October 31, 2017, accessed April 9, 2019, https://www.csa.fr/Proteger/Droits-des-femmes/Mediatiser-le-sport-feminin/Image-des-femmes-dans-la-publicite-televisee-les-decalages-et-stereotypes-persistent.

53 Gender Equality Measure™ (GEM™), https://seeher.com/gender-equality-measure.

SARAH ZOUAK

54 "Rapport 2019 Du CCIF," CCIF—*Collectif contre l'islamophobie en France*, March 15, 2019, www.islamophobie.net/en/2019/03/15/rapport-2019-du-ccif.

On Image and Representation

55 The group has been called Kering since 2013.

56 Mona Chollet, *Beauté Fatale: les Nouveaux Visages d'une Alienation Feminine* (Paris: Éditions La Découverte, 2012) 13-14.

57 Idem, 14.

58 Idem, 221.

59 Anne Sogno, "Baromètre de la diversité du CSA: les chaines peuvent mieux faire," *TéléObs*, January 10, 2019, accessed January 28, 2019, https://www.nouvelobs.com/tv/20190110.OBS10362/barometre-de-la-diversite-du-csa-la-representation-de-la-population-a-la-television-reste-assez-eloignee-de-la-realite.html.

60 Aïssa Maïga, *Noire n'est pas mon métier* (Paris: Éditions du Seuil, 2018), 9.

61 Idem, 21.

62 Hua Hsu, "*Crazy Rich Asians* and the End Point of Representation," *The New Yorker*, August 20, 2018.

63 Grace Ly, "Pourquoi *Crazy Rich Asians* Ne Changera Rien en France," *La Petite Banane*,"

August 21, 2018, accessed May 22, 2019, http://lapetitebanane.com/index.php/2018/08/21/pourquoi-crazy-rich-asians-ne-changera-rien-en-france.

64 Jennifer Padjemi, Les Lesbiennes, *Femmes Invisibles?*, interview with Marie Kirschen, *Miroir Miroir*, podcast audio, December 25, 2018, https://www.binge.audio/les-lesbiennes-femmes-invisibles.

65 "Les 1000 de la Presse Francaise 2018 (6eme Edition)," *Press'Edd*, December 20, 2018, accessed April 9, 2019, https://www.edd.fr/les-1000-de-la-presse-francaise-2018-6eme-edition.

66 Les Expertes, https://expertes.fr/le-projet.

On Motherhood

67 Diksha Basu, "Rebranding Motherhood," *New York Times*, August 10, 2018, accessed February 5, 2019, https://www.nytimes.com/2018/08/10/well/rebranding-motherhood.html.

68 In comparison, paid parental leave still isn't mandatory in the United States, and there is nothing approximating this level of state support for new mothers.

69 Lynda Gratton, "It's Time to Make Paternity Leave Work," *MIT Sloan Management Review*, January 8, 2019, accessed February 5, 2019, https://sloanreview.mit.edu/article/its-time-to-make-paternity-leave-work/

70 The United States has also been at the forefront of IVF access to the LGBTQ community and "a pioneer of the social egg-freezing revolution."

71 Charis Thompson, "IVF Global Histories, USA: Between Rock and a Marketplace," *Reproductive Biomedicine & Society Online 2* (June 2016): 128-35, https://www.sciencedirect.com/science/article/pii/S2405661816300235.

72 Pauline Delage, *Droits des Femmes, Tout Peut Disparaître* (Paris: Editions Textuel, 2018), 98.

The Visionaries

RAHAF HARFOUSH

73 Harfoush is also the author of *The Decoded Company*, a *New York Times* bestseller, and *Hustle & Float: Reclaim Your Creativity and Thrive in a World Obsessed with Work*, published in 2019.

KAT BORLONGAN

74 Exits refer to when a company is sold or when the founders or investors sell their shares.

NIDA JANUSKIS

75 Ania Nussbaum, "Air France to Name Its First Female Chief Executive Officer," *Bloomberg*, December 12, 2018, accessed April 7, 2019, https://www.bloomberg.com/news/articles/2018-12-12/air-france-is-said-to-name-its-first-female-chief-executive.

Editor: Laura Dozier
Designer: Sarah Gifford
Production Manager: Denise LaCongo

Library of Congress Control Number: 2019939715

ISBN: 978-1-4197-4281-1
eISBN: 978-1-68335-878-7

Printed and bound in China
10 9 8 7 6 5 4 3 2 1

Abrams books are available at special discounts when purchased in quantity for premiums and
promotions as well as fundraising or educational use. Special editions can also be created to
specification. For details, contact specialsales@abramsbooks.com or the address below.

Abrams® is a registered trademark of Harry N. Abrams, Inc.

ABRAMS The Art of Books
195 Broadway, New York, NY 10007
abramsbooks.com